101 Ways To Cut
Business Insurance Costs
without Sacrificing Protection

William S. McIntyre IV
Jack P. Gibson

Third Edition

International Risk Management Institute, Inc.
Dallas, Texas

PRINTED IN THE UNITED STATES OF AMERICA

"This publication is designed to provide accurate and authoritative information in regard to the subject matter covered. It is sold with the understanding that the publisher is not engaged in rendering legal, accounting, or other professional service. If professional advice is required, the services of a competent professional should be sought."

—From a Declaration of Principles jointly adopted by a Committee of the American Bar Association and a Committee of Publishers and Associations.

ISBN 1-886813-95-7

International Risk Management Institute, Inc.®
12222 Merit Drive, Suite 1660
Dallas, Texas 75251-2217
(214) 960-7693
Fax (214) 960-6037

International Risk Management Institute, Inc.,® and *IRMI*® are registered trademarks.

Contents

Preface

DO YOU THINK YOUR ORGANIZATION PAYS TOO MUCH FOR INSURANCE? If you are like most business managers, your answer to that question is a resounding "Yes!" You may also feel that you are totally at the mercy of your insurance company because you just do not understand insurance jargon, complicated policies, and how premiums are determined. To many business people, insurance is a mysterious but necessary evil.

This does not have to be the case. You probably manage your taxes on a proactive basis to control your tax burden as best you can. If you take the same approach with your insurance program, you can also control your insurance premiums!

However, there is one major stumbling block—not usually faced by tax managers—to taking control of property and liability insurance costs. While the Internal Revenue Code is a published document in the public domain, the insurance industry's "rating manuals," which govern how your premiums are calculated, are not so easily obtainable. And, like the tax laws, you would probably need an interpreter to explain how to apply them to your business if you were to obtain them.

101 Ways To Cut Business Insurance Costs does this for you. As your personal insurance interpreter, it summarizes and explains how your premiums are calculated. More important, it tells you about the "tricks of the trade" used to calculate your organization's premiums. Knowledge of these approaches and of the important risk management techniques reviewed in this book can save your organization thousands of premium dollars. It is based on our experience over the years as consultants for numerous commercial and public entities, as insurance agents and underwriters on behalf of commercial insureds, and as researchers into insurance industry practices and procedures. We have attempted to explain in plain English how you can reduce or control your business insurance costs without exposing your organization to uninsured losses that it cannot handle. If your business, public, or nonprofit organization can benefit from just a few of these ideas, our efforts will have been worthwhile.

William S. McIntyre IV
Jack P. Gibson

About the Authors

WILLIAM S. MCINTYRE IV, CPCU, ARM, is chairman of American Contractors Insurance Group, Ltd., a construction-industry-owned insurance company. For over 40 years, Mr. McIntyre has been involved in the insurance industry. He has been very active over the years with the Associated General Contractors of America, writing articles, reviewing contract documents, and serving on AGC's Insurance and Safety/Health Committees. Mr. McIntyre has written many articles on insurance and risk management for construction and insurance industry trade journals. He cochairs the annual IRMI Construction Risk Conference and is a technical adviser for IRMI's reference manual for contractors, *Construction Risk Management.*

JACK P. GIBSON, CPCU, CLU, ARM, is president of International Risk Management Institute, Inc. Mr. Gibson is the coauthor of 11 reference works on insurance and risk management, all of which have been published by IRMI. Included among these are *Contractual Risk Transfer, Commercial Liability Insurance,* and *The Additional Insured Book.* He is also editor-in-chief of IRMI.com, which is a Web-based risk and insurance magazine, and *IRMI Update,* its companion e-zine. Mr. Gibson cochairs the annual IRMI Construction Risk Conference and has been a highly rated presenter at all of them. He has also been very active in the CPCU Society, having served as president of the Dallas chapter, as a national director, and on three national committees. Mr. Gibson majored in risk management at the University of Georgia where he received a bachelor of business administration degree, *cum laude,* in 1977 and a master of business administration degree in 1979. In 1996, he was honored as the University of Georgia's Outstanding Insurance Alumnus of the year.

1

MANAGING INSURANCE COSTS

INSURANCE, PARTICULARLY IN RECENT TIMES, has become a major cost item to American business. For most business people, the method by which insurers determine their premiums for property and liability insurance is a complete mystery. Thus, we have written *101 Ways To Cut Business Insurance Costs* to shed some light on the insurance industry's approach to pricing its product and to alert you to ways you can manage your organization's property and casualty insurance costs.

Determining Insurance Premiums

The premium for an insurance policy is calculated by determining a *rate* which is then applied to some measurement of the business's propensity to have losses or claims (called the *exposure base*). For many types of insurance, the rate is found by simply looking it up in a manual published by an insurance company or insurance industry rating organization. Although members of the public can obtain these rating manuals much more easily than in the past, they are certainly not available in bookstores across the nation. Depending on the type of insurance, the rates applicable to a particular organization will vary according to (1) geographic location (some regions have more automobiles on the road, poorer fire departments, or a more litigious social environment), (2) the type of property or operation being insured (wood frame buildings cost more to insure than masonry structures; drivers of sports cars tend to have more accidents than do those who drive other types of vehicles), (3) protective safeguards in place (it costs less to insure a building with a sprinkler system than one without), and (4) other similar types of variables that influence the probability of losses. For most lines of insurance, the rating manuals that contain rules and rates are prepared by for-profit or not-for-profit *rating organizations*.

While in the past, rating organizations developed recommended rates for insurers to use, in recent years this practice has changed. Rating organizations now develop loss costs on behalf of insurers. Loss costs are the portion of the rate that is intended to develop adequate premium to cover only the insured's losses. An additional amount must be added to the loss cost to cover the insurer's expenses and provide for a profit. Since different insurers have different expense structures and profit requirements, the rates they charge can vary, even though they began with the same loss costs.

Rating Organizations

Some rating organizations are nonprofit organizations that serve their member insurance companies. Some others are for-profit companies. They collect statistical data for the insurance

1

companies and use this data to determine recommended insurance loss costs. They file these loss costs with state insurance regulators on behalf of their member insurance companies. Each individual insurance company then files either a multiplier to be applied to the loss cost to develop the final rate or a schedule of actual rates based on the loss costs.

The most important insurance industry rating organizations are the National Council on Compensation Insurance (NCCI), the Insurance Services Office, Inc. (ISO), the American Association of Insurance Services (AAIS), and the Surety Association of America (SAA).

NCCI collects statistical data, provides rating information, and promulgates "standard" policy forms for workers compensation insurance.

ISO provides virtually the same types of services for nearly every line of insurance with the exception of workers compensation insurance and surety bonds. ISO provides insurers with rating data and promulgates standard policy forms for such lines of insurance as homeowners, personal automobile, commercial property, commercial automobile, commercial crime, boiler and machinery, inland marine, and commercial general liability. ISO is a for-profit company that serves most insurers in the United States.

AAIS is ISO's chief competitor. It provides policy forms and rating data for most of the coverage lines serviced by ISO, including inland marine, commercial liability, commercial package policies, and commercial property.

SAA provides rating information and promulgates standard policy forms for fidelity insurance (such as employee fidelity policies, public official bonds, financial institution bonds, etc.) and surety bonds (such as performance and payment bonds).

New Trends in the Rating Process

In the past decade, two developments have had a significant impact on the way rates for property and liability insurance are determined, regulated, and distributed. These two developments are a change from regulated rates to open rating and a change from promulgated rates to promulgated "loss costs." These changes, and their effect on insurance buyers, are discussed in the paragraphs that follow.

Open Rating

Previously, insurance rates had been heavily regulated. Rating organizations would compile industrywide loss and exposure information for each classification for the various lines of coverage, estimate losses for each classification, add an allowance for insurer expenses and profits, seek approval from regulators, and issue advisory rates that all insurers were required to use in a particular state. Deviations from state-made rates had to be approved by state insurance regulators prior to use. By the mid-1990s, however, most states had changed this system to one known as "open rating," whereby insurers are allowed to determine their own rates. The goal of open rating is to promote competition in the commercial insurance markets. In many states advisory data is provided for insurers to use as benchmarks or starting points in determining rates. But unlike previous years, insurers no longer need approval to deviate from them. In effect, pricing of coverage is on a market-driven, rather than a regulation-driven, basis.

The net effect of the trend from regulated rates to open rating is increased variation between insurers' prices for comparable coverage, a fact that requires you to take an even more proactive purchasing approach. First, it makes it important to shop and compare prices from insurer to insurer. Second, open rating sets up increased negotiating possibilities with individual insurers.

Loss Costs

Previously, ISO and NCCI published *rates* for coverage. Now in most states, these organizations publish *loss costs*. The difference is that prospective loss costs contemplate only expected losses and loss adjustment expenses, whereas rates included loadings for catastrophic losses, insurer expenses, and underwriting profit, as well.

To develop a final rate for a particular line of insurance, an insurer must determine how much to add to the loss costs to cover its expenses and provide for a profit. Each insurer develops its own "multiplier" that is applied to the loss costs to derive rates. This allows more competition than the previous system, which included these factors in the rates all insurers were supposed to charge—since insurers with the most efficient and cost-effective operations should be able to charge lower rates.

Another effect of the change from rates to loss costs is that it requires additional work for insurance agents and brokers. Previously, a rating manual or set of rates provided a single rate applying to all of the companies they represented. To determine premiums now, agents and brokers must obtain rates (or multipliers) from every company. (Insurers provide their representatives with rates in some cases; in others, agents/brokers apply a different set of insurer-specific multipliers for each of the individual insurance companies that they represent.)

Ultimately, the change from rates to loss costs increases the importance of the partnership with your agent/broker. The agent/broker must now perform additional work and possess additional expertise to ascertain and compare price differences from insurer to insurer, which underscores the need for a positive working relationship and effective communication with your agent/broker.

Proactive Approach to Insurance Purchasing

While the insurance rating process sounds—and really is—simple, there is much more to it than simply looking up the loss costs or manual rate in a book and multiplying it by an exposure base. There are published "rules" in the insurance industry's rating manuals that guide the insurance underwriters and rating technicians in determining the exposure base to use, in choosing the most appropriate loss costs or rate from the manual, and in deviating from these costs or rates. If you knew all of these rules, you would know what actions to take to ensure that the loss cost/rate chosen for your business was the lowest one possible. The two key rating manuals used by the insurance industry are the *Commercial Lines Manual* (*CLM*), published by ISO, and the *Basic Manual for Workers Compensation and Employers Liability Insurance*, published by NCCI. You should be aware that these publications supply much of the information needed to determine and compare prices for the various lines of insurance coverage that will be discussed in this book. A detailed discussion of these manuals is beyond the scope of this chapter and we have cross-referenced many of the book's recommendations with the rating manual rules upon which they are based.

This book supplies you with the knowledge to understand how these manuals are used to determine insurance premiums and to verify the accuracy of those premiums. It provides a list of actions that you can take to ensure that the lowest possible insurance costs/rates are used in pricing your organization's policies. It examines the areas where the insurance industry frequently makes mistakes in calculating business insurance premiums, allowing you to verify that these mistakes are not being made or correct them if they are. Finally, the book also points out areas in which business managers frequently make mistakes that cost them money.

For too many years, businesses have allowed insurance companies to calculate their premium costs with virtually no audit function in place and with no accountability as to whether or not these costs were properly determined. This approach is very similar to asking the Internal Revenue Service (IRS) to determine your tax liability without your input or even your understanding of how income taxation is derived. Given the competitive pressures confronting all types of firms, this is a costly way of doing business. In contrast, by proactively managing your insurance program and practicing the art and science of *risk management*, you will be assured that your organization is paying no more than it should for its property and casualty insurance. As a result, the competitive position of your company will be enhanced.

Saving Money with Risk Management

Risk management is a common sense approach to handling the potential ways in which an organization could suffer losses other than those solely attributable to business operations. In other words, risk management is an approach to protecting an organization from losses caused by fire, theft, flood, earthquake, liability lawsuits, work-related injuries to employees, and similar events. It attempts to effectively handle these "loss exposures" or "risks" at the lowest possible cost to the organization.

The process involves the following logical steps that you can apply to manage risks.

- Identify risks.
- Analyze risks.
- Select the best methods for handling the risks.
- Implement the chosen alternatives.
- Monitor the results.

Risk Identification

Identifying risks is the most important step in the process because risks that are not identified may not be contemplated in the risk management program. The result may be large, unexpected, and uninsured losses. Risk identification is accomplished by carefully reviewing your organization's operations and assets to determine the ways that losses may occur. These identified risks are then analyzed in an attempt to determine the magnitude of the losses if they did occur and the potential effects on the organization. Your insurance agent or broker should take an active part in this process but cannot do it without your help and cooperation.

Risk Management Techniques

Once these loss exposures are identified and their potential effects on the organization are analyzed, determine which risk management techniques will best handle each loss exposure. The various risk management techniques seek to keep losses from occurring, reduce the effects of those that do occur, and/or finance the cost of losses. The most commonly used risk management techniques are the following.

- Avoidance
- Loss control
- Retention

- Contractual risk transfer
- Insurance transfer

Risk Avoidance

Avoidance involves not engaging in operations that may lead to unacceptable losses. For example, many contractors decided not to enter into the pollution cleanup business because of the high potential for catastrophic, uninsurable liability losses. Similarly, pharmaceutical companies have discontinued production of certain drugs because of the liability suits associated with possible side effects.

Risk Control

Risk control involves reducing the potential for losses to occur and/or the effects of those that do occur. For example, the use of protective eyeglasses by workers in a manufacturing plant reduces the possibility that eye injuries to employees will occur. Installing a building sprinkler system, to give another example, reduces the amount of damage from a fire that does start. An insured loss will cost your business substantially more than the amount you will recover from your insurance in lost productivity, management time, and other hidden costs. For this reason, risk control is a very important risk management technique.

Risk Retention

Retention involves the organization's paying for all or part of the losses it suffers out of operating income or, in some cases, out of a dedicated fund, rather than transferring them to another party, such as an insurer. It can be achieved by assuming deductibles, using rating plans that provide premium returns when losses are lower than expected or surcharges when they are higher, or by simply not buying insurance. Retention is almost always less expensive than insurance in the long run. In the short run, however, large retentions can cause severe budgeting and cash flow problems if a firm suffers losses, as well as the loss of an immediate tax deduction that would have been available had the organization purchased first-dollar insurance coverage.

Three rules are often considered in the process of selecting a retention level.

1. Do not risk a great deal (of loss) for a small premium saving.
2. Do consider the odds (of a large loss, or many small ones, occurring).
3. Do not risk more than your organization can afford to lose.

These three rules, when followed, will generally cause the organization to retain losses that happen frequently and/or do not potentially involve large dollar amounts. These types of losses are budgetable and do not impair the financial viability of the organization when they occur. Risks that present the possibility of large, catastrophic losses should almost always be insured.

As an example of how these concepts apply, assume a large manufacturer, The Widget Company, decides to self-insure its workers compensation insurance. After carefully studying Widget's loss patterns for the past 5 years, the risk manager determines that Widget will typically experience $750,000 per year in workers compensation losses. Of course, she recognizes that a plant explosion or other unusual event could occur in any particular year, resulting in much higher losses. With this in mind, she decides to seek quotes for excess insurance with retentions ranging between $500,000 and $1 million. By purchasing the insurance, Widget will be self-insuring the so-called working layer, which is relatively predictable (and thus, budgetable). The catastrophic exposure above this will be transferred to an insurer.

Contractual Risk Transfer

Contractual risk transfer (sometimes called *noninsurance risk transfer*) involves passing your organization's risks to others by use of hold harmless or indemnity clauses and insurance requirements in business contracts, such as leases. A hold harmless clause requires one party to hold the other party harmless for losses to a member of the public arising from operations covered by the contract. For example, a lease may require the tenant to hold the landlord harmless for lawsuits brought against the landlord by members of the public injured in the part of the premises rented to the tenant. Similarly, a business may transfer potential liability to another organization by contractually requiring that it be named as an additional insured on the transferee's insurance policy. In these ways, you may be able to pass some of your risks on to others, thereby reducing the need for, or cost of, liability insurance. You should review contracts entered into with other parties to (1) determine what risks the other party is attempting to pass to your firm and how you will handle these risks if you accept them, and (2) determine if you can transfer some of your risks to the other party.

Insurance

For those risks not handled by the previous techniques, you buy insurance. This involves an insurance company financing the organization's losses. For all but the smallest organizations, insurance is an income-smoothing device that spreads the financial consequences of losses out over a period of time. The erratic, unbudgetable losses are traded for a budgetable insurance premium. However, all but the very smallest commercial insureds will, over time, reimburse their insurers for most, if not all, losses they pay on these insureds' behalf, plus a factor to cover the insurers' expenses and profits. As a general rule, approximately 70 to 75 percent of insurance premiums are used to pay losses, with the remainder applied to overhead and profits. Reducing your insured losses will reduce your insurance premiums. This fact justifies expending time and effort using the previously mentioned risk management techniques even if they do not eliminate the need for insurance.

Monitoring the Results

Once the alternatives are chosen and implemented, you must monitor the results. Remember that changes in the organization, the insurance marketplace, and society will affect the continued appropriateness of your past decisions. The organization's risk management program should be periodically fine-tuned as these changes occur.

Summary

Risk management is a practical process for handling an organization's risks of loss other than business risks. The primary goal of the process is to ensure that the organization's income stream and/or assets are not impaired by a loss or losses to an extent that threatens the organization's survival. The second goal of risk management is to employ the least expensive risk management techniques possible to meet the primary goal. The risk management process can be applied by business managers for whom insurance purchasing is one of many responsibilities or by professional, full-time risk managers. Contemplating possible losses and taking cost-effective steps to handle them before they occur will save your organization substantial amounts of money.

How To Use this Book

This book is divided into chapters that correspond to the various lines of insurance purchased by most businesses. It includes chapters on several risk management topics that can also lead to cost savings. The various ways of cutting business insurance costs are numbered sequentially throughout these chapters. Not all of the 101 ways will be applicable to every organization, and some of them are mutually exclusive. We suggest that you first scan this book to develop a feel for its contents. Then read the related insurance coverage chapter(s) approximately 150 days prior to renewing a particular insurance policy. This will allow time for applying the various techniques before the policy's renewal. The chapters on agent/company relationships, claims, loss control, risk financing, competitive bidding, and the general recommendations can be applied at any time.

Also note that each chapter presents an overview of the subjects it covers before discussing specific ways to cut costs. This is to provide background information on some important aspects of the topic. For example, the chapters dealing with specific insurance policies provide brief descriptions of their scope and application. Those chapters dealing with risk management techniques, claims, and industry relationships provide background information on the importance of claims, the insurance distribution system, or the risk management concept. These discussions should be particularly informative for readers who have not had extensive experience with insurance.

Read the book as you would read any other book and then use it as, in essence, a reference for cost control. In advance of renewing any particular type of insurance policy, review the chapter related to that policy. For assistance in scanning the book, Figure 1.1 gives you a checklist of the cost-cutting methods that are discussed.

Figure 1.1

The 101 Ways To Cut Costs

The following is a list of the 101 ways to cut business insurance costs that are discussed in this book. The various headings correspond with the titles of chapters in the book.

Chapter 2: *Automobile Insurance*

1. Determine Proper Classifications for Vehicle Use
2. Determine Proper Classifications for Vehicle Location
3. Determine Proper Classifications for Vehicle Use Radius
4. Determine Proper Classifications for Vehicle Weight
5. Avoid Premiums on Mobile Equipment
6. Use Contractors Equipment Floater Policies
7. Obtain Personal Vehicle Rating Credits
8. Reduce Recreational Vehicle Premiums
9. Consider Specified Causes of Loss Coverage
10. Use Deductibles
11. Self-Insure Collision
12. Self-Insure Bodily Injury and Property Damage Liability
13. Obtain Schedule Credits, Dividends, and Deviations
14. Use Experience Rating
15. Use the Suspension of Insurance Endorsement
16. Understand the "Stated Amount" Approach
17. Discontinue Medical Payments and Personal Injury Protection Coverage Where Possible
18. Discontinue Uninsured/Underinsured Motorists Coverage Where Possible
19. Think Twice about Rental Car Physical Damage Loss Waivers
20. Reject Accident and Health Coverages on Rental Cars

Chapter 3: *Commercial General Liability Insurance*

21. Use Proper Classifications
22. Use Lessor's Risk Only Classification
23. Delete Nonapplicable Exposures
24. Apply the Executive Officer Payroll Limitation
25. Look Twice at Intercompany Sales
26. Obtain Schedule Credit/ Dividends
27. Use Deductibles
28. Negotiate Premium Credits for Coverage Limitations
29. Use Experience Rating
30. Drop Medical Payments Coverage
31. Obtain Insurance Certificates from Contractors

Chapter 4: *Umbrella Liability Insurance*

32. Consider Alternative Primary Limits and Obtain Quotes for Buffer Layers

Figure 1.1 (cont.)

The 101 Ways To Cut Costs (cont.)

33. Obtain Competitive Pricing
34. Submit Well-Prepared Specifications
35. Determine the Premium Basis
36. Select Reasonable Umbrella Limits
37. Provide for Automatic Extensions
38. Use Care with Adjustable Rate Policies

Chapter 5: *Workers Compensation*

39. Obtain Correct Classifications
40. Delete Overtime Payroll Surcharge
41. Use a "First-Aid" Folder
42. Consider a Deductible Plan
43. Take Advantage of Dividends and Flexible Rates

Chapter 6: *Workers Compensation Experience Rating*

44. Review Reserves
45. Prepare a Test Modifier
46. Review Final Modifier
47. Correct Calculation Errors
48. Recognize the Effect of Ownership Changes on Experience Modifiers

Chapter 7: *Property Insurance*

49. Obtain Rate Deviations/ Dividends
50. Use Deductibles
51. Invest in Fire and Loss Prevention

52. Obtain Duplicate Records Credit
53. Use the Business Interruption Reporting Form
54. Obtain Coinsurance Credits
55. Report Proper Builders Risk Values

Chapter 8: *Insurance Industry Relationships*

56. Choose a Knowledgeable Agent or Broker
57. Use a Limited Number of Agencies/Brokerages
58. Use a Written Scope of Engagement
59. Maintain Communication
60. Know Your Underwriter
61. Use Consultants

Chapter 9: *Claims*

62. Request Advance Payment of Property Claims
63. Retain Public Adjusters for Large Property Losses
64. Have Periodic Meetings with Insurance Company Adjusters
65. Obtain the Right To Approve Workers Compensation and Liability Claims Payments
66. Audit Claims Departments and Adjusting Firms
67. Maintain Loss Records
68. Manage Litigation Costs Aggressively

Figure 1.1 (cont.)

The 101 Ways To Cut Costs (cont.)

Chapter 10: *Risk Control*

69. Obtain Senior Management Support for Risk Control
70. Allocate Costs on a Loss-Sensitive Basis
71. Involve Workers in the Safety and Risk Control Process
72. Motivate Safe Work Habits with Incentives
73. Use Prehire Measures To Control Claims
74. Communicate with Workers before Injuries
75. Investigate "Near-Miss" Incidents
76. Commission an Independent Safety Program Audit
77. Use Medical Bill Reviewers
78. Use Managed Care Arrangements
79. Implement Visitation and Return-to-Work Programs

Chapter 11: *Risk Financing*

80. Carefully Select Retrospective Minimum and Maximum Factors
81. Negotiate the Agent's Commission Outside the Rating Plan
82. Negotiate Other Retrospective Rating Factors
83. Explore a "Paid Loss" Retrospective Rating Plan
84. Consider Other Cash Flow Programs

85. Examine the Self-Insurance/Captive Option
86. Consider Alternative Risk Financing Facilities

Chapter 12: *Saving with Competitive Proposals*

87. Don't Bid Too Frequently
88. Allocate Insurers to the Agents/Brokers
89. Allow Adequate Time To Secure Proposals
90. Provide Adequate Information
91. Don't Bid "Excess and Surplus Lines" Coverages Among Agents

Chapter 13: *General Recommendations*

92. Consolidate Effective Dates
93. Maximize Purchasing Power with One Insurer
94. Buy Package Policies
95. Consider Multiyear, Noncancellable Policies
96. Prepare or Verify Premium Audits
97. Defer Premiums
98. Develop a Comprehensive Insurance Database
99. Prepare Early for Renewals
100. Hire a Risk Manager
101. Implement Contractual Risk Transfer Programs

2 AUTOMOBILE INSURANCE

THE TWO TYPES OF COVERAGE automobile insurance provides are liability for injuries to others and/or damage to their property ("bodily injury liability and property damage liability") and damage to the insured's own vehicles. The liability coverage is generally referred to as *automobile liability insurance*, while damage to owned vehicles is referred to as *automobile physical damage* coverage. Most organizations are covered under a policy called the *business auto policy* (BAP), or the business auto coverage form. Automobile dealerships, parking garages, and auto repair shops use the garage policy, and coverage for trucking firms is written either on a truckers or motor carrier form.

Besides covering exposures associated with owned vehicles, liability insurance may cover your company's liability arising out of operation of nonowned vehicles in cases such as when an employee uses a personal car to run an errand. It can also cover liability arising from a hired auto—one that your company leases, hires, rents, or borrows.

There are two basic types of physical damage coverage usually provided for owned autos: collision and comprehensive. The *collision coverage* insures against damage from collision with another vehicle or object as well as from overturning. The *comprehensive coverage* provides protection against damage from other types of perils such as hail, fire, vandalism, and flood. Additionally, there are several secondary coverages such as medical payments, personal injury protection (PIP), and towing.

Before 1960, many insurance companies issued a separate policy for each vehicle owned by the insured. With the introduction of the comprehensive auto liability policy, coverage was afforded automatically with respect to liability for all owned vehicles and, subject to certain conditions, for auto physical damage. While some insureds report fleet additions and deletions during the year, the preferred approach is to report all fleet changes at the end of the year with the insurance company making the necessary premium adjustment at that time. This saves substantial administrative costs for you, your insurance agent, and your insurance company.

Ways To Cut Costs

This chapter offers 20 ways to cut automobile insurance costs.

1. Determine Proper Classifications for Vehicle Use

The first step in developing the premium for a commercial vehicle is to determine its "use" classification from the following categories.

1. Service use
2. Retail use
3. Commercial use

Service use refers to the transportation of employees or property to and from job locations. Generally, it applies to contractors and those service firms that perform work away from their own premises. Retail use involves the pickup of property from, or delivery to, individual households—usually by vans or trucks. Commercial use covers any use other than service or retail use.

The service use classification is usually subject to the lowest rate. Depending on whether a truck is classified as light (up to 10,000 pounds), medium (10,001–20,000), or heavy (20,001–45,000), vehicles falling into the retail or commercial use classification are subject to the highest rate. (Refer to Figure 2.4 on page 16).

Given the nature of the classification system, it is important that you review the actual usage of vehicles to determine if your company's vehicles can be rated in a lower classification. Agents can be very helpful in this area. Unless you provide proper information, insurance underwriters tend to apply the old adage, "When in doubt, use a higher rate." As with all rules and regulations, there are many gray areas. During times of restrictive insurance markets, insurance companies tend to use the higher classifications. These use classifications are summarized in Figure 2.1.

Figure 2.1

Summary of Use Classifications

Most Expensive

> *Retail Use:* Vehicles used to pick up property from, or deliver property to, individual households

Moderately Expensive

> *Commercial Use:* Vehicles not classified as retail use (above) or service use (below)

Least Expensive

> *Service Use:* Vehicles used for transportation of insured's personnel, tools, equipment, and incidental supplies

---

Another important technique in determining the proper classification of vehicles, especially those dispersed over a large geographical area, is to photograph the vehicles and build a file that includes the pictures, license receipts, and invoices. This enables the insurance representative to classify the vehicles more accurately and to provide a record of the actual property insured (which can be of great value after a theft).

2.   Determine Proper Classifications for Vehicle Location

The second step in determining an auto premium is based on the location in which a vehicle is garaged. The insurance industry develops loss statistics for each state and even breaks each state into rating territories. For instance, Texas—being one of the larger states—has more than 40 territories. The reason for these territorial classifications is that experience in densely populated areas differs from that in less populated areas. Areas with high population density tend to have more accidents, because of traffic congestion, than do less dense areas. In other words, more cars produce more wrecks.

People in urban areas are also more prone to litigate. They tend to sue more frequently, pursue their claims for a longer period of time, and sue for more money. This increases claims and legal costs in heavily populated areas.

You can use these territorial rating classifications to your advantage. If vehicles are used and garaged in rural areas where rates are low, the insured that reports them as being garaged in those rural areas—rather than in the urban area where its home office is located—gains an advantage by avoiding the higher urban rates. A question arises: "Does the policy have to be revised every time there is a change in a vehicle's location?" The answer is, "No." Instead, review the automobile schedule at each policy anniversary date to determine changes in the location of vehicles and report accordingly.

Rates differ substantially from state to state. For example, average rates are higher in New York than in Texas. By planning as much as possible where automobiles will be garaged, and by being sensitive to variations in rates from territory to territory and from state to state, you can substantially reduce the premiums for business automobiles.

3.   Determine Proper Classifications for Vehicle Use Radius

A vehicle's radius of use is the third variable that determines premium. Since longer driving distances increase the probability of accidents, insurers consider driving distances in rating auto insurance. Distance surcharges—based on the number of miles driven to and from a particular location—usually apply. The first surcharge usually applies at distances over 50 miles. A second, higher, surcharge generally applies to vehicles driven over 200 miles. This is summarized in Figure 2.2.

Figure 2.2

Summary of Distance Surcharges

Local	Up to 50 miles
Intermediate	51 to 200 miles
Long Distance	Over 200 miles
"Regular and Frequent Travel"	Meaning of term varies

The theory is that the more miles the vehicle travels, the greater the chance of loss. Therefore, the insurance company should receive additional premiums based on the longer distances driven. However, there are some questions as to how these surcharges are applied. For example, the surcharges are not to be applied until a vehicle exceeds the specified distance on a regular and frequent basis. The Illinois Supreme Court once ruled that the term "regular and frequent" may mean 26 times a year between the same two points over that certain distance. Some insurance companies deem regular and frequent use to be once a month. As a result, there is great discussion and latitude in this area.

Also, the distance does not have to be measured in road miles but can be "as the crow flies," or the straight-line distance between two points. A location that is 60 miles away by road may be only 50 air miles away and, therefore, not subject to a surcharge.

To avoid overcharges, you must ask, "What distance surcharges are being applied? Are these charges really valid?" In this somewhat gray area, underwriters will be more liberal during a soft market. In a tight market, however, underwriters looking for any basis to increase premiums will be less willing to negotiate this point.

While the territory classification will usually not affect the applicability of coverage, some companies add a limitation of use endorsement, suspending coverage outside a given radius. Therefore, you must ask whether any territorial limitation in the policy affects the coverage. If the insurance company adds a limitation of use endorsement, coverage may be severely impaired. In the past, courts have voided these limitation of use endorsements. Consequently, most insurance companies will not attach them to their policies, but some will.

When faced with the question of whether to have vehicles designated local with the limitation of use endorsement or have a distance surcharge added without a limitation of use endorsement, it is usually better to pay the surcharge rather than limit the coverage. Again, most companies negotiate coverage and cost based on operations and will not attach limitation endorsements.

4. Determine Proper Classifications for Vehicle Weight

The fourth variable in rating commercial automobiles is the gross weight of the vehicle, usually based on the manufacturer's capacity rating. The logic behind this approach is that the heavier the vehicle, the more damage it can cause. Heavy vehicles also cost more to repair. Therefore, owners of heavier vehicles pay more in premiums.

This sounds very simple, but there is potential for quite a few errors. You must be certain that the underwriter gets proper weight information. A common error occurs when a large truck becomes unreliable and is removed from its primary service. The configuration of the truck might be changed so that it can be used as an on-premises vehicle or in some similar operation. This is especially true of remanufactured vehicles for which weight capacity is changed because the cargo-carrying capability has been reconfigured. Again, if underwriters are not sure of the vehicle's actual weight, they assume higher weight levels and charge higher premiums. The different weight classifications are summarized in Figure 2.3.

Figure 2.3

Summary of Weight Classifications

Light Trucks	0–10,000 lbs. Gross Vehicle Weight (GVW)
Medium Trucks	10,001–20,000 lbs. GVW
Heavy Trucks	20,001–45,000 lbs. GVW
Extra-Heavy Trucks	Over 45,000 lbs. GVW
Heavy Truck Tractors	0–45,000 lbs. Gross Combination Weight (GCW)
Extra Heavy Truck Tractors	Over 45,000 lbs. GCW

Importance of Classifications

Figure 2.4 is taken from the *Commercial Lines Manual* section that contains scheduled factors for classification and rating. Examining the table gives an idea of the cost variations that might occur as a result of misclassifications. If we assume that a base liability coverage rate for a heavy truck is $1,000, the rate gets modified by a factor from the schedule, depending on use and distance. For example, if it qualifies as a service vehicle that is used locally (under 50 miles), a 1.10 factor is applied to develop a premium of $1,100.

However, an underwriter might find this vehicle subject to the intermediate mileage charge (51 to 200 miles) and consider it a commercial vehicle. This intermediate distance surcharge, combined with a change in the vehicle's "use" category, demands a 2.25 factor that makes the premium $2,250. This example illustrates the magnitude of savings to be realized by paying attention to these classifications. Remember, the territory classification variable might create greater saving.

Most commercial insurance buyers do not understand or remember all these rating techniques. However, understanding the fundamentals prompts you to ask important questions of the insurance producer or company. There is really nothing magical about this approach, but you must pay particular attention to all details to get optimum cost and coverage.

The main point to remember is that cost is *negotiable*. The more the underwriters know about your particular business, the more secure they will feel about taking risks and charging reasonable premiums.

Rating

The source of the various classifications and the rates (or loss costs) for these classifications is the *Commercial Lines Manual* (*CLM*) published by the Insurance Services Office, Inc. (ISO), or a state-specific manual, such as those for Texas and California. The *Manual* provides rules and rates/loss costs for all commercial lines, including automobile.

Figure 2.4

Truck and Tractor Rating Classes

Size Class	Business Use Class		Radius Class	
			Local Up to 50 Miles	
			Liability	Phys. Damage
Light Trucks (0–10,000 Lbs. GVW)	Service	Factor	1.00	1.00
		Code	011--	011--
	Retail	Factor	1.60	1.20
		Code	021--	021--
	Commercial	Factor	1.30	1.15
		Code	031--	031--
Medium Trucks (10,001–20,000 Lbs. GVW)	Service	Factor	1.05	.85
		Code	211--	211--
	Retail	Factor	1.65	1.00
		Code	221--	221--
	Commercial	Factor	1.35	.95
		Code	231--	231--
Heavy Trucks (20,001–45,000 Lbs. GVW)	Service	Factor	1.10	.75
		Code	311--	311--
	Retail	Factor	1.70	1.15
		Code	321--	321--
	Commercial	Factor	1.80	1.00
		Code	331--	331--
Extra-Heavy Trucks (Over 45,000 Lbs. GVW)		Factor	2.50	1.15
		Code	401--	401--
Heavy Truck-Tractors (0–45,000 Lbs. GCW)	Service	Factor	1.50	1.05
		Code	341--	341--
	Retail	Factor	2.40	1.45
		Code	351--	351--
	Commercial	Factor	2.10	1.25
		Code	361--	361--
Extra-Heavy Truck-Tractors (Over 45,000 Lbs. GCW)		Factor	2.60	1.25
		Code	501--	501--
Trailer Types				
Semitrailers		Factor	.25	.85
		Code	671--	671--
Trailers		Factor		.65
		Code	.15 681--	681--
Service or Utility Trailer (0–2,000 Lbs. Load Capacity)		Factor		.40
		Code	0 691--	691--

Source: *Commercial Lines Manual,* Insurance Services Office, Inc., 1997.

Loss costs associated with a classification vary from state to state. An individual insurer may develop its own rates or loss costs or join with others by subscribing to those developed by ISO. Such insurers may modify these "bureau" loss costs or rates but will often use them as a starting point. This is accomplished by multiplying the "basic limits rate" by an appropriate "increased limits factor."

Finally, since basic company loss costs are based on statutory limits of liability, which is different for each state, they must be adjusted for the higher limits of liability you will want to purchase. They are found in a table in the *Commercial Lines Manual*.

5.   Avoid Premiums on Mobile Equipment

The commercial general liability (CGL) policy insures against property damage and bodily injury liability arising out of the operation, ownership, and use of mobile equipment, just as the auto policy insures against liability from autos. However, no additional premium is charged in the CGL to cover individual units considered to be mobile equipment. As will be shown in Chapter 3, other types of exposure indicators are used in the CGL rating process.

Since the auto policy requires a specific liability insurance charge for each vehicle and the CGL policy does not include a unit charge for mobile equipment, the distinction between "autos" and "mobile equipment" is important.

Mobile equipment is specifically and precisely defined in both the CGL and the auto policy. The definition is shown in Figure 2.5. Mistakes are often made in determining what vehicles are mobile equipment and what vehicles are autos. Unnecessary auto liability premiums are often paid as a result of these mistakes.

As Figure 2.5 shows, most construction and farm equipment should be classified as mobile equipment, as should a truck or automobile maintained and used solely on or next to owned premises. Trucks and similar vehicles that are maintained primarily to move permanently mounted power cranes and other specified equipment—as well as street and road construction or resurfacing equipment—should be classified as mobile equipment. Air compressors, pumps, and other items mentioned in paragraph 6(c) in Figure 2.5 are considered mobile equipment only if they are not self-propelled (e.g., mounted on trailers).

You should carefully review the automobile schedule to determine whether your company is paying auto liability premiums on mobile equipment. Correcting these errors may eliminate a considerable amount of liability premiums. A word of caution: the commercial general liability policy does not insure against physical damage to the mobile equipment. Physical damage of the equipment can be insured under an equipment floater policy.

6.   Use Contractors Equipment Floater Policies

Mobile equipment such as that discussed in the above recommendation may be insured against physical damage in a contractors equipment policy. This policy can cover both the vehicle and the specialized equipment mounted on it.

Figure 2.5

Mobile Equipment Definition

"Mobile equipment" means any of the following types of land vehicles, including any attached machinery or equipment:

1. Bulldozers, farm machinery, forklifts, and other vehicles designed for use principally off public roads;

2. Vehicles maintained for use solely on or next to premises you own or rent;

3. Vehicles that travel on crawler treads;

4. Vehicles, whether self-propelled or not, maintained primarily to provide mobility to permanently mounted:

    a. Power cranes, shovels, loaders, diggers, or drills; or

    b. Road construction or resurfacing equipment such as graders, scrapers, or rollers;

5. Vehicles not described in 1, 2, 3, or 4 above that are not self-propelled and are maintained primarily to provide mobility to permanently attached equipment of the following types:

    a. Air compressors, pumps, and generators, including spraying, welding, building cleaning, geophysical exploration, lighting, and well servicing equipment; or

    b. Cherry pickers and similar devices used to raise or lower workers;

6. Vehicles not described in 1, 2, 3, or 4 above maintained primarily for purposes other than the transportation of persons or cargo. However, self-propelled vehicles with the following types of permanently attached equipment are not "mobile equipment" but will be considered "autos":

    a. Equipment designed primarily for:

        (1) Snow removal;

        (2) Road maintenance, but not construction or resurfacing;

        (3) Street cleaning;

    b. Cherry pickers and similar devices mounted on automobile or truck chassis and used to raise or lower workers; and

    c. Air compressors, pumps, and generators, including spraying, welding, building cleaning, geophysical exploration, lighting, and well servicing equipment.

Source: Business Auto Coverage Form, Insurance Services Office, Inc., Copyright 1993.

Often, automobile physical damage rates will run 2 to 3 percent of the market value of the unit in question. If it qualifies, however, this equipment may be covered under a contractors equipment policy for a rate ranging between $.40 to $1.25 per $100 of value. This is a substantial savings over using the automobile policy for such coverage. Generally, the more equipment insured under a contractors equipment policy rather than an auto policy, the lower the premium cost.

7. Obtain Personal Vehicle Rating Credits

Privately owned companies often provide vehicles to spouses or others and insure them under the business auto policy. If the major use of these vehicles is for nonbusiness purposes, the insurance company will sometimes agree to classify them as being for personal use and charge rates much lower than those applying to commercial vehicles.

8. Reduce Recreational Vehicle Premiums

Many corporations own recreational vehicles such as campers, hunting vehicles, and the like. Obviously, if the vehicles are garaged in an urban area and designated in a high-use category, the premium can be quite high. It is often possible to garage them in the rural areas where they are used and have them classified as farm vehicles to establish a lower premium.

9. Consider Specified Causes of Loss Coverage

As mentioned at the beginning of this chapter, *comprehensive coverage* is one of two types of physical damage insurance usually provided by the policy for owned autos. Comprehensive covers any and all perils that might damage the automobile except collision, overturn, and certain excluded perils. The coverage is *all risk* and will even cover damage caused in very unusual situations such as when an oil well spews acid that eats away the paint, a dog gets upset and rips the upholstery, or a sandstorm sandblasts the windows. As one might expect, this coverage is fairly expensive.

Specified causes of loss (formerly called fire, theft, and combined additional coverage) is a substantially less expensive alternative approach to purchasing comprehensive coverage. It is known as *named perils* coverage, which provides protection against specified perils such as the following.

- Fire
- Theft
- Windstorm
- Earthquake
- Hail

- Lightning
- Explosion
- Flood
- Vandalism

- Sinking, burning, collision, or derailment of a conveyance transporting the covered auto

Exposures not covered are very unusual, seldom occurring events such as those mentioned earlier. In addition, damage to windshields from flying rocks, often encountered on roadways, would be excluded. If there is low exposure to these perils or if your company can afford to retain some of the exposure, such as windshield damage, you should use this approach. In most cases, choosing the alternative specified causes of loss coverage will result in reduced premium dollars.

To determine the potential savings, obtain alternative quotes for comprehensive and for specified causes of loss. If the premium difference is large enough, you can assume some reasonable risk, which will not be large enough to cause financial hardship.

10. Use Deductibles

You can agree to assume deductibles for collision, comprehensive, and even bodily injury and property damage liability coverage.

Physical Damage Deductibles

Some minimum deductibles are usually required for collision and comprehensive coverage. Therefore, under these coverages, the question is not really whether to take the deductible but how much of a deductible to assume. It is usually beneficial to assume at least a $500 collision deductible on private passenger automobiles and pickups and a $1,000 deductible on larger vehicles. On larger fleets, even higher collision deductibles may be desirable.

The basic loss analysis should be similar to the following example. Assume that your firm wants to determine whether to change from a $500 collision deductible to $1,000 on private passenger vehicles. Also suppose that this will save $2,000 in premium for these particular vehicles.

Past experience shows that at least two accidents causing over $1,000 damage should occur during the year. This means an additional $1,000 (2 × $500) in deductible expense is expected to be sustained. Therefore, if $2,000 in premium is saved and an additional $1,000 is assumed in higher deductibles, a net $1,000 of savings will be realized in addition to the investment income on the $2,000 of premiums not paid to the insurance company. This savings merits shifting to a higher deductible.

The same analysis can be applied to comprehensive coverage. The shift from a $250 comprehensive deductible to a $500 comprehensive deductible will probably be well worth the increase in loss assumption.

On larger fleets, consider moving to an annual aggregate deductible program. This means the insured will pay deductibles up to an annual aggregate level, say $50,000, and after that, the insurance company will reimburse all losses. Often, this annual aggregate deductible program can be expanded to cover nonautomotive equipment (such as contractors' equipment) as well.

Liability Deductibles

Deductibles may also be used with liability coverages. For bodily injury, however, the deductible credit is often not large enough to warrant the risk. Also, underwriters worry that the insured may fail to promptly report a potentially severe claim, initially believing that no injury occurred; therefore, many insurers will not allow a bodily injury liability deductible. However, property damage liability deductibles ranging from $250 to $2,500 can save a considerable amount of money. Every insured who owns more than five vehicles should seriously consider assuming at least a $250 property damage liability deductible for each.

An interesting twist to liability deductibles is that your company does not have to adjust its own claims below the deductible level. Claims can be handled on a "reimbursement basis." The insurance company will settle the claim and then bill your firm for the deductible. This approach bypasses the problem of adjusting and researching the claim. However, insurance companies may resist this approach because they are highly computerized and may want to avoid the additional accounting caused by "backcharging" the insured for the deductible portion.

It is important to distinguish between the two types of liability insurance deductibles: *"per occurrence"* basis deductibles and *"per claim"* basis deductibles.

A per occurrence basis deductible applies only one time for all claims arising from a particular accident. Consider a highway accident caused by a company employee involving 12 automobiles. The per occurrence property damage liability deductible of $500 would apply only once to the accident.

On the other hand, a per claim basis deductible would apply to each of the 12 claims. In other words, the insured would have to pay $6,000 in deductibles instead of $500. Of course, per claim deductibles provide greater reductions of premiums than per occurrence deductibles. But the potentially higher retained loss amounts must be considered. Small businesses should probably stick to the per occurrence basis deductibles.

In summary, you should strongly consider deductibles in the area of physical damage liability. A loss analysis combined with alternative premium quotes can usually determine whether the use of higher deductibles can be cost-effective in the long run.

11. Self-Insure Collision

Additional dollar savings are available if your firm self-insures a portion of its collision exposures.

As the number of owned vehicles increases, self-insuring collision becomes more desirable, especially for vehicles more than 3 years old. You should seriously consider self-insurance when premiums equal the average value of owned vehicles. It is quite improbable that more than one owned vehicle will be involved in a single collision. Therefore, collision is a good area to self-insure. An analysis identical to that used in selecting a collision deductible can be used to determine the feasibility of insuring collision.

Some firms will continue to purchase collision coverage on new vehicles but will drop this coverage after 2 or 3 years. This approach assumes that the vehicle's value will approach the sum of the premium and the deductible after 2 or 3 years.

Self-insurance with respect to specified causes of loss and/or comprehensive coverage should normally be avoided by all but the largest organizations. Vehicles are often garaged together during off-hours or on weekends; as a result, many owned vehicles can be damaged by a single event such as a fire, an explosion, or a hailstorm. The total losses in such an event could far exceed the premium savings. However, if your organization has a large fleet spread over many states, you may want to look at self-insuring this exposure as well as collision.

12. Self-Insure Bodily Injury and Property Damage Liability

Self-insuring bodily injury and property damage liability is an alternative for large firms and may lead to substantial savings. It should be noted, however, that many states have financial responsibility laws requiring the organization to buy insurance. In those states, your company can file with regulatory authorities, usually the Department of Public Safety, to become a qualified self-insurer. To become a qualified self-insurer, you are required to meet certain minimum qualifications. If you are considering self-insurance of this exposure, allow adequate time for regulatory approval.

Given the catastrophic loss potential of auto liability, you should assume only low levels of loss (for example, the first $100,000 to $1 million). Excess insurance should be purchased above this level. Obviously, this alternative is only for large organizations, and statistical analysis of past loss experience can be helpful in determining the optimum retention level.

13. Obtain Schedule Credits, Dividends, and Deviations

So far, this chapter has discussed the development of *manual premium*, the premium determined solely by applying the rules and factors specified in the industry's rating manuals.

Once an insurance underwriter has determined the manual premiums for automobile liability and physical damage, the premiums can be further adjusted by applying schedule credits, deviations, or paying dividends. A discount or deviation can be as much as 25 percent. Moreover, insurance companies have the option of paying dividends on premiums that range from 10 to 15 percent. Subjective factors are often used in developing a credit or deviation and are noted in Figure 2.6.

Figure 2.6

Automobile Schedule Rating Factors

- Motor vehicle records (MVRs)
- Prior loss experience
- Age of vehicles
- Driver selection and training program
- Vehicle maintenance program
- Percent of young and old drivers to total number of drivers
- Weather conditions common to area
- Vehicles driven in urban versus rural areas
- Types of terrain traveled

You should review these factors, determine whether cost-effective improvements can be made to reduce premiums, and make sure that all positive factors are communicated to the underwriter. During a "buyer's market," insurance is readily available and insurance companies are competing for the consumer's premium dollar. In such times, schedule credits are fairly easy to obtain. When the market begins to tighten, a "seller's market" develops and buyers will see their schedule credits disappear; they may be subject to debits instead. While the application of schedule rating may fluctuate based on the existing market, many underwriters continue to use this rating approach in a logical fashion. Therefore, you should ascertain the credits or surcharges currently being applied and the basis for them. If the maximum 25 percent credit is not being applied, ask underwriters what you must do to obtain the maximum credit. Understanding this important rating factor can substantially reduce your long-term premium costs.

You should also be aware that in most states, each insurance company develops its own rates or loss costs and then applies schedule rating. It is important, then, to obtain the manual unit rates as well as to determine the percentage of deviation from them. This will provide a means of verifying that the correct rate is being applied when an automobile policy is being rated.

Finally, recognize that another area of potential cost savings lies in the differential between various insurers' multipliers. As was noted in Chapter 1, page 3, the multipliers, which take into account individual insurers' overhead and profit, will vary. Thus, insurers with the most efficient and cost-effective operations should have the lowest multipliers and, ultimately, the lowest premium rates.

14. Use Experience Rating

Experience rating is not mandatory for automobile insurance and is not frequently used. However, you should consider experience rating if you have a large fleet and good loss experience. If your organization has few losses, additional discounts may also result from a scheduled credit approach to rating your firm. In a soft market, credits of 35 to 50 percent (schedule and experience rating combined) off the manual rate are not uncommon. For extremely large risks, credits will be even larger. If the underwriter views past loss experience as unsatisfactory, experience rating will develop substantial surcharges. Often, this past bad experience can be mitigated by assuming deductibles. Although the experience rating is calculated using reduced premiums (or, premiums after deductible credits), the deductible is subtracted from losses. If the deductible eliminates a larger dollar amount of losses than the deductible credit reduces the premium used in the calculation, the net effect will be an even greater savings than just the deductible credit.

15. Use the Suspension of Insurance Endorsement

Liability and physical damage rates generally contemplate year-round use of a vehicle, but some vehicles may not be used year-round because of the seasonal nature of operations. For instance, an ice plant may store some vehicles during the winter. Another example might be a street contractor in the Northwest that uses its vehicles only during the warmer months. Other situations may involve slowdowns of a particular business or labor strikes that force equipment to be taken out of service.

If the automobiles are not being used, your firm can save money by suspending the insurance coverage on these vehicles while they are out of service if these periods exceed 30 days.

Once a piece of equipment has been out of service for more than 30 days, attempt to negotiate credits on the premium rates for that particular automobile for the period of time during which the automobile has been out of service. You may negotiate a direct return or be reimbursed through schedule credits.

The policy can be endorsed for this inactivity by means of the Suspension of Insurance Endorsement (CA 02 40, 07 97), to indicate that coverage has been suspended. Of course, if an accident does occur, no coverage is provided. As a result, you must take great care to prevent a loss by making sure the equipment is not used.

Automobiles on which coverage is suspended should be scheduled under the general liability policy as "mobile equipment." This will provide liability (not physical damage) coverage should someone somehow be injured by the vehicle.

In summary, if full rates are presently being paid for automobiles that are not used the entire year, credits may be negotiated to reflect the suspension of insurance.

16. Understand the "Stated Amount" Approach

Automobile physical damage coverage applies on an *actual cash value* basis, which applies depreciation factors to the original, new cost of the vehicle. The depreciation factor is determined by the age group classification for a given vehicle. Basically, as a vehicle gets older, the rates get lower. However, with respect to specified causes of loss coverage or comprehensive coverage, there is an alternative approach. The insured can request coverage on a *stated amount* basis. For vehicles with a long life, this approach might be desirable to, in effect, increase the depreciation amounts used in valuing the vehicle. For instance, if a truck's new cost is $80,000 and the actual cash value is based on a lower amount of depreciation than the insured thinks is appropriate, the insured might elect to use the stated amount basis. Under this arrangement, a higher depreciation factor can be used to reduce the insured value. The insurance rates will then be applied to lower stated value, resulting in a net lower premium.

A word of caution: you can collect no more than the lesser of the stated amount or the actual cash value in the event of a loss. This can cause a problem in times of severe inflation, when the replacement cost of the vehicle may be much higher. However, unless the entire vehicle is subject to a *total* loss, such as by theft, this should be of no great concern.

Usually, the savings produced by this approach are not enough to justify the effort to employ it if only three or four vehicles are involved. For large fleets of vehicles, however, this type of coverage may be appropriate. In summary, if vehicles are over 5 years old and have a substantially high new cost, the stated amount approach may save a significant amount of money.

17. Discontinue Medical Payments and Personal Injury Protection Coverage Where Possible

There are several types of automobile coverage that apply to exposures for which coverage is available elsewhere and/or present relatively low levels of potential financial loss.

Because of concern about injury to customers and employees, many businesses choose to buy medical payments coverage as well as personal injury protection (PIP) for their commercial vehicles (nonprivate passenger vehicles). This coverage pays the cost of medical care incurred by nonemployees as a result of an accident and is in addition to any claims paid to these persons under the bodily injury liability coverage.

In general, medical payments or PIP coverage is advisable for a family automobile. Commercial risks, though, are different. Losses that generally range from $2,500 to $5,000 in this category will be considered in arriving at rates and premiums in future policy periods. For that reason, a $2,000 loss paid under this coverage would generate a premium in later years that could approach $4,000 to $5,000. Since the limits are very low on this coverage and the exposures are not that great, it may be better to pay the losses if and when they occur rather than have the insurance company pay them and then increase the premiums later. In many cases, the payments will be made on behalf of nonemployees or customers. Depending on the circumstances, your firm may feel no responsibility for the injuries and elect not to pay the medical expenses. Self-insurance preserves the option with the insured. Employees will be covered under workers compensation or group medical insurance.

Therefore, it may be best not to insure this exposure. If someone riding in the owned vehicle has no workers compensation or hospitalization coverage, a very rare situation, then it is generally best for your company to pay the loss out of its own pocket. The company's payment would be well received and would definitely save premiums in the long run.

18. Discontinue Uninsured/Underinsured Motorists Coverage Where Possible

Uninsured/underinsured motorists coverage applies when the insured vehicle is involved with an uninsured/underinsured or hit-and-run motorist, and insurers are required to provide it under most state laws. Such coverage requires your firm to sue its own insurer as if its insurance company were the insurer for the other motorist.

There are, of course, drawbacks to this type of coverage. First, it is not much fun to sue your own insurer. While uninsured/underinsured motorists coverage may be good for family autos, it should usually not be purchased for commercial vehicles. Consider rejecting this coverage—and saving the related premium—if your state's law will allow you to do so. If desirable, savings in this area can be used to improve health and accident coverages to remove any negative ramifications from dropping this coverage. An exception to this point might be in those states that allow high limits of uninsured motorists coverage.

19. Think Twice about Rental Car Physical Damage Loss Waivers

When renting a vehicle, you are usually given an option to accept or decline the loss damage waiver (LDW). The loss damage waiver is not insurance, although people often equate it with the purchase of physical damage insurance from the rental company and without the usual deductible that accompanies most types of physical damage coverage. Instead, the LDW, subject to all the terms of the rental contract, is one of the optional broadening features of the contract that are available for an extra charge.

Rejection of the LDW means that you accept full responsibility for loss or damage to the rental vehicle, up to its full market value, plus towing and storage and loss of use. Acceptance (or purchase) of the LDW means that in exchange for the LDW per-day charge, the rental company will assume all loss or damage, subject to certain exceptions (e.g., driving the vehicle recklessly or while under the influence of alcohol). Since LDW is subject to all terms of the rental contract, violation of any of the contract's terms can negate the benefits of accepting the LDW. Unfortunately, daily LDW charges are usually quite high. If the charge is multiplied by 365 days, the equivalent annual "premium" runs into the thousands of dollars.

If your firm is willing to assume the risk of physical damage in its own fleet policy, you would do well to take the same approach for rental cars. Exceptions might be where the cost of the loss damage waiver could be passed back to a customer, as in a law firm or an accounting firm that is reimbursed for expenses, or where the total risks of loss would exceed some predetermined amount, such as $35,000.

Remember that a number of credit cards automatically provide some coverage, if the card is used to rent the automobile. Therefore, use of a company credit card that provides such protection is an effective method of handling this exposure at virtually no cost. It should be recognized, however, that such coverage applies as excess over any other available coverage.

Another lower cost alternative if you carry any physical damage coverage on your own autos is to ask your commercial auto insurer to cover physical damage to hired autos as well. In most states, this coverage is available for an additional premium. If you rent cars with any frequency, this premium will be much less than would be LDW charges.

20. Reject Accident and Health Coverages on Rental Cars

You should also reject accident and health insurance coverages. Such protection is provided by your firm's workers compensation and/or employee benefits program. All the additional rental coverages should usually be rejected by medium-sized and large businesses unless there is a specific reason to do otherwise. Small businesses that do not frequently rent vehicles should review the rental agreement and purchase the collision waiver if the deductible is greater than some prespecified amount (such as $500).

For further research and study

An extensive treatment of automobile liability exposures, coverages, and rating approaches can be found in *Commercial Auto Insurance*, published by IRMI. A more abbreviated IRMI publication on this topic is *Commercial Auto Insurance Guide*. Visit the Products and Services section of IRMI.com for more information.

The definitive source for rating automobile coverage is Insurance Services Office's *Commercial Lines Manual*. This publication contains the rules, classification codes, and rates not only for automobile insurance but also for commercial general liability and property insurance. Contact Insurance Services Office, Inc., 545 Washington Blvd., Jersey City, NJ 07310–1686; telephone 1–800–888–4ISO (1–800–888–4476); www.ISO.com.

3

COMMERCIAL GENERAL LIABILITY INSURANCE

THE COMMERCIAL GENERAL LIABILITY (CGL) policy protects the insured against lawsuits alleging bodily injury or property damage. In other words, the policy covers defense costs, awards, or settlements associated with lawsuits brought by third parties who are injured by the insured's premises, operations, products-completed operations, or independent contractors. The policy also automatically includes contractual liability insurance, meaning that it provides protection to other parties whom the insured agrees in a business contract to "hold harmless and indemnify." The CGL policy does not cover liability arising from aircraft, most watercraft, or automobiles. Separate policies must be purchased to cover these risks.

Personal and Advertising Injury Coverage

In addition to coverage for bodily injury and property damage liability, the policy also provides "personal injury and advertising injury" liability coverage. The personal injury portion of CGL insurance protects against suits brought by others alleging libel, slander, defamation of character, false arrest, disparagement of goods, and similar allegations.

The advertising injury coverage insures against disparagement of goods, slander, copyright infringement, and similar allegations that may arise in connection with the advertising activities of the organization. As a word of caution, however, this advertising liability coverage applies only to organizations advertising their own products; it does not provide errors and omissions coverage for advertising agencies, publishers, or broadcasters.

Medical Payments Coverage

A CGL policy also provides a type of "no fault" medical payments coverage. This coverage will reimburse the insured for medical bills paid on behalf of others who are injured on the insured's premises or by the insured's operations, subject to a $5,000 per person limit. Taking this approach to medical expenses is thought to reduce the likelihood that injured parties will bring a lawsuit.

Classifications and Rating

As in other lines of insurance, the *manual premium* for the CGL policy is determined by multiplying an appropriate rate by the number of exposure units. Therefore, the first step in

27

determining the premium is to calculate the appropriate rate. Begin by classifying your firm's operations. Depending on the procedure used in your state, the classification(s) dictates either a manual rate or a loss cost for your business. If it is the latter, the next step is to apply the particular insurer's "multiplier" to the loss cost to obtain the rate (see Chapter 1). The rate is then adjusted once more to reflect the policy limits that you are purchasing. Once the final rate is obtained, it is multiplied by an estimate of the appropriate exposure base for your business (usually payroll, sales, or square footage) to indicate the annual premium.

The source of the various classifications and the rates (or loss costs) for these classifications is the *Commercial Lines Manual (CLM)* published by the Insurance Services Office, Inc. (ISO). The *Manual* provides rules and rates/loss costs for all commercial lines including general liability, automobile liability, property, and professional liability insurance coverages in all 50 states.

Loss costs associated with a classification vary from state to state. An individual insurer may develop its own rates or loss costs or join with others by subscribing to those developed by ISO. Such insurers may modify these "bureau" loss costs or rates but will often use them as a starting point.

Finally, since basic company loss costs are based on limits of liability of only $25,000 each "occurrence" for bodily injury and property damage, $25,000 per person or organization for personal injury and advertising injury, and $50,000 general aggregate and products-completed operations aggregate limits, they must be adjusted for the higher limits of liability you will want to purchase. This is accomplished by multiplying the "basic limits rate" by an appropriate "increased limits factor," which is found in a table in the *Commercial Lines Manual.*

Mistakes that may lead to premium overcharges can be made in choosing classification codes and/or the amount of the exposure base to use in rating the policy; they can also be made in applying certain other rating rules, discussed in the following "Ways To Cut Costs."

Ways To Cut Costs

This chapter gives you 11 ways to cut general liability insurance costs.

21. Use Proper Classifications

The first step in rating a CGL policy is to determine the classification that *best* describes your business operations. The purpose of the classification system is to group insureds with similar operations together to facilitate a statistical analysis of losses so that loss costs can be determined for all insureds in that business class. As shown in Figure 3.1, there are four general categories of classification codes: (1) mercantile, (2) manufacturing, (3) buildings, and (4) contracting. In addition, there is a "miscellaneous" category that includes various types of codes that do not fit into the four primary classification groupings. Each individual classification is assigned a unique classification code number within the rating manuals published by ISO. Figure 3.2 gives some examples of these classification codes.

Figure 3.1

CGL Classification Summary

Industry Group	Numerical Sequence	Exposure Base
Mercantile	10000–19999	Gross Sales*
Manufacturing/Processing	50000–59999	Gross Sales*
Buildings/Premises	60000–69999	Area, Units, or Gross Sales*
Contracting/Servicing	90000–99999	Payroll*
Miscellaneous	40000–49999	Various

* These exposure bases usually apply on a per 1,000 basis.

The loss cost for a particular classification code within a particular state can be determined by looking up the classification code in the *Commercial Lines Manual* state rate pages. Rates/loss costs are then adjusted to reflect increases in policy limits and multiplied by the exposure base. Note that the exposure base is usually on a per 1,000 basis, meaning that the actual amount of sales, area, or payroll is divided by 1,000 before being multiplied by the rate.

Spend time with your agent or broker studying the classification code(s) used to rate your organization's CGL. Carefully consider the business operations and the extent to which they fit within the scope of the classification code. Look in particular for classification codes that carry lower rates that might be more appropriate for your organization's operations. In addition, more than one classification code may be applicable if the organization has multiple business operations. For example, a manufacturer that makes both powered and unpowered hand tools would rate its business with two classification codes: 59782, "tool manufacturing—hand type—not powered"; and 59783, "tool manufacturing—hand type—powered." The difference in the products and completed-operations rate for these two classification codes can be substantial, and it may be to the insured's benefit to separate the two types of products for rating purposes.

Figure 3.2

Commercial Lines Classification Codes Example

DESCRIPTION	Fire	CPP	Businessowners Policy			General Liability		Crime/Fidelity	Contents, Fire		Company Use Only
	Class Code	PMA	Class Code	Rate No.	Rate Group	Class Code	Premium Base	Class Code	Rate Group	Class Limit	
Building Material Dealers—											
secondhand material	(3)	M	52114	2	4	10256 (5)	s	4440	1	5,000	
other than secondhand material	(3)	M	52114	2	4	10255 (4)	s	4440	1	15,000	
Building Material Distributors	(3)	M		NA	NA	10257 (6)	s	4213	*		
Building Structure—raising or moving	(8)	(8)		NA	NA	91280 (9)	p	2330	1 (10)	5,000	
Buildings or Premises—bank and other financial institutions	0702	0	(1)	(1)	(1)	61223 (3) (4) (8)	a+	NA	(2)		
Buildings or Premises—bank or office—mercantile or manufacturing (lessor's risk only) —											
Not-for-Profit only	(5)	(5)	(6)		(6)	61216 (3) (7)	a+	5310	(5)		
Other than Not-for-Profit	(5)	(5)	(6)		(6)	61212 (3) (7)	a+	5310	(5)		
maintained by the insured—Not-for-Profit only	(5)	(5)	(6)		(6)	61218 (3)	a+	5310	(5)		
maintained by the insured—Other than Not-for-Profit	(5)	(5)	(6)		(6)	61217 (3)	a+	5310	(5)		
Buildings or Premises—office—											
Not-for-Profit only	0702	0	(1)	(1)	(1)	61227 NOC (3)	a+	NA	(2)		
Other than Not-for-Profit	0702	0	(1)	(1)	(1)	61226 NOC (3)	a+	NA	(2)		

Source: *Commercial Lines Manual,* Insurance Services Office, Inc., 1999.

22.   Use Lessor's Risk Only Classification

When an organization owns a building and leases a substantial amount of that building to other businesses, the organization's liability exposures arising from such premises are reduced because the tenants will maintain liability insurance for the portions of the building they are leasing. The owner should also insert a *hold harmless* clause into the lease agreement whereby the tenants hold the owner of the building harmless for liability arising from parts of the premises they lease as well as for liability arising from their operations. In conjunction with the hold harmless clause, the lease should require the tenants to purchase general liability insurance, including contractual liability coverage. Finally, if the owner is named as an additional insured on the tenant's CGL policy, this should further reduce the exposure to loss and ultimately lower the company's premium for this coverage.

Recognizing the reduced exposures associated with these actions, a substantial rate credit is available to insureds who occupy less than 90 percent of an owned building. The portion of the premises occupied by the insured is classified and rated according to the insured's business operations. The remainder of the premises falls under one of four classification codes.

Classification	Class Code
Buildings or Premises—bank or office—mercantile or manufacturing (lessor's risk only)—not-for-profit	61216
Buildings or Premises—bank or office—mercantile or manufacturing (lessor's risk only)—other than not-for-profit	61212
Buildings or Premises—bank or office—mercantile or manufacturing—maintained by the insured (lessor's risk only)—not-for-profit	61218
Buildings or Premises—bank or office-mercantile or manufacturing—maintained by the insured (lessor's risk only)—other than not-for-profit	61217

These classifications carry much lower loss costs or rates than the regular "buildings or premises" codes. For example, the loss costs for code 61212 in Texas at the time of this writing is $23.20, versus loss costs of $121.00 per 1,000 square feet for code 61226, "buildings or premises—bank or office—other than not-for-profit." As you can see, substantial premium savings can be obtained through the use of this rating rule.

23.   Delete Nonapplicable Exposures

A number of items are sometimes mistakenly included in the exposure base reported to insurers, which should not be included when computing a premium for CGL coverage.

Truck Drivers and Pilots

Contractors and service companies with payroll as their exposure base should not include the *payroll* of drivers and their helpers whose primary duties are to work in or on automobiles or trucks. The liability exposure of these persons is connected with driving, which is covered by the automobile policy rather than the general liability policy (which excludes liability arising from owned autos). These payrolls, then, should not be included in the exposure base for the general liability policy. For the same reason, wages paid to aircraft pilots and copilots whose principal duties involve work on or in connection with aircraft should not be included in the payroll used as an exposure base for general liability insurance.

Clerical Office Employees

Contractors and other firms providing services for which *payroll* is used as the exposure base should not include the payroll of clerical office employees. This rule applies only if these employees are physically separated from other work areas of the insured and if their duties are strictly clerical in nature.

Overtime Surcharges

Extra pay for overtime is also not included in the payroll of contractors and other service providers that use *payroll* as an exposure base. In other words, the extra 50 percent of the hourly wage paid to an employee who works overtime should not be included in the payroll exposure base. (This rule does not apply to stevedores.) The insured must maintain records to indicate overtime pay separately by employee and in summary by classification code. For many insureds, this additional record-keeping requirement will be more than justified by the premium dollars saved.

Sales/Excise Taxes

For those organizations rated using a gross sales exposure base, sales and excise taxes paid to governmental entities should not be included in the exposure base. Likewise, finance charges for items sold on an installment basis should also not be included in the exposure base.

24. Apply the Executive Officer Payroll Limitation

For contractors and other service organizations whose exposure base is *payroll,* the payroll of executive officers, individual owners, and partners is included in the exposure base. However, most states limit the amount of payroll for each of these individuals. For example, at the time of this writing, Kentucky includes only the first $27,000 of annual individual payroll for each executive officer. In Alabama, only the first $18,300 is included. Make certain only the limited payroll amounts for executive officers are included instead of the entire amount of each officer's annual salary. Your insurance agent or broker should be able to

Figure 3.3

Workers Compensation and Commercial General Liability Executive Officers, Partners, and Sole Proprietors Payroll Limitations as of July 2002

| State | Executive Officers Weekly Payroll Limit for WC or Annually if so indicated | | Executive Officers Annual Payroll Limit for CGL or Weekly if so indicated | | Partners and Sole Proprietors for WC and CGL | | | |
| | | | | | Can Partners Be Covered for WC? | Can Sole Proprietors Be Covered for WC? | Annual Remuneration Included* | |
	Min.	Max.	Min.	Max.			WC	CGL
AL	250	2,100	18,300		Yes	Yes	41,200	18,300
AK	300	1,300	36,400		Yes	Yes	22,100	36,400
AZ*	286	2,300	26,400		Yes	Yes	600/ 2,100 mo.	26,400
AR	200	1,800	24,000		Yes	Yes	25,100	24,000
CA	26,000 yr.	74,100 yr.	33,600		Yes	Yes	Same As Exec. Off.	33,600
CO	41,100		31,500		Yes	Yes	41,100	31,500
CT	342	500	100 wk.	300 wk.	Yes	Yes	46,300	10,400
DE*	300	1,500	25,300		Yes	Yes	Same As Exec. Off.	25,300
DC	300	2,600	30,000		No	No	N/A	30,000
FL	250 (125–Construction)	1,600	16,700		Yes	Yes	35,200	16,700
GA	300	2,200	24,400		Yes	Yes	43,400	24,400
HI	300	2,100	100 wk.	1,000 wk.	Yes	Yes	31,300	15,600
ID	300	2,000	26,300		Yes	Yes	13,000	26,300
IL	300	2,500	33,500		Yes	Yes	42,000	33,500
IN	294	2,400	27,300		Yes	Yes	40,100	27,300
IA	273	2,200	28,800		Yes	Yes	28,800	28,800
KS	300	2,200	30,300		Yes	Yes	31,800	13,300
KY*	269	2,200	27,000		Yes	Yes	37,500	27,000
LA*	100	1,100	15,600		Yes	Yes	27,300	15,600
ME	263	2,100	22,600		Yes	Yes	27,400	22,600
MD	300	2,500	28,100		Yes	Yes	42,200	28,100
MA*	200	1,000	28,600		No	No	N/A	28,600
MI	357	1,400	29,700		Yes	No	15,600	29,700

continued

Figure 3.3 (cont.)

Workers Compensation and Commercial General Liability Executive Officers, Partners, and Sole Proprietors Payroll Limitations as of July 2002 (cont.)

State	Executive Officers Weekly Payroll Limit for WC or Annually if so indicated		Executive Officers Annual Payroll Limit for CGL or Weekly if so indicated		Partners and Sole Proprietors for WC and CGL			
	Min.	Max.	Min.	Max.	Can Partners Be Covered for WC?	Can Sole Proprietors Be Covered for WC?	Annual Remuneration Included*	
							WC	CGL
MN*	180 204 – Spouse, parent, or child	1,285 - No maximum for spouse, parent, or child	30,800		Yes	Yes	Same as Exec. Officers	30,800
MS	100	1,600	100 wk.	500 wk.	Yes	Yes	15,900	10,400
MO	300	500	28,400		Yes	Yes	15,600	28,400
MT*	200	700	18,800		Yes	Yes	10,800–34,710	15,700
NE	262	2,100	27,400		Yes	Yes	27,300	27,400
NV*	6,000 year 500 per month noncompensated	36,000 year 6,000 year—noncompensated	29,300		Yes	Yes	300—deemed wage per month 1,800—elective wage per month 500—as subcontractor, deemed wage per month	29,300
NH	301—Corporation 155—Unincorporated Association	2,500—Corporation 1,200—Unincorporated Association	26,800		Yes	Yes	46,500	26,800
NJ*	400	1,610	32,300		Yes	Yes	N/A	32,300
NM	300	2,000	27,900		Yes	Yes	26,000	27,900
NY*	425—Corporation 200—Not-for-profit Unincorporated Association	1,275 3,375—non-executive officers	27,500		Yes	Yes	Same as Exec. Officers	27,500
NC	281	1,100	24,800		Yes	Yes	29,500	24,800
ND	Monopolistic		24,200		N/A	N/A	N/A	24,200
OH	Monopolistic		36,900		N/A	N/A	N/A	36,900
OK	250	1,900	10,400	38,100	Yes	Yes	24,600	19,200
OR*	300	2,300	31,100		Yes	Yes	20,800	31,100
PA*	300	1,550	40 wk.	200 wk.	No	No	N/A	5,200
RI	231	1,800	26,700		No	No	N/A	26,700
SC*	250	1,900	24,100		Yes	Yes	24,500	24,100

continued

Figure 3.3 (cont.)

Workers Compensation and Commercial General Liability Executive Officers, Partners, and Sole Proprietors Payroll Limitations as of July 2002 (cont.)

State	Executive Officers Weekly Payroll Limit for WC or Annually if so indicated		Executive Officers Annual Payroll Limit for CGL or Weekly if so indicated		Partners and Sole Proprietors for WC and CGL			
					Can Partners Be Covered for WC?	Can Sole Proprietors Be Covered for WC?	Annual Remuneration Included*	
	Min.	Max.	Min.	Max.			WC	CGL
SD*	200	1,800	25,800		Yes	Yes	33,800	25,800
TN	300	2,200	100 wk.	500 wk.	Yes	Yes	42,200	13,300
TX*	150	1,200	31,900		Yes	Yes	31,200	31,900
UT*	273	2,200	30,700		Yes	Yes	2,400 mo.	30,700
VT	260	2,100	100 wk.	300 wk.	Yes	Yes	27,400	10,400
VA	150	500	26,300		Yes	Yes	15,700	26,300
WA*	Monopolistic		17,800		N/A	N/A	N/A	17,800
WV	Monopolistic		31,800		N/A	N/A	N/A	31,800
WI*	175	873	31,600		Yes	Yes	30,300	31,600
WY	EL Cov. Only 164 1,300		19,500		No	No	EL Only 17,400	16,200
PR	Monopolistic		28,000		N/A	N/A	N/A	28,000

NOTES TO CHART

All States—Board, lodging, and tips are included for WC and CGL only if an amount is included in payroll records of insured.

Arizona—See State Rate pages for WC exceptions.

Delaware—Overtime is not deducted.

Kentucky—Pay or allowance for hand tools is excluded for WC.

Louisiana—Unanticipated bonus is excluded for WC. Employee $300/weekly payroll limitation: CGL (old program only)

Massachusetts—CGL—See Massachusetts State Rate pages for exceptions.

Minnesota—Pay for sickness, holiday, and vacation is excluded for WC. Applicable in assigned risk plan only.

Montana—See State Rate pages for WC exceptions.

Nevada—Effective 7–1–99. Payroll limitation program extended until further notice for GL.

New Jersey—See State Rate pages for WC exceptions.

New York—In accordance with Manual Rule V–F, for employees other than executive officers whose classification notes indicate a payroll limitation, the maximum weekly remuneration is $2,775.

Oregon—Pay for vacation, unanticipated bonus, and profit sharing are excluded for WC.

Pennsylvania—CGL—See Pennsylvania State Rate pages for exceptions. Overtime is not deducted.

South Carolina—Employee $300/weekly payroll limitation: CGL (old program only).

South Dakota—Pay for sickness, holiday, and vacation is excluded for WC.

Texas—See State Rate pages for WC exceptions.

Utah—Overtime is not deducted.

Washington—Employee $600/weekly payroll limitation: CGL.

Wisconsin—See State Rate pages for WC exceptions.

specify the payroll limitation in the state(s) where operations are conducted. The specific payroll limitations that currently apply in each of the 50 states appear in Figure 3.3.

25.   Look Twice at Intercompany Sales

The CGL policy will cover a suit against one insured brought by another insured. For this reason, the money paid to one company by a sister company for goods or products is included in the *gross sales* exposure base of insureds in the manufacturing, processing, or mercantile businesses. This coverage for intercompany suits can, however, be excluded by endorsement, specifically by attaching the Intercompany Products Exclusionary Endorsement (CG 21 41). When this is done, intercompany sales should be deleted from the applicable exposure base.

Determine what dollar volume of intercompany sales is being included in the general liability exposure base. The ultimate effect on premium can then be calculated by multiplying the applicable rate times the intercompany sales amount divided by 1,000. The exposure to intercompany suits and the need for general liability insurance coverage by one organization being sued by another should then be analyzed. Usually, it is best not to exclude such coverage. Nevertheless, some organizations with subsidiaries will not feel the need to cover the liability suits brought by one subsidiary against the other subsidiary and will be willing to exclude coverage in return for a lower premium expenditure.

26.   Obtain Schedule Credit/Dividends

Schedule rating allows the underwriter to modify filed loss costs/manual rates either upward (debits) or downward (credits) to reflect the individual risk characteristics of the insured. The characteristics generally given consideration for general liability insurance include the following.

- Care and condition of premises
- Geographic location
- Type of equipment used in operations, including maintenance
- Product quality control programs
- Employee selection, training, supervision, experience

In a few states, underwriters are not permitted to use schedule credits/debits. Underwriters in these states often have the option of paying dividends to general liability insurance policyholders. Although it is to the insured's advantage to be eligible to receive dividends, it is important to remember that they cannot be guaranteed. Do not count on receiving a dividend until it has actually been paid.

27.   Use Deductibles

As with other lines of insurance, assuming a deductible can significantly reduce the premium charged for coverage. Commercial general liability insurance can be written subject to a bodily injury liability deductible, a property damage liability deductible, or a combined bodily injury and property damage deductible. These deductibles can range in amount from $250 into the thousands of dollars. The deductibles may be written on either a *per claim* or *per occurrence* basis, with the per claim basis deductible providing the largest reduction of premium. However, keep in mind that a single accident can lead to the imposition of several per claim deductibles, whereas only one per occurrence deductible would apply. When evaluating deductibles, always compare an estimate of the additional amount that will be paid in deductibles to the premium savings.

28. Negotiate Premium Credits for Coverage Limitations

Some insurance coverages currently included in the commercial general liability policy that in previous years had to be purchased for additional premiums can now be deleted from the policy by exclusionary endorsements. The coverages that can be deleted from the policy by exclusionary endorsements include blanket contractual liability; personal injury liability; advertising injury liability; medical payments coverage; fire legal liability; "explosion, collapse, and underground property damage"; and employees as insureds. In a tight insurance marketplace, some underwriters may require the deletion of one or more of these coverages. While such coverage restrictions should be resisted, a fallback position might be to negotiate for reduced rates in recognition of the restricted coverage.

The insurance industry has not established any guideline rate credits to be applied when these coverage restrictions are imposed, so that these premium reductions are negotiable.

29. Use Experience Rating

Experience rating of CGL insurance is optional in all states and is not frequently used. It involves the use of a formula that compares the insured's past loss experience to that of other insureds with similar operations to calculate an experience modifier. The experience modifier is then applied to decrease or increase the manual premium. If, based on your company's loss history, an experience rating plan would lower premiums, you should insist on it.

Experience rating tends to be more sensitive to loss frequency than to loss severity. Therefore, an insured with 10 $5,000 losses would be penalized more than an insured with one $50,000 loss. So if your firm has experienced a low frequency of losses, you may be able to reduce general liability insurance costs by encouraging the underwriter to experience rate the premium.

30. Drop Medical Payments Coverage

One of the "fringe" coverages automatically provided by the commercial general liability policy is *medical payments coverage* and you should consider having it deleted. This coverage reimburses the insured for money spent for first aid or other medical treatment of third parties injured on an insured's premises. In effect, it is "goodwill" insurance. Any losses paid by the medical payments coverage will affect your loss experience. Of course, premiums are charged for this coverage. Deleting this coverage from the policy should result in reduced premiums and will remove some claims from your firm's loss experience.

While accidents should be reported to the insurer to preserve your protection if a liability claim is filed against your organization, you can decide to pay these medical expenses to injured individuals on a case-by-case basis when the coverage is not purchased. In many situations, those persons should be paid (without, of course, admitting liability) to preserve a customer relationship and/or reduce the customer's incentive to make a liability claim.

31. Obtain Insurance Certificates from Contractors

The CGL policy automatically covers suits brought against the insured arising from the operations of its independent contractors. As an example, assume you hire a service to maintain the grounds around your office building. The service company injures a pedestrian while mowing the lawn and that pedestrian sues both your independent contractor and your company. Your CGL policy will cover your business for this claim. This is called *independent contractor's coverage.*

A fairly low rate applies to this coverage, recognizing a reduced exposure because of the liability insurance carried by the contractors. However, the low rate applies only if the insured obtains proof that its contractors are carrying "adequate insurance." This is done by obtaining and keeping on file certificates of insurance showing that they have liability insurance. If certificates are not obtained, a much higher rate can be charged by the insurer when the annual audit is performed. To avoid this extra premium charge, all contractors and subcontractors should be required to purchase liability (and workers compensation) insurance and provide certificates of insurance showing such coverage is in place. Figure 3.4 provides a list of applicable Subcontracted Work Codes under CGL policies.

Other than immediately avoiding the additional premium charged by the insurer, requiring liability insurance from independent contractors and including a hold harmless clause in the contract will help insulate your organization's insurance from paying losses the contractors cause. This preserves your liability limits, which can be very important when there is a major disaster and everyone involved has potential liabilities. It also keeps claims that could cause future premium increases out of your loss experience. At the minimum, require contractors to purchase commercial general liability insurance, including coverage for personal injury, bodily injury, property damage, completed operations, and contractual liability subject to a specified minimum limit. The amount to set as a minimum limit will depend on the work to be performed by the contractor. There may also be additional coverages that should be requested. Your agent or broker should assist in determining appropriate insurance requirements to use in contracts.

Figure 3.4

CGL Subcontracted Work Codes

Description	General Liability Class Code
Contractors—subcontracted work—in connection with construction, reconstruction, repair or erection of buildings	91585 NOC[1]
Contractors—subcontracted work—in connection with oil and gas field construction, reconstruction or repair	91586[1,2]
Contractors—subcontracted work—in connection with pipeline (other than oil or gas), or communication or power line construction, reconstruction or repair	91587[1]
Contractors—subcontracted work—in connection with street or highway construction, or repair, not elevated	91589[1]

[1]This classification applies to that portion of the operations performed by adequately insured subcontractors of the insured. Operations performed by subcontractors without adequate insurance shall be classified and rated under the specific classification description for each operation.

Determination of the adequacy of insurance shall be made in accordance with criteria established by the company prior to policy inception.

[2]This classification includes oil or gas pipeline construction, reconstruction, or repair.

Source: *Commercial Lines Manual,* Insurance Services Office, Inc., 1999.

For further research and study

For more information concerning general liability coverage provisions and rating explanations, refer to *Commercial Liability Insurance,* a three-volume reference manual published by IRMI. A less extensive IRMI publication on this topic is *CGL and Umbrella Insurance Guide.*

The definitive source concerning rating CGL coverage is ISO's *Commercial Lines Manual.* This publication contains the rules, classification codes, and rates not only for CGL insurance, but also for automobile and property insurance, as well. Contact Insurance Services Office, Inc., 545 Washington Blvd., Jersey City, NJ 07310–1686; telephone 1–800–888–4ISO (1–800–888–4476).

A handy means of tracking down CGL codes is IRMI's *Classification Cross-Reference.* The book is especially useful if you do not wish to obtain and maintain classification rating manuals for workers compensation and CGL codes and it can assist you in accurately and inexpensively classifying CGL risks.

A detailed analysis of issues relating to additional insureds can be found in *The Additional Insured Book. Contractual Risk Transfer* is a reference manual that guides you through the process of transferring risk in contracts and even provides boilerplate contract language. These are also published by IRMI.

The IRMI Web site, www.IRMI.com, also contains many articles on CGL insurance. Access is free.

UMBRELLA LIABILITY INSURANCE

AFTER WORLD WAR II, Lloyd's of London developed a special policy for business organizations with ocean-related (wet marine or blue water marine) liability risks. These policies were referred to as "bumbershoots" and provided substantially higher policy limits over the limits normally provided by primary markets. In addition, these policies offered substantially broader coverage.

In the late 1950s, Lloyd's and American insurance companies began offering specific excess policies for land-related liability risks. The term *umbrella* became popular to differentiate these policies from the marine-related policies. Again, these policies were often much broader than the primary policies written by traditional insurance companies.

All businesses should purchase additional liability limits in an umbrella policy. Because it covers catastrophic claims—those that could shut down the company—this is probably the most important policy your company buys.

Coverage

Figure 4.1 illustrates the various functions of an umbrella policy. The umbrella provides excess coverage over the limits of the underlying, or primary, policies. The applicable primary coverages generally include the commercial general liability (CGL) policies, the liability coverage of the business auto policy, and the employers liability coverage of the workers compensation policy. Sometimes an umbrella can be arranged to provide excess coverage over professional liability insurance as well. In those areas where the umbrella provides broader coverage, coverage would drop down to a self-insured retention of usually $10,000 or $25,000. In other words, the insured would be required to pay the first $10,000 or $25,000 and then the umbrella would pay amounts in excess of this self-insured retention.

The application of the umbrella policy is fairly simple. Assume that the liability limit of an insured's auto policy is $1 million, and the umbrella provides a $3 million limit. An automobile loss occurs that involves an ultimate claim of $2 million. The auto policy would exhaust its per accident limit by paying $1 million and then the umbrella would pay the $1 million of loss that exceeds the first $1 million. But if a loss occurred that was not covered by a primary liability policy, the insured would be responsible for the first $25,000 (a self-insured retention) and the umbrella policy would pay the next $975,000.

The umbrella policy became very popular in the 1960s; by 1975, virtually every business organization of any size carried an umbrella of at least $1 million. As a result, an entirely new specialty market developed to meet the demand for these policies. Unlike the standard commercial general liability, business auto, and workers compensation policies, however, there is no standard umbrella form. In fact, International Risk Management Institute, Inc., has identified more than 180 types of variations in the wording of umbrella forms

Figure 4.1

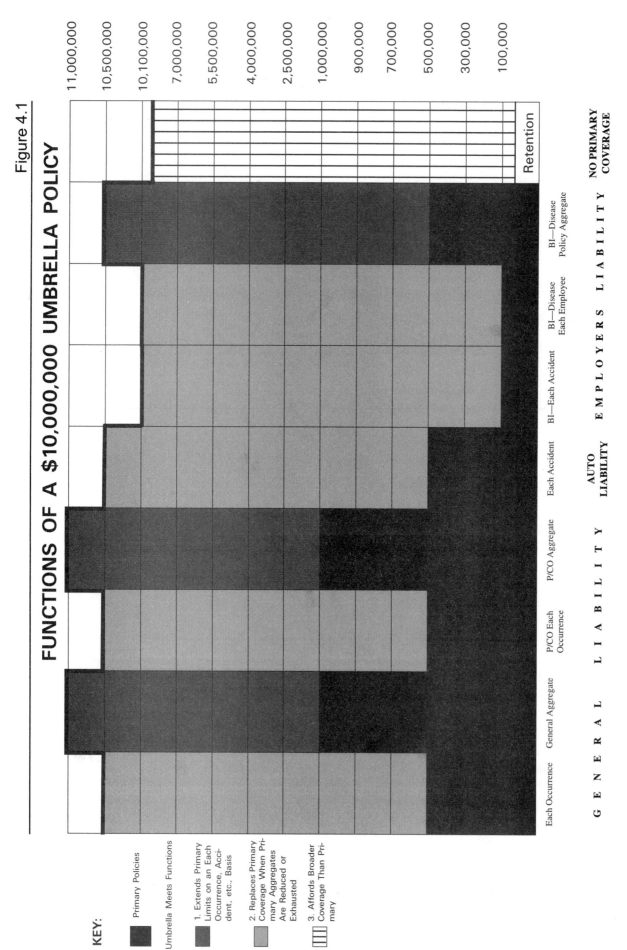

FUNCTIONS OF A $10,000,000 UMBRELLA POLICY

KEY:

Primary Policies

Umbrella Meets Functions

1. Extends Primary Limits on an Each Occurrence, Accident, etc., Basis

2. Replaces Primary Coverage When Primary Aggregates Are Reduced or Exhausted

3. Affords Broader Coverage Than Primary

Source: Reprinted from *Commercial Liability Insurance*, published by International Risk Management Institute, Inc., Copyright © 1986.

used in the current marketplace. Therefore, these forms must be carefully reviewed and compared when they are purchased.

In summary, the primary function of umbrella policies is to provide high limits of liability above general, auto, and employers liability insurance for catastrophic losses. They also usually "drop down" to become first-dollar insurance if the aggregate limits of these primary policies are exhausted because of loss frequency.

Ways To Cut Costs

This chapter presents seven ways to cut umbrella liability costs.

32. Consider Alternative Primary Limits and Obtain Quotes for Buffer Layers

As the insurance market progresses through its cycles, the umbrella and primary insurance markets develop ever-changing attitudes to the *intermediate risk layer*, which might be defined as that layer between $300,000 and $1 million. For instance, during a buyer's market, when pricing is soft, umbrella insurers will normally develop an aggressive pricing posture for this risk layer as compared to the primary markets. As a result, a general rule is that umbrella insurers will be more competitive in this risk layer than the standard, well-known primary insurers.

Figure 4.2

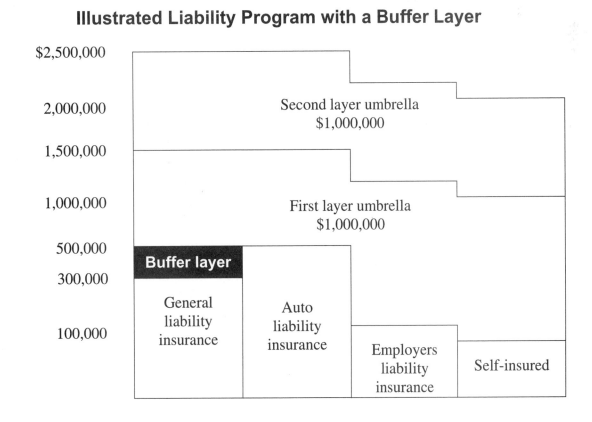

Illustrated Liability Program with a Buffer Layer

On the other hand, as the market evolves into a tight, seller's market, umbrella insurers will pull back and provide coverage only in excess of higher underlying limits. While some umbrella insurers may agree to provide the intermediate layer, the pricing will normally be substantially higher than primary insurers charge for higher limits. At the same time, the primary insurers normally pursue a more stable pricing approach and their pricing will be much more competitive than the umbrella markets.

Therefore, the preferred approach is to obtain quotes for alternative primary limits from the primary insurer, as well as for varying attachment points from umbrella insurers, to see which market segment will be more competitive in the intermediate risk layer.

In summary, primary insurers will be more competitive in an intermediate risk layer during tight markets while umbrella insurers will be more competitive during soft markets.

The intermediate risk layer is often described as a buffer layer. For a brief period during the transitional periods of the market, it often pays to obtain quotes for this buffer layer from a third market. Figure 4.2 shows the appearance of such an insurance program.

When neither primary nor umbrella insurers want to be involved in the buffer layer and, as a result, both are charging substantially higher premiums, it may be better to determine the limits and attachment points at which both will become most comfortable and competitive. Since the umbrella insurer will want to attach at a higher level and the primary insurer will want to provide lower limits, a third market must be used to provide the buffer layer. For example, a buffer layer might be used to fill the gap between $500,000 and $1 million. Usually, the premiums for this buffer layer will border on being exorbitant. However, the premium saved by removing pressure from both the primary and umbrella insurers may far exceed the additional cost of the buffer layer.

Again, depending on the volatility of the market, the buffer window may be open for only 3 to 6 months during a transitional period of the marketplace.

33. Obtain Competitive Pricing

To say that the umbrella market is volatile is a gross understatement. Umbrella markets come and go almost as quickly as other markets change their pricing philosophy. In addition, markets' attitudes for certain risk categories, such as contractors, oil risks, and manufacturers, will change as underwriters move from one company to another. Therefore, it is extremely important that all the potential markets for your risk be contacted.

However, extreme care should be taken in approaching the marketplace. It is usually preferable to use one insurance agent to contact all of the specialty markets since these markets work on a "brokerage" basis and will work with any financially viable insurance agent or broker. On the other hand, no one agent represents all the primary companies that will write umbrellas only over their own primary policies. Therefore, it may be necessary to do some market research to determine which primary companies are competitive in your geographical area and type of business and to contact one or two other agents who have access to these markets and who are generally regarded as profitable and desirable agents by those markets. At that point, the various markets should be allocated between these agents, to avoid having more than one agent approach the same insurer.

At the same time, loyalty usually pays off in the insurance business. Therefore, if your umbrella insurer is still actively seeking umbrella business, special emphasis should be placed on approaching that particular market.

34. Submit Well-Prepared Specifications

Bank loan officers and insurance company underwriters are amazingly similar. Since most organizations deal directly with banks, they are more familiar with making presentations to banks. For instance, two organizations approach a bank for a line of credit. One delivers a very polished presentation concerning its financial position, its business opportunities, and its risks. It will probably receive better terms than the other business organization, which walks in with a handwritten yellow sheet of paper, intending to simply promise to pay back the money at some indefinite point in the future.

The careful approach of the former should be taken with insurance underwriters. Approaching the insurer market with well-prepared insurance specifications that outline the operations and risks of your organization is best. If the premiums are large enough, consider having your chief financial officer or president make a personal presentation to the underwriters who are most likely to offer the best proposal. This personal approach can save thousands of premium dollars and obtain important coverages.

While you may be capable of preparing the submission, it is usually prepared by insurance agents or brokers. Either way, you should demand an opportunity to review the submission before it is given to underwriters. This puts pressure on your agent or broker to do a superior job. Be sure to verify the accuracy of the data provided and make suggestions to improve it. Time spent in this area pays great dividends.

35. Determine the Premium Basis

Umbrella premiums are generally determined by applying a percentage to the premiums charged by the primary insurer for the underlying limits. During a tight insurance market, umbrella underwriters often use manual premiums before any discounts apply to their rating percentages to develop the umbrella premium. Since these umbrella underwriters may not be entirely familiar with your business operations, erroneous manual premiums may be developed through the use of improper classifications. Therefore, it is usually desirable to develop the estimated manual premiums based on correct rating classifications and provide them to underwriters.

Most of the time, umbrella underwriters apply their rating percentages to the actual premium to be charged by the auto and general liability insurers. For instance, in a soft market the first $1 million of umbrella coverage will range between 9 and 12 percent of the primary premium, but during a tighter market, the percentage will range from 17.5 to 27.5 percent. At the same time, the premiums charged by the primary insurer will increase or decrease based on the market. This results in great volatility in umbrella premiums.

Generally, the $4 million layer above $1 million will cost approximately 50 to 60 percent of the first $1 million while $5 million excess of $5 million will be 40 to 60 percent of the premium paid for the $4 million excess of the $1 million underlying umbrella limit.

Therefore, it is critical to negotiate the very best price possible for the auto and general liability coverage. Keep in mind that while cost reduction tools—such as deductibles—also pose a degree of extra risk, their use also saves umbrella premiums.

In a soft, buyer's insurance market, primary liability *and* umbrella liability premiums can often be reduced by purchasing lower primary limits ($750,000 instead of $1 million, for example). The primary insurers charge less because they are providing lower limits. The umbrella insurer should charge more, because of the lower attachment point, but actually charges less when the umbrella premium is determined by applying a flat percentage to the primary premiums. This approach does not work in a tight market because umbrella insurers refuse to drop down over lower primary limits. Based on the above percentages, for every dollar saved in the general liability/auto liability area, another 25 to 35 cents may be saved, assuming a $10 million umbrella is purchased.

36. Select Reasonable Umbrella Limits

It is surprising how few umbrella claims are actually paid. Those that are paid normally involve large businesses. However, when suits are filed, the damages requested far exceed actual damages. So without higher limits the insured will become fearful of a possible settlement over its limits while financial institutions providing credit may become concerned and may begin reducing available credit.

Therein lies a very difficult question. What limits of coverage should your organization carry? You cannot expect your insurance agent to give you a concrete answer. Agents have their own errors and omissions liability exposure to worry about. They may think that if they recommend that you drop your limits from $5 million to $3 million, the next day one of your employees may be involved in an automobile accident with a carload of highly paid surgeons on the way to a medical convention. Agents have a tendency to play it safe and recommend higher limits. As usual, the buck stops with the president of your organization.

Figure 4.3

Rules of Thumb for Umbrella Liability Coverage Limits
(In Thousands)*

Sales	Limits
Under 2,000	1,000
2–5,000	2,000
5–10,000	3,000
10–15,000	4,000
15–25,000	5,000
25–50,000	10,000
50–100,000	15,000
100–250,000	20–25,000
250–500,000	25–50,000
500,000–1,000,000	50–100,000
Over 1,000,000	Subject to availability

*Many insurance professionals believe $5 million is the minimum amount any business should purchase.

Figure 4.3 is a sample of limits suggested by some insurance professionals. Note its recommendation that all organizations purchase at least a $1 million umbrella over the primary policies. Many insurance professionals think that $5 million should be the absolute minimum for any organization. Obviously, the nature of operations must be taken into consideration. For instance, a petrochemical plant operating close to a populated area needs higher limits than a small manufacturer of relatively safe products located in a rural town.

In some cases, customers will dictate the limits required. Sometimes these required limits will be excessive, reflecting a soft insurance market. If so, simply asking the customer to reduce the requirements in view of the current market conditions may result in a desired reduction, thereby making the organization more competitive and saving the customer unnecessary costs.

In any event, reducing limits can be a gut-wrenching decision, and it is preferable to cut coverages for noncatastrophic exposures. However, reducing limits is a tool sometimes used for containing umbrella costs during tight markets.

37. Provide for Automatic Extensions

During soft markets, plenty of umbrella capacity can be found at extremely low pricing. Just about the time that the average purchaser of insurance comes to expect this approach, the market changes and capacity dries up while prices go through the roof. This becomes very frustrating to the average buyer of insurance, who often becomes hostile in the process.

In soft markets, insurers cut back on personnel to contain costs. When the market turns, most insureds and agents begin contacting more insurers with greater frequency. This, in turn, overloads the system that underwriters have maintained in producing quotations and, as a result, quotations—particularly from the better insurers—may not be received by the agents and their customers until a week before renewal. In some cases, it may only be the day before renewal. Usually, the closer to expiration that the insured receives a quote, the worse it will be. Therefore, you should press your agent/broker to provide quotes earlier. With all the best intentions and efforts, however, this may not happen.

Many insureds will negotiate an agreement to provide automatic extensions during the competitive phase of the market. For instance, the existing insurance company agrees ahead of time that if it does not provide a renewal quote within 30 days of expiration, it will automatically extend the existing policy for 30 or 60 days beyond the expiration date at the same terms, conditions, and cost. Therefore, if a shocking quote is received a week or a day before renewal, the buyer has time to reenter the market and try to find a better quotation.

This same approach is desirable for other major coverages such as general and auto liability policies. Again, this agreement will be available only in a buyer's market, but it will help avoid surprises and the need to make last-minute decisions regarding the first renewal that takes place after the market tightens.

38. Use Care with Adjustable Rate Policies

Some underwriters will quote premiums that are "flat." These nonadjustable premiums apply whether the business grows or decreases in size. In other words, the premium is not inflation-

or volume-sensitive. If a new company is formed or acquired, however, a pro rata charge may be made. In softer markets, flat premiums are usually used as a competitive tool, especially if the economy is in an upswing that will result in a greater volume of business for the insured. Generally, then, during soft markets it is more desirable to seek flat premiums based on conservative estimates of business volume.

On the other hand, during a tight market, underwriters will favor adjustable rate policies that are based on rates per $100 of payroll, receipts, mileage, or, possibly, hours worked. If the company is growing, these policies can result in some very undesirable surprises at the end of the policy term when the insurance company asks for a substantial additional premium after auditing the insured's books. Alternatively, adjustable rate umbrella policies are usually subject to a minimum premium, which allows the insurer to avoid returning significant amounts of premium if the business contracts.

Generally, the larger the business organization, the lower the composite rate per unit. Perhaps the best approach is to supply an optimistic estimate of the business volume, which should result in a lower rate per unit. Likewise, a high minimum premium based on the higher estimated volume should be avoided. Preferably, the minimum premium should be 50 to 75 percent of the premium that would be incurred at the estimated business volume.

The unit to which the rate will be applied can be very important. For instance, in times of inflationary pressures, it is desirable to avoid the use of receipts or payroll. The more desirable approaches are hours worked for contractors, mileage for trucking companies, number of employees for service firms, or manufactured units for manufacturers. A similar approach might be taken with the underlying auto and general liability policies, as well.

For further research and study

For in-depth analyses of most available umbrella policy forms, as well as a thorough discussion of umbrella policy coverage, see *Commercial Liability Insurance,* Volume II, a reference manual published by IRMI.

A less extensive IRMI publication on this topic is *CGL and Umbrella Insurance Guide.* Visit the Products and Services section of IRMI.com for more information on these publications.

5 WORKERS COMPENSATION

AT THE BEGINNING OF THIS CENTURY, the United States was emerging as an industrialized nation while society was developing a social conscience. In those days, employees who were injured on the job had to sue their employer under common law to obtain benefits. Employers had basic common law defenses that were very difficult to overcome in court. Since average employees had very little, if any, savings, it was virtually impossible for them to hire an attorney. As a result, injured employees and their families often ended up in the poorhouse.

The Workers Compensation System

Starting in 1911 with Wisconsin, each state began to pass workers compensation statutes that amounted to a trade-off between the employer and the employee. Under these statutes, the employers agreed to give up their common law defenses and, in return, enjoyed a limitation on their liability for weekly indemnity and medical benefits. Employees gained by receiving "no fault" benefits if injured on the job. Each state individually passed its own workers compensation statute and, in 1927, Congress passed the U.S. Longshore and Harbor Workers Compensation Act, providing benefits to longshoremen, who were not considered covered under the individual states' statutes.

The United States is the only major industrialized nation that has a private workers compensation system. In most countries, workers compensation is part of a social security program. There are five U.S. states that do not allow the private insurance industry to fund benefits. Instead, monopolistic state funds have been established in the states of North Dakota, Ohio, Washington, West Virginia, and Wyoming. If you have operations in these states, you must purchase coverage from the monopolistic state fund.

In Arizona, California, Colorado, Hawaii, Idaho, Kentucky, Louisiana, Maine, Maryland, Minnesota, Missouri, Montana, New Mexico, New York, Oklahoma, Oregon, Pennsylvania, Rhode Island, Texas, and Utah, competitive state funds compete in the open marketplace with private industry.

If your firm is engaged in stevedoring or has employees working on stationary platforms—such as oil rigs located over navigable bodies of water—you may be subject to the U.S. Longshore and Harbor Workers Compensation Act, which allows substantially higher benefits than most state acts. A specific endorsement is required to provide this coverage under the standard policy.

The Workers Compensation Policy

Benefits provided to employees are covered by the standard workers compensation and employers liability policy in most states. This standard form was drafted by the National Council on Compensation Insurance (NCCI) and filed with most states on behalf of insurers. Today's workers compensation policy has three basic coverage parts.

Part One provides coverage for the statutory liability of the employer under the specified state statutes. Rather than insuring a specific individual or a class of individuals, the employer insures the liability created by state statutes. However, some employees—such as domestic help and agricultural employees—as well as sole proprietors/partners are often excluded under the law and have to be specifically added to the policy for coverage to apply.

Part Two provides coverage for any liability to an employee presented to the employer under common law. Such coverage is known as employers liability insurance. It applies in those few situations where the employee can elect not to come under the workers compensation statute. In most states, if the employee decides to press a common law liability suit, benefits under Part One are forfeited.

Part Three provides for statutory benefits when employees can press claims in states other than those where they are working. This *other states coverage* may come into play when, for example, an employee is injured while traveling in a state that provides higher benefits than the state in which he or she normally works. This coverage should be structured to apply to all states except those specified in Part One and the monopolistic fund states listed on the previous page.

Workers Compensation Rating

During the past 2 decades, there has been a significant shift in the way that rates have been developed, used, and marketed by the various insurers. Prior to the 1990s, the NCCI, or an alternate rating bureau approved by the state, would compile industrywide loss and payroll information for each employee classification, project estimated losses for each classification, add an allowance for insurer expenses and profits, and issue advisory rates that all insurers were required to use in that state. Any deviations from state-made rates had to be approved prior to use in most states.

Although some states still operate on the basis of this "administered pricing" system, the trend in the 1990s was toward "competitive rating" or "open rating," which allows insurers to determine their own rates. The goal of open rating is to promote competition in the workers compensation insurance market.

Most open rating states still provide some form of advisory data for insurers to use as benchmarks or starting points in determining rates. Some competitive rating states continue to publish advisory rates, but insurers do not need approval to deviate from the published rates. However, most competitive rating states now publish only the loss costs or "pure premium" component for their respective states. Each insurer then determines a multiplier that will be applied to the loss costs to determine a final rate. For NCCI states, the advisory rates or advisory loss costs appear in the state's "rate pages" of the *Basic Manual for Workers*

Compensation and Employers Liability Insurance. The manner in which workers compensation rates are determined for the various states is noted in Figure 5.1.

Figure 5.1

_____

State Rating Methods

Competitive Rating States

Alabama[1]	Kansas[1]	New Mexico[1]
Alaska[1]	Kentucky	North Carolina[1]
Arkansas[1]	Louisiana	Oklahoma
California	Maine	Oregon[1]
Colorado	Maryland	Pennsylvania
Connecticut[1]	Michigan	Rhode Island
Delaware	Minnesota	South Carolina[1]
District of	Mississippi[1]	South Dakota[1]
Columbia[1]	Missouri[1]	Tennessee[1]
Georgia[1]	Montana	Texas
Hawaii	Nebraska	Utah
Illinois[2]	Nevada[1]	Vermont[1]
Indiana[3]	New Hampshire[1]	Virginia[1]

Administered Pricing States

Arizona	Iowa	New York
Florida	Massachusetts	Wisconsin
Idaho	New Jersey	

Monopolistic States

North Dakota	West Virginia
Ohio	Wyoming
Washington	

_____

[1] Issues both advisory loss costs for voluntary market and separate assigned risk rates.

[2] Issues both advisory rates and loss costs. Insurers can use either in developing final rates.

[3] Issues both advisory rates and loss costs. Insurers in the voluntary market can use either in developing final rates. Advisory rates must be utilized for assigned risk policies.

Workers Compensation Classification

Although the workers compensation classification system has been standardized in most states, monopolistic states have their own classification systems, and a few nonmonopolistic states—California, Delaware, Pennsylvania, and Texas—also have their own classification systems. The system that applies nationally is administered by NCCI. The states that do not use the NCCI system have their own bureaus.

The various rating jurisdictions collect data for each classification, such as payrolls and losses to develop pure loss costs for each type of activity. Added to these pure loss costs are nonloss expenses such as premium taxes, agent's commissions, insurance company overhead, and other similar expenses to develop the manual rate. These manual loss costs are listed in the various workers compensation rating manuals.

Review Current Classification(s) and Look for Alternatives

The first step in determining (or confirming) the proper classification(s) for your particular business is to sit down with your insurance agent, consultant, or insurance company representative—and the applicable workers compensation manual—and develop a list of all classifications that might apply to your particular business. At the same time, look up the manual rates or loss costs for each classification in each state where you do business.

Then, review the current classification approach to determine if any new classifications might be applied or if some classifications are being used erroneously. Often, there will be gray areas, which can be negotiated with the insurance company; or perhaps a favorable ruling can be requested from the applicable rating bureau. Again, an insurance agent, broker, or consultant can be of great help in this process.

If you are certain your operations can be reclassified to effect lower premium costs, a meeting should be scheduled with the insurance company to obtain its concurrence. If the insurance company disagrees, and you feel that you have a good case, you may request an inspection and ruling by the bureau having jurisdiction. If the insurance company disagrees, this does not mean that its representatives are being unduly arbitrary. It simply reflects the many gray areas in payroll classification and the fact that reasonable disagreements can arise.

In any event, after the appropriate classification procedures are developed, they should be confirmed in writing and, preferably, put into a simple workbook to be followed by accounting personnel. Many classification errors occur after a turnover of employees. The trained employee leaves, and the replacement begins to misclassify the payrolls.

If you discover a gross misclassification in your favor, many states will allow you to recover past overcharges subject to the statute of limitations for written contracts in that particular state.

Preferably, the classification process should not be approached in an adversarial manner. Careful communication with your insurance underwriter and insurance company auditor, assisted by your insurance agent or consultant, normally will produce the best possible results.

Workers Compensation Manuals

A key source of information concerning workers compensation classification and rating is NCCI's *Basic Manual for Workers Compensation and Employers Liability Insurance.* This publication includes rules, regulations, and rates for all but the monopolistic states and territories (North Dakota, Ohio, Washington, West Virginia, Wyoming, Puerto Rico, U.S. Virgin Islands, St. Thomas, St. Croix). Delaware, Hawaii, Massachusetts, New Jersey, New York, Pennsylvania, and Texas follow the rules established by the independent rating bureaus published in their respective manuals. California and Michigan require that insurers file their own manuals. Among other topics, the NCCI manual explains coverages, classification methods, special conditions affecting coverage and premiums, cancellation approaches, and the U.S. Longshore and Harbor Workers Compensation Act. While the NCCI manual is still available in print, NCCI has published it on the Internet and is strongly encouraging people to subscribe to the online version. Their Web site is at www.ncci.com.

An understanding of the classification process is central to minimizing workers compensation costs. Toward this end, the basic and other NCCI manuals explain and provide rules for the manner in which payrolls should be classified. To illustrate, there are some instances in which, if a number of people work in the same room, performing various tasks, all of the employees must be classified under the highest rated classification. On the other hand, some classes, such as construction, will allow a division of payroll. There are also rules as to how certain payrolls—such as overtime—can be excluded and how payrolls of owners and partners and other exempt employees might be treated. Since workers compensation is the most expensive policy for many businesses, it is important to read the rules and regulations. Fortunately, they are not very lengthy. The applicable manual(s) might be borrowed from an insurance agent or consultant or, if continued use is contemplated, a personal copy can be purchased. (See "For further research and study" at the end of this chapter for more information.) The industrial commission or bureau in non-NCCI states must be contacted directly to obtain such manuals.

Unless you are armed with an up-to-date copy of the applicable workers compensation manual, proper classification of payroll may be very difficult.

Other Key Factors Influencing Workers Compensation Costs

In addition to the manner in which your company's various operations are classified, there are a number of other factors that have an impact upon the dollar amount of premiums that you pay to cover (or self-insure) your company's workers compensation exposure. These areas, which are discussed in other sections of this book, include experience rating (Chapter 6), claims (Chapter 9), risk control (Chapter 10), and risk financing (Chapter 11). These chapters should be reviewed along with this chapter.

Experience Rating

An experience modification factor is developed by measuring the difference between your firm's *actual* past loss experience and the *expected* loss experience for your type of business.

This factor produces either a premium debit (a higher premium) or a premium credit (a lower premium), after the initial manual premium is developed by multiplying the applicable rates by the applicable payrolls based on your company's specific operations. The process of arriving at an experience modifier is not purely mechanical, however. Thus, an entire chapter of this book has been devoted to explaining methods that can legitimately reduce your firm's experience modifier, and thus, minimize the amount of workers compensation premium that you will pay.

Risk Control

Given the fact that every company of any size—even those that buy coverage on a so-called guaranteed cost basis—is subject to experience modification, it is incumbent on your company to control claims, both from the standpoint of preventing claims from occurring as well as in minimizing the dollar amount of those claims after a loss has occurred. There are a variety of ways to accomplish this, and Chapter 10 provides a number of effective risk control suggestions.

Claims

Once workers compensation claims have occurred, the manner in which they are handled can have a dramatic effect on their ultimate cost to your organization. Various litigation cost control strategies, methods of dealing with your insurance company's claims department, record-keeping approaches, and periodic audits of adjusting firms are a few of the ways discussed in Chapter 9 that can assist you in optimizing the claim-handling function and ultimately reduce the cost of workers compensation claims.

Risk Financing

Within the broad scope of providing workers compensation coverage, a number of options are available in addition to a traditional guaranteed cost insurance policy. For example, firms have the option of using retrospectively rated plans that are truly "loss-sensitive," large or small deductible programs, self-insurance, and even captive insurance companies (a form of "do-it-yourself coverage"). Chapter 11 provides details about these many options that can result in meaningful cost savings.

Ways To Cut Costs

This chapter covers five important ways to cut workers compensation costs.

39. Obtain Correct Classifications

The first step toward controlling workers compensation costs is to be sure that your payrolls are being properly classified. To rate workers compensation insurance, the insurance industry uses classification codes that are similar to the Standard Industry Classification (SIC) codes developed by the government. Figure 5.2, an excerpt from the *Basic Manual's* workers compensation classification table, is an example. Each classification code has its own corresponding loss cost or rate that is multiplied by the payroll (per $100) associated with the operations included in the code. (As was noted in Chapter 1, many states now publish only the actual loss costs associated with the different classification codes and leave it up to individual insurers to provide a multiplier that increases the loss cost to reflect their individual administrative costs associated with writing the coverage.)

Of course, you will want to use the code(s) with the lowest rate(s) and the insurance underwriter will opt for the code(s) with the highest rates. While some operations are easy to classify because there is only one "governing code" (playing card manufacturers, for example), others are very difficult because numerous codes can apply. For example, over 60 classifications might apply to construction operations. The various classifications are arranged in more than 130 groups of industry classifications.

Figure 5.2

Basic Manual Classification Page Example

FURNITURE ASSEMBLY—WOOD—from manufactured parts   2881

   Includes finishing. Codes 2881 and 2883 furniture mfg. and 2735 furniture stock mfg. shall not be assigned to the same risk unless the operations described by these classifications are conducted as separate and distinct businesses.

FURNITURE MANUFACTURING (MFG)—METAL   3076

FURNITURE MFG—WOOD—Not Otherwise Classified (NOC)   2883

   Includes assembling or finishing.

FURNITURE MOVING & storage, Drivers   8293

FURNITURE or Fixtures INSTALLATION—portable—NOC   5146

   Applies to installation in offices or stores.

FURNITURE STOCK MFG   2735

FURNITURE UPHOLSTERING   9522

Source: *Basic Manual for Workers Compensation and Employers Liability Insurance,* National Council on Compensation Insurance, 2000.

40. Delete Overtime Payroll Surcharge

All states, with the exception of Delaware and Pennsylvania, allow for the deletion of the premium portion (in other words, the portion of the payroll that represents the additional 50 percent of wages paid) of overtime in developing payrolls used in rating workers compensation insurance. For instance, if the hourly wage rate is $12, an employee will be paid this rate for the first 40 hours; for each hour thereafter, a 50 percent premium generally applies. So, an hourly rate of $18 will be paid.

From a workers compensation risk standpoint, there is no greater risk at the 41st hour than at the first hour of work during that particular week. Therefore, for insurance purposes, if the employee works 50 hours, the 50 hours are multiplied by the $12 hourly rate and, in turn, the employer reports $600 of ratable payroll to the insurance company. The overtime premium of $60 (10 hours x $6) is deleted from the rating base.

To qualify under this rule, you must maintain your books in a manner that allows overtime premium to be easily verified. You cannot use averages to estimate the amount of payroll to exclude.

41. Use a "First-Aid" Folder

The majority of workers compensation claims involve "medical only" claims. These are instances where an employee suffers a minor injury and is taken to an industrial clinic or emergency room. Although medical treatment may continue, very little time is lost. If these claims are reported to the insurance company with a request for payment, the doctor will be required to complete lengthy insurance forms and submit individual bills. In addition, it will be necessary for the insurance company to process the claim.

As a result, the doctor may add as much as 50 percent to the medical bill for processing the claim, while the insurance company may incur as much as $100 in processing the payment. In the long run, this expense is charged back to the employer through insurance experience rating or reduced dividends.

You may be able to establish an arrangement with your insurer whereby small medical only claims up to a predetermined amount of, generally, $250 to $500 will be paid directly by your firm, unless you request otherwise. (However, these plans are not allowed by regulators in every state.)

You can then make an arrangement with one or more clinics to treat injured employees. Ask clinics to submit monthly billings to you for all services rendered. You will continue to complete injury reports and file these with your insurer with the notation, "This report is for information purposes only." Therefore, the doctors will not charge for their paperwork and the administrative cost of the insurer will be avoided. On the other hand, if a claim develops and is more serious than originally thought, then the insurer can be requested to activate a file.

42. Consider a Deductible Plan

In recent years, workers compensation deductible programs have become increasingly popular. Deductibles can be applied in either of two forms—large or small deductibles. In both cases, they may help you control escalating workers compensation premiums.

Small Deductible Plans

Small deductible plans, developed and filed on behalf of insurers by NCCI, are available to all insureds in states that have approved the particular plans. Although there is no formal definition of what constitutes a "small" deductible, such programs are generally considered to apply in the range of $100 to $10,000 per claim.

There is a great deal of variety among states in their small deductible plans as to whether the deductible applies to both medical and indemnity or one of them alone, range of deductibles available, range of deductible discounts, and whether losses are reported gross or net for experience rating and ratemaking purposes. Figure 5.3 provides a list of the states in which small deductibles can be included in workers compensation programs.

Large Deductible Plans

In contrast, large deductible plans are individually filed by insurers. These plans are available to insureds whose workers compensation insurers have large deductible plans submitted and approved by individual states. Such insureds usually have to meet specified financial requirements mandated by the individual states to qualify for a large deductible program. Large deductibles are generally considered to be in excess of $10,000 (or above whatever is the highest small deductible offered in the jurisdiction) per claim. These plans are permitted in most states. Since they are developed by individual insurers, they vary greatly from one insurer to another. Figure 5.4 beginning on page 61 indicates the states in which large deductible programs are available.

From a cash flow perspective, large deductible plans operate in essentially the same manner as retrospectively rated programs. The insured pays a deposit premium that compensates the insurer for services (such as loss control and loss adjustment) and insurance coverage for losses that exceed the deductible. The insurer handles, litigates, settles, and pays covered losses and bills the insured periodically for reimbursement of payments within the deductible. The premium payable on a large deductible plan may be funded in a number of ways. In some cases, the insured will pay in an amount equal to what the guaranteed premium would be (given the chosen deductible) and the insurer adjusts the premium based on incurred losses, much like an incurred loss retro. Some insurers will bill premiums on a paid-loss basis, which usually requires a deposit of 2–2½ months' expected losses, with the remainder secured by a letter of credit, surety bond, or trust agreement.

Advantages and Disadvantages of Deductible Plans

Both large and small deductible plans can offer significant benefits to a company. First, large deductible plans provide many of the benefits of self-insurance without the administrative

Figure 5.3

States with Small Workers Compensation Deductibles

The following 36 states' rating manuals allow for small deductibles to be offered according to state-approved deductible rules, which are outlined in this exhibit. States highlighted in bold do not require deductibles to be offered. In addition to these states, insurers are *permitted* to file small deductible programs in **Arizona, Idaho, Louisiana, Michigan,** and **Mississippi.**

State	Type of Deductible	Range of Deductible	Range of Discount
AL	Medical & Indemnity	$100–2,500	0.4–12.6%[1]
AR	Medical & Indemnity	$1,000–5,000	8.6–31.7[1]
	Medical Only	$1,000–5,000	8.1–26.5[1]
	Indemnity Only	$1,000–5,000	2.1–15.5[1]
CA	Medical & Indemnity	$500–100,000 or 50% of the estimated annual workers compensation standard premium (whichever is less)	Varies
CO	Medical & Indemnity	$500–5,000	2.4–19.1%[1]
CT	Medical & Indemnity	$1,000–10,000	4.3–34.9%[1]
DE	Medical & Death	$500–5,000	4.0–12.0%
FL[2]	Medical & Indemnity	$500–75,000	1.4–31.1%
GA	Medical & Indemnity	$100–2,500	1.3–8.9%[1]
HI	Medical Only	$100–10,000	1.1–20.7%[1]
IL	Medical Only	$1,000	4.5%
IN[3]	Medical & Indemnity	$500–5,000	5.0–25.2%
IA	Medical Only	$100–2,500	No policy credits
KS[4]	Medical & Indemnity	$100–10,000	0.9–28.9%
KY	Medical & Indemnity	$100–10,000	0.9–30.5%[1]
ME	Medical or Indemnity[5]	Medical: $250–500 Indemnity: $1,000–5,000	2.5–5.5% 1.4–5.6%
MD	Medical & Indemnity	$500–2,500	1.8–9.7%
MA	Medical & Indemnity (Benefits Deductible)	$500–2,500 (required) $5,000 (optional)	3.0–7.1% 10.6%
	Medical & Indemnity[6] (Benefits Claim & Aggregate Deductible)	$2,500 (per claim) $10,000 to 5% of est. annual standard premium (aggregate)	4.3–7.0% based on size of aggregate deductible

Figure 5.3 (cont.)

States with Small Workers Compensation Deductibles (cont.)

State	Type of Deductible	Range of Deductible	Range of Discount
MN	Varies with filing. However, most plans cover medical & indemnity.	$100–10,000	Filed by insurer
MO	Medical & Indemnity	$100–25,000	0.5–53.9%[7]
MT[8]	Medical & Indemnity Medical Only	$1,000–10,000 $500–2,500	4.0–29.6%[1] 2.9–13.0[1]
NE	Medical Only	$500–2,500	2.0–10.8%
NV	Medical & Indemnity	$100–20,000[9]	0.7–41.6%
NH	Medical & Indemnity	$500–5,000	per accident or disease deductible 2.9–23.0%[1] per claim deductible 2.9–23.1%[1]
NM	Medical & Indemnity	$500–10,000	3.9–37.0%[1]
NY[10]	Medical & Indemnity	$100–5,000	0.1–10.5%
NC	Medical & Indemnity	$100–5,000	0.5–17.8%[1]
OK	Medical Only	$500–2,500	2.7–14.6%[1]
OR	Medical Only	$500	No premium credit
PA	Medical & Indemnity	$1,000–10,000	2.4–31.5%[1,11]
RI	Medical & Indemnity	$250–5,000	0.8–14.0%
SC	Medical & Indemnity	$100–2,500	1.2–17.6%[1]
SD	Medical & Indemnity Medical Only	$500–2,500 $500–2,500	5.5–23.4%[12] 0.5–2.5%[13]
TN	Medical & Indemnity	$100–2,500	0.6–15.2[1]
TX[14]	Medical & Indemnity	$1,000–25,000	3.0–59.0%
UT	Medical & Indemnity	$500–5,000	6.2–36.7%[1]
VA	Medical & Indemnity	$100–10,000	0.7–28.0%[1]

Figure 5.3 (cont.)

States with Small Workers Compensation Deductibles (cont.)

[1]These figures represent advisory loss elimination ratios (LERs) provided by NCCI; insurers calculate deductible discounts using these LERs and their own expense ratios.

[2]Florida has four programs: (1) a coinsurance program, with coinsurance of $5,000–21,000 per claim, with a range of 1.5–3.4 percent premium reductions; (2) a deductible program with $500–2,500 deductible per claim with a range of 1.4–4.5 percent premium reductions; (3) a deductible with coinsurance program with a $500–2,500 per claim deductible and a $21,000 per claim coinsurance limit with a range of 4.5–7.1 percent premium reductions; and (4) a flat $2,500 medical and indemnity deductible with no premium credit where losses are reported net rather than gross. Premium discount percentages for intermediate deductibles (which are permitted but not required) (those between $5,000–75,000) range from 7.3–31.1 percent and are advisory only. Insurers can file for deviations with the Florida Department of Insurance.

[3]Indiana has three programs: (1) a coinsurance program, with coinsurance of up to $21,000 per claim, with a range of 5.0–7.7 percent premium reductions; (2) a deductible program with $500–5,000 deductible per claim with a range of 5.0–21.1 percent premium reductions; and (3) a deductible with coinsurance program with a $500–5,000 per claim deductible and a $21,000 per claim coinsurance limit with a range of 9.0–25.2 percent pure premium reductions.

[4]Small deductibles permitted on voluntary markets, required in residual market.

[5]In addition to the optional medical and/or indemnity deductibles available in the voluntary market, Maine has a mandatory $1,000 indemnity deductible for all nonretrospectively rated residual market policies with annual premium of at least $12,000; no premium credit applies.

[6]Employers with an estimated standard premium of $200,000 or less are offered a program with a medical and indemnity claim deductible of $2,500 and aggregate deductible of $10,000. Employers with a premium in excess of $200,000 are offered a medical and indemnity deductible of $2,500 and an aggregate deductible amount of 5 percent of the estimated annual standard premium.

[7]These figures represent advisory loss elimination ratios (LERs) per occurrence provided by NCCI. The applicable premium reduction percentage is determined by the insurer for the deductible selected by the employer. Insurers determine the percentage and provide actuarial justification with the filings to the Missouri Department of Insurance.

[8]Medical loss deductible programs are mandatory. Total loss deductible programs are optional.

[9]Deductible options at $10,000, $15,000, and $20,000 are applicable for new business on July 1, 2001 and at the anniversary rating date for renewal business. Deductibles are optional in the voluntary market and must be offered in the residual market.

[10]Deductibles must be offered to a policyholder with an estimated annual premium at inception of $12,000. Offering a deductible to policyholders below the $12,000 premium level is optional.

[11]Insurers can offer different deductible levels and/or premium credits with the approval of the Pennsylvania Insurance Department.

[12]These figures represent premium reduction percentages provided by the NCCI; insurers may use these or file their own credits with the South Dakota Department of Insurance based upon their expense assumptions in the past.

[13]These percentages do not represent final percentage premium reductions to be applied to policy premium.

[14]Texas has three programs: (1) Per accident deductibles of $1,000, $2,500, $5,000, $10,000, and $25,000, not to exceed 50 percent of a policyholder's estimated annual workers compensation premium must be offered by all insurers; (2) an annual aggregate deductible option must be offered in amounts ranging from $2,000 to 100 percent of the policyholder's estimated annual workers compensation premium, not to exceed $100,000; and (3) a per accident deductible of the amounts listed above in option 1; must be offered in conjunction with an aggregate deductible of the amounts specified above in option 2 to create a combined per accident/aggregate deductible option.

Figure 5.4

States Allowing Large Workers Compensation Deductibles

The following states allow insurers to develop and offer workers compensation large deductible programs. Minimum premium levels are required in some states before an insured is eligible for a large deductible program. Some states also specify minimum deductible levels before a deductible program is a large deductible rather than a small deductible. The state requirements, where applicable, are shown in this Exhibit. Keep in mind that insurers may set out their own minimum premium and deductible levels.

State	Minimum Premium	Minimum Deductible	Loss Report Gross/Net
AL	$100,000	$25,000 per claim min.	Gross
AZ	No restrictions	No restrictions	Gross
AR	No restrictions	No restrictions but must exceed $5,000 per claim, the largest small deductible option available.	Gross
CA	$500,000 of either California or country-wide estimated annual standard workers compensation premium	$100,000 per accident or employee	Gross
CO	No restrictions	No restrictions but must exceed $5,000 per claim, the largest small deductible option available.	Net[1]
CT	No restrictions	No restrictions but must exceed $10,000 per claim, the largest small deductible option available.	Gross
DE	No restrictions	No restrictions but must exceed $5,000 per claim, the largest small deductible option available.	Gross
DC	No restrictions	No restrictions	Gross
FL	$500,000	$100,000 per claim min.	Gross
GA	No restrictions	No restrictions but must exceed $2,500 per claim, the largest small deductible option available.	Gross
HI	No restrictions	No restictions but insurer must file plans.	Gross
ID	No restrictions	No restrictions	Gross
IL	No restrictions	No restrictions	Gross
IN	No restrictions	Must exceed $5,000 per claim, the largest small deductible option available	Gross
IA	$100,000	$25,000 per claim min.	Gross
KS	No restrictions	No restrictions but must exceed $10,000 per claim, the largest small deductible option available.	Net[2]
KY	No restrictions	No restrictions but must exceed $10,000 per claim, the largest small deductible option available.	Gross

continued

Figure 5.4 (cont.)

States Allowing Large Workers Compensation Deductibles (cont.)

State	Minimum Premium	Minimum Deductible	Loss Report Gross/Net
LA	No restrictions	No restrictions	Gross
ME	No restrictions	Must be in excess of $5,000 for per occurrence and excess of $500 for a medical deductible which are the largest deductible options available under the small deductible plan.	Gross less 1st $5,000
MD	No restrictions	No restrictions but must exceed $2,500 per claim, the largest small deductible option available.	Gross
MA	$1 million interstate with a MA premium of $50,000 or $500,000 MA only	$100,000 min.; annual aggregate cap must be applied on all large deductibles	Gross
MI	No restrictions	No restrictions	Gross
MN[3]	$250,000	No min. specified but must exceed $10,000 per claim, the largest small deductible option available; max. may not exceed insurer's retention limit with the Workers Compensation Reinsurance Association	Gross
MS	No restrictions	No restrictions	Gross
MO	$100,000 (before deductible credits)	$25,000 per claim min.; max. may not exceed 40% of standard premium;[4] may offer annual aggregate cap	Either[5]
MT	No restrictions	Must be in excess of $10,000 for per occurrence and excess of $2,500 for a medical deductible which are the largest deductible options available under the small deductible plan.	Gross
NE	$125,000	$50,000 min.; max. may not exceed 40% of standard premium. Insurers may offer annual aggregate cap.	Gross
NV	No restrictions	$25,000 per claim min.	Gross
NH	No restrictions	No restrictions but must exceed $5,000 per claim, the largest small deductible option available.	Gross
NJ	$200,000[6]	$25,000 per accident or employee. May not exceed 40% of standard premium.	Gross
NM	$500,000	$100,000 per claim min.	Gross
NY	No restrictions	No restrictions but must exceed $5,000 per claim, the largest small deductible option available.	Gross
NC	No restrictions	No restrictions, but insurer must file a range of deductibles	Gross
OK	$25,000	Above $2,500[7]	Gross

continued

Figure 5.4 (cont.)

States Allowing Large Workers Compensation Deductibles (cont.)

State	Minimum Premium	Minimum Deductible	Loss Report Gross/Net
OR	$750,000	$75,000 per claim minimum. Insurer may offer an aggregate limit but it may not be less than the deductible limit per claim.	Gross
PA	Varies	No restrictions	Gross
RI	No restrictions	No restrictions, but large deductibles are any amount over highest small ded. available ($5,000)	Gross
SC	$100,000	$50,000 per claim min.	Gross
SD	No restrictions	No restrictions but must exceed $2,500 per claim, the largest small deductible option available.	Gross
TN	No restrictions	No restrictions but must exceed $2,500 per claim, the largest small deductible option available.	Gross
TX	Excess of $50,000–$100,000[8]	Must exceed the highest promulgated per accident deductible of $25,000 and/or the highest promulgated annual aggregate deductible of $100,000.	Gross
UT	No restrictions	No restrictions but must exceed $5,000 per claim, the largest small deductible option available.	Gross
VT	No restrictions	No restrictions	Gross
VA	$250,000	$100,000 per claim min.	Gross

[1]Net reporting for first $5,000 of experience rating; gross for ratemaking and loss based assessments.

[2]Net reporting for experience rating; gross for rate making and loss based assessments.

[3]Insurers are required to offer deductible plan (large or small) unless insured is not sufficiently financially stable to be able to reimburse.

[4]An exception can be made if the policy deductible amount is secured by collateral as required by statute and the NAIC in connection with credit for unauthorized reinsurance.

[5]Insurer may report losses for experience rating on gross or net basis; must indicate gross or net reporting for a particular risk and when using gross reporting, must document that the insured chose gross reporting. Assessments based on gross losses.

[6]$200,000 of New Jersey or countrywide estimated annual standard premium except $500,000 premium threshold necessary for large construction projects.

[7]Oklahoma has a five-tier large deductible plan with deductible options ranging from in excess of $2,500 per claim to 40 percent of the estimated annual standard countrywide workers compensation premium. Annual aggregates are required for deductible programs in tiers 1 through 3 with the aggregate not greater than three times the deductible amount in tier 1 and 5 times the deductible in tiers 2 and 3.

[8]Minimum deductible is either excess of $50,000 when a per accident deductible is chosen or excess of $100,000 when either the annual aggregate deductible option is chosen or the insured has an estimated annual policy premium before the application of the deductible credit of more than $100,000.

burden of obtaining regulatory approval to begin or conclude operations as a self-insurer. This is especially important for businesses that operate on a multistate basis. Second, given the long payout patterns characteristic of workers compensation claims, insureds enjoy substantial cash flow advantages from these plans. Third, deductible plans also afford an organization the benefit of insurer services in conducting its program. Fourth, deductible plans allow a company to operate similarly to a self-insurer, but without the need to pay fronting fees, which can sometimes be as high as 8 percent of the policy's annual premium. Fifth, since a firm will be paying less premium under a deductible plan, it can realize savings (in most states) because residual market charges are assessed as a percentage of annual premiums. Finally, in a few states, a firm's experience modifier will improve because under deductible plans, some or all portions of each loss will not be included in calculating the modifier.

One meaningful disadvantage associated with deductible plans is the risk of higher-than-expected losses if a company does not purchase an aggregate deductible. (It should be recognized, however, that such aggregates may not always be available or available at a reasonable premium.) Nevertheless, such a risk arises from a frequency problem, which is generally much more controllable than a severity problem.

Figure 5.5

Advantages and Disadvantages of Large Deductible Programs

Advantages to Employer

- Advantages of self-insurance without having to obtain regulatory approval, especially in multistate operations

- Advantages of self-insurance, but with easy entry and easy exit

- Significant cash flow advantage

- Maintain all services of insurer

- No fronting fees

- Potentially lower cost from residual market load (RML) savings (may be negated by some states)

- Ability in some states to improve experience modifier

Disadvantages to Employer

- Risk of large losses, especially if no aggregate deductible applies

- Unpredictable timing of reimbursements

- Low or immediate tax deductions for paid premiums

Another disadvantage associated with deductible plans is the loss of an immediate tax deduction for payment of an insurance policy premium. This is especially true with regard to large deductible programs under which up-front premium payments are substantially lower compared to guaranteed cost or retrospective plans.

These advantages and disadvantages of large deductible programs are summarized in Figure 5.5.

43. Take Advantage of Dividends and Flexible Rates

Until 15 years ago, virtually every state required all insurance companies to use the same rates for specific industry classifications. In recent years, most states began allowing insurance companies to use insurance rates based on their own experience to encourage more competition. Other states required use of the same base rates but allowed insurance companies to apply credits or surcharges to these standard rates. Figure 5.6 shows the range of credits/debits that are allowed in states where schedule rating is permitted.

Figure 5.6

Schedule Rating Table

Range of Modification
(Credit to Debit)

State	Maximum Modification	Premises	Classification Peculiarities	Medical Facilities	Safety Devices	Employee Selection Training Supervision	Management Cooperation w/Insurer	Management Safety Organization
AL	15%	+6% to −6%1	+6% to −6%	+3% to −3%	+3% to −3%	+6% to −6%	+3% to −3%	+3% to −3%
AZ	25%	+10% to −10%	+10% to −10%	+5% to −5%	+5% to −5%	+10% to −10%	+5% to −5%	+5% to −5%
CO	25%	+10% to −10%	+10% to −10%	+5% to −5%	+5% to −5%	+10% to −10%	+5% to −5%	+5% to −5%
DC	25%	+10% to −10%	+10% to −10%	+5% to −5%	+5% to −5%	+10% to −10%	+5% to −5%	+5% to −5%
IN	50%	+10% to −10%	+10% to −10%	+10% to −10%	+10% to −10%	+10% to −10%	+5% to −5%	+5% to −5%
MS	25%	+10% to −10%	+10% to −10%	+5% to −5%	+5% to −5%	+10% to −10%	+5% to −5%	+5% to −5%
MT	25%	+10% to −10%	+10% to −10%	+5% to −5%	+5% to −5%	+10% to −10%	+5% to −5%	+5% to −5%
NH	25%	(See state special rules: + or −25%)						
NM	25%	+10% to −10%	+10% to −10%	+5% to −5%	+5% to −5%	+10% to −10%	+5% to −5%	+5% to −5%
OK	25%	+10% to −10%	+10% to −10%	+5% to −5%	+5% to −5%	+10% to −10%	+5% to −5%	+5% to −5%
RI	25%	+10% to −10%	+10% to −10%	+5% to −5%	+5% to −5%	+10% to −10%	+5% to −5%	+5% to −5%
SC	25%	+10% to −10%	+10% to −10%	+5% to −5%	+5% to −5%	+10% to −10%	+5% to −5%	+5% to −5%
SD	25%	+10% to −10%	N/A	+5% to −5%	+10% to −10%	+5% to −5%	N/A	+5% to −5%
TN	25%	+10% to −10%	+10% to −10%	+5% to −5%	+5% to −5%	+10% to −10%	+5% to −5%	+5% to −5%
UT	25%	+10% to −10%	+10% to −10%	+5% to −5%	+5% to −5%	+10% to −10%	+5% to −5%	+5% to −5%
VT	25%	+10% to −10%	+10% to −10%	+5% to −5%	+5% to −5%	+10% to −10%	+5% to −5%	+5% to −5%

In the states where competitive rating is not used and schedule credits are unavailable, dividend plans may be used to adjust premiums. These dividend plans typically fall into three categories: flat dividends, retention plans, and sliding-scale plans.

Flat Dividends

A flat dividend is usually paid regardless of the insured's loss experience. However, it should be recognized that underwriters will not agree to place an insured with poor past loss experience in a dividend plan. Dividends will range between 6 and 9 percent.

Retention Plans

A retention plan is more of a cost-plus program. The insurance company develops a cost factor, called a retention factor, based on its operating expenses, reinsurance premiums, agents' commissions, premium taxes, and loss-handling fees. The remaining funds are used to pay losses, with any surplus returned to the insured at the end of the year as a dividend. For example, assume that all of these expenses amount to a percentage factor of 30 percent of the premium. Further assume that the insured sustains losses equal to 50 percent of the premium. Therefore, the insurance company will retain 30 percent of the premium for expenses and 50 percent for losses; it will return the balance of 20 percent to the insured in the form of a dividend about 12 to 24 months after expiration of the insurance policy.

Sliding Scale Dividend Plans

A sliding scale dividend plan is similar to a retention plan in that it is based on losses. However, the insurance company will use a table that indicates a percentage of return based on the loss ratio (losses divided by premiums). For instance, if the insured has a 25 percent loss ratio, a return of 20 percent might be paid. On the other hand, if the loss ratio was higher, say 50 percent, the dividend paid might be approximately 13 percent.

Generally speaking, retention plans will return more money at low loss ratios, while the sliding scale plan will allow more returns at higher loss ratios.

Overall, dividend plans have the effect of rewarding insureds for controlling losses, as well as allowing the insurance company some flexibility in adjusting the premium rates to reflect its individual operating expenses and investment programs.

An important caveat to the buyer is that dividends are not guaranteed. In fact, most states have laws that prohibit such guarantees. Therefore, an insured may earn a dividend, but if the insurance company's board of directors decides not to declare dividends, no such dividend will be forthcoming.

In summary, loss costs, schedule credits/debits, and dividends have an important impact on the net cost of workers compensation insurance. Therefore, you should understand how these programs operate and know what options are offered by the insurance industry.

For further research and study

For the interstate rating manual that applies in the state(s) where your operations are located, contact NCCI at the following address.

National Council on Compensation Insurance
901 Peninsula Corporate Circle
Boca Raton, Florida 33487
(800) 622–4123
www.ncci.com

NCCI requires subscribers to buy their *Basic Manual for Workers Compensation* to subscribe to the state rates. Service to one state is included with the purchase of this manual.

For rating information in the independent jurisdictions, contact the following.

California
Workers Compensation Insurance Rating Bureau
  of California
525 Market St., Suite 800
San Francisco, CA 94105–2716
Tel.: 415–777–0777 or 888–229–2472
Fax: 415–778–7007
http://www.wcirbonline.org

Delaware
Delaware Comp. Rating Bureau
The Widener Building, 6th Floor
1 S. Penn Square
Philadelphia, PA 19107–3577
Tel.: 302–654–1435; Fax: 215–564–4328
http://www.dcrb.com/shared/d_contents.htm

Hawaii
NCCI, Inc.
901 Peninsula Corporate Circle
Boca Raton, FL 33487
Tel.: 800–622–4123; Fax: 561–893–1191
http://www.ncci.com

Michigan
The Compensation Advisory Organization
  of Michigan
P.O. Box 3337
Livonia, MI 48151–3337
Tel.: 734–462–9600; Fax: 734–462–9721
http://www.caom.com

New Jersey
Compensation Rating and Inspection Bureau
60 Park Place
Newark, NJ 07102
Tel.: 973–622–6014
http://www.njcrib.com

New York
New York Compensation Insurance Rating Board
200 East 42nd St.
New York, NY 10017
Tel.: 212–697–3535; Fax: 212–972–1393
http://www.nycirb.org

Pennsylvania
Pennsylvania Compensation Rating Bureau
The Widener Building, 6th Floor
1 S. Penn Square
Philadelphia, PA 19107–3577
Tel.: 215–568–2371; Fax: 215–564–4328
http://www.pcrb.com/shared/p_contents.htm

Texas
Department of Insurance
P.O. Box 149104
Austin, TX 78714–9104
Tel.: 512–463–6169; 800–578–4677
http://www.tdi.state.tx.us

Two manuals published by IRMI provide valuable information about the ways in which workers compensation costs are determined and can be minimized. These manuals include *IRMI Workers Compensation* and *Risk Financing*. Two less extensive IRMI publications to consider are *Blueprint for Workers Compensation Cost Containment* and *IRMI Workers Compensation Insurance Guide*. In addition, IRMI's *Classification Cross-Reference* is a handy, inexpensive listing of workers compensation and general liability classifications cross-indexed in various ways. Visit the Products and Services section of IRMI.com for more information on these publications.

6
WORKERS COMPENSATION EXPERIENCE RATING

EXPERIENCE RATING IS A SYSTEM for recognizing an insured's past loss experience when determining premiums. It uses a formula to generate an "experience rating modifier" (ERM). An insured that has historically experienced higher losses than the average for its industry group will have a "debit modifier." Conversely, an insured with better-than-average experience will have a "credit modifier."

The purpose of experience rating plans is for the premium charged for coverage to reflect the past experience of individual policyholders. If the prescribed formula develops a 20 percent credit, then the insured's ERM will be .80 and it will pay 80 percent of the applicable manual rates. On the other hand, if the insured has had poor loss experience and develops a modifier of 1.20 or a 20 percent debit, the applicable standard rates are surcharged by 20 percent. Assuming there are no major shifts in payroll, the credits applied to all policies written should equal the debits applied so that the insurance industry, as a whole, earns premiums based on payrolls multiplied by the standard rates. This system of credits and debits is designed to encourage safety practices by rewarding employers who control their losses, while penalizing employers who have adverse loss experience.

The National Council on Compensation Insurance (NCCI) administers a master experience rating plan that is applicable to workers compensation insurance in most states. However, there are a number of experience rating plans that apply to the individual states. In "monopolistic" states, only the state itself is authorized to provide workers compensation coverage, and each of these five states develops its own individual experience rating plan. Other states—such as California and Texas—have their own individual experience rating plans that apply if all of the insured's operations are exclusively within those particular states.

The definitive source of information on the topic of workers compensation experience rating is the *Experience Rating Plan Manual for Workers Compensation and Employers Liability Insurance,* published by NCCI. The manual contains both general rules of experience rating as well as rules that apply in individual states. The recommendations in this chapter are based on the information found in the NCCI publication.

Experience Rating Overview

Unfortunately, most insurance buyers and many insurance agents do not thoroughly understand how the experience rating process works. To effectively control insurance costs, it is very important to closely monitor the development of experience modifiers.

To calculate an experience modifier, the individual loss experience of an insured is compared to the expected experience of the insured's industry group. It is important to note that modifiers are not a function of loss ratios, or past losses divided by past premiums. Instead, current expected loss rates are multiplied by past payrolls and compared to past losses. Therefore, as long as your organization can maintain low losses, it can earn substantial credits.

Figure 6.1

Experience Rating Premium Eligibility Requirements

State	Column A Total Premiums 2 Years or Less	Column B Average Premium More than 2 Years	State	Column A Total Premiums 2 Years or Less	Column B Average Premium More than 2 Years
Alabama	$10,000	$ 5,000	Montana	$ 5,000	$ 2,500
Alaska	$ 5,000	$ 2,500	Nebraska	$ 6,000	$ 3,000
Arizona	$ 6,000	$ 3,000	Nevada	$ 6,000	$ 3,000
Arkansas	$ 8,000	$ 4,000	New Hampshire	$11,000	$ 5,500
California	$26,200[1]		New Jersey	$ 3,900[1]	
Colorado	$ 8,000	$ 4,000	New Mexico	$ 9,000	$ 4,500
Connecticut	$11,000	$ 5,500	New York	$10,000	$ 5,000
Delaware	$ 3,161[2]		North Carolina	$ 5,000	$ 2,500
D.C.	$ 7,000	$ 3,500	Oklahoma	$10,000	$ 5,000
Florida	$10,000	$ 5,000	Oregon	$ 5,000	$ 2,500
Georgia	$10,000	$ 5,000	Pennsylvania	$10,000[1]	
Hawaii	$ 5,000	$ 2,500	Rhode Island	$ 7,500[3]	$ 3,750[3]
Idaho	$ 6,000	$ 3,000	South Carolina	$ 9,000	$ 4,500
Illinois	$10,000	$ 5,000	South Dakota	$ 7,500	$ 3,750
Indiana	$ 5,000	$ 2,500	Tennessee	$ 9,000	$ 4,500
Iowa	$ 7,500	$ 3,750	Texas	$10,000	$ 5,000
Kansas	$ 4,500	$ 2,250	Utah	$ 7,000	$ 3,500
Kentucky	$10,000	$ 5,000	Vermont	$ 8,000	$ 4,000
Louisiana	$10,000	$ 5,000	Virginia	$ 7,000	$ 3,500
Maine	$ 9,000	$ 4,500	Wisconsin	$10,000	$ 5,000
Maryland	$10,000	$ 5,000			
Massachusetts	$11,000	$ 5,500			
Michigan	$ 8,000	$ 4,000			
Minnesota	$ 6,000	$ 3,000			
Mississippi	$ 9,000	$ 4,500			
Missouri	$ 7,000	$ 3,500			

[1] Total for all years of the experience period
[2] Based on a 2-year prior policy exposure extended at current residual market rates
[3] Effective September 1, 2002, eligibility requirements increase to $10,000/$5,000.

One of the basic experience rating concepts to understand is that the experience rating formula penalizes insureds that have *high frequency* of losses more than it does insureds that have *high severity* of losses. In other words, an insured with $100,000 in past workers compensation losses will have a higher modifier if there were 100 losses of $1,000 each than if there were two losses of $50,000 each. The rationale for this is that it is easier to reduce the number of on-the-job accidents than it is to reduce the severity of the injuries that result from the accidents that do occur. Therefore, when implementing a safety program for the first time, focus first on techniques that will reduce the number of on-the-job accidents.

Experience Rating Period and Eligibility

The experience period used in developing experience modifiers is 3 years, but the most current year is not counted. Assume, for example, that your workers compensation policy will renew on February 1, 2003. The policy years to be used begin February 1 of 2001, 2000, and 1999. The latest year, which began on February 1, 2002, and ended on January 31, 2003, will not be used because the expiring period has not been audited to determine exact payrolls by classification. In addition, some of the losses to be covered by the 2001 policy year may (not) be reported until after policy expiration. Therefore, the 3 "mature" years that ended just prior to the expiring policy period are used.

Workers compensation experience rating is mandatory in most states for insureds that meet minimum workers compensation premium requirements. The minimum premium requirements range from $2,500 to $5,500 annually or from $4,500 to $11,000 for the entire experience period. As more small insureds meet the minimum requirements, NCCI has gradually increased minimum requirements. At this point, the most common requirement for experience rating is: (a) payrolls developed during the last year or the last 2 years of the experience period that are enough to produce a manual premium of at least $10,000; or (b) payrolls developed during more than 2 years of the experience period that are enough to produce an average annual manual premium of at least $5,000. Note that these minimum premium requirements can be expected to continue to rise over time. A list of all the current requirements by state can be found in Figure 6.1.

Ways To Cut Costs

This chapter covers five ways to cut workers compensation costs by understanding experience rating.

44. Review Reserves

The insurer(s) involved during the 3-year experience period to be used is required to report payrolls and incurred losses (paid claims and case reserves) for each year. On the older second and third years, insurers report any changes in claims and claim reserves since the last modifier was calculated. It is important to note that reserves for unpaid claims are used and count as if they have been paid. These losses are "valued" 6 months after the end of the policy period or 18 months after inception. Therefore, for an October 1 renewal, the valuation date used to compute the experience modifier is April 1. This chronology is illustrated in Figure 6.2.

It is best to negotiate an arrangement allowing you to review reserves before they are reported to NCCI. The usual procedure is to meet with the claims manager of the insurance company just before the 6-month evaluation. Before the meeting, prepare an analysis of open claims. During the meeting, these outstanding claims will be reviewed with you and the reserved amounts should be evaluated and adjusted, based on the consensus. In some instances, the eventual outcome of many cases may be known; but because it takes an insurer 90 days to process paperwork, the adjusted reserve may not yet be reflected in the company's records. Shortly after the review, the insurer should make changes as agreed on in the meeting, so that the actual filings with NCCI will reflect the most current status of the claims.

Figure 6.2

Experience Rating Chronology

Payrolls and losses for the 1999, 2000, and 2001 policy years are used to calculate the insured's modifier for the 2003 year. Any changes in reserves made prior to the April 1, 2002, "valuation date" should be reflected in the new modifier.

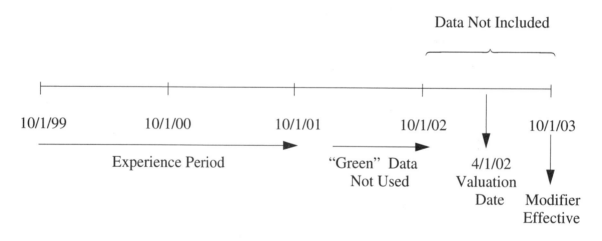

45. Prepare a Test Modifier

After the claims have been reviewed, the insurance agent or insurance company should prepare a "test rating" for you. This will allow you to budget your estimated insurance cost for the 12-month period beginning approximately 5 months hence. Just as important, it allows you and your advisers to develop a renewal strategy. For instance, if the experience modifier is expected to drop substantially, consider purchasing a guaranteed cost program with a flat dividend. But if there is going to be an increase in the modifier, especially in the debit range, you should work on improving your safety program, as well as giving serious thought to assuming a more aggressive cost-plus plan, such as a dividend retention plan, a retrospective rating plan, or a deductible plan.

The bottom line is that you cannot make an intelligent purchase of workers compensation without a forecast of your next experience rating modifier.

46.　Review Final Modifier

Theoretically, the official modifier should be promulgated and issued by the appropriate board or bureau within 6 weeks prior to the anniversary date. Unfortunately, this is not usually the case because rate changes may be pending, insurers involved in the experience period may not have filed their information in a timely manner, or—in some cases—the rating organization is simply behind in its paperwork. This, again, underscores the importance of test ratings.

Usually, the official modifier will be received within 90 days after the expiration date. When it is published, obtain a copy of the calculation. If the official modifier is the same as the test modifier, no further action is indicated. However, if there is a difference between the two, additional action is necessary. Payrolls should be checked, losses in the test rating should be compared to those in the promulgated rating, and so forth.

One reason for a difference could simply be the fact that rates changed during the period between the test rating and the official rating. Rating factors used in the experience rating process invariably change at the time of a manual rate change.

However, it is also possible that the rating organization made errors in calculating the modifier. Payrolls may have been left out, some other employer's experience may have been included, or a number of other clerical errors may have been made. When notified of such errors or mistakes, the applicable rating bureaus are usually very cooperative in recalculating the modifier.

47.　Correct Calculation Errors

There is a potential for several different kinds of errors to be made when calculating experience modifiers. Some of the most common are reviewed below.

Check Payroll and Losses Used

Experience modifiers are calculated by rating bureaus. Each insured employer has a risk identification number. In the process of keypunching information, it is possible for the data entry clerk to simply transpose two numbers, so that you may lose some of your experience, have another firm's experience included in your calculation, or simply have a higher loss amount included than should be (say, $17,000 instead of $1,700). There have even been instances in which payrolls for an entire year have been omitted. If losses are included without the payroll to offset such losses, there is a substantial negative effect on the experience modifier.

To summarize, actual payrolls and losses should be checked during the test rating process and then payrolls and losses used in the test rating should be compared to the official data.

Subrogation Recoveries

Many injuries to workers are caused by the negligence of third parties. The standard process for handling these claims is for the workers compensation insurer to pay workers compensation benefits while joining with the injured employee in a liability suit against the party that caused the injury. Meanwhile, the outstanding claim is charged to you under the experience rating plan. However, the experience rating rules allow for immediate revision of the current modifier at the time a successful recovery is made through the suit against the third party.

For instance, assume that a $90,000 claim has been included in your experience rating calculation. The ensuing third-party suit is quite serious and takes 4 years to resolve. In the meantime, the claim has been included in two experience rating modifiers. When the claim is resolved, you can ask the insurance company to revise your current experience rating data to reflect the recovery made so that the modifier would be reduced. In this case, if the entire $90,000 is recovered, with the exception of $15,000 in attorneys' fees, the ratable amount will be reduced from $90,000 to $15,000 to reflect the net expense to the insurance company including legal fees.

Given the length of time required to resolve certain claims, an agreement with the insurer should be sought concerning the possibility of revising experience modifiers prior to the current year. The need for such an agreement is demonstrated by the fact that complex cases of this kind often require as many as 6 years to conclude.

Noncompensable Claims

Some claims presented to employers by employees may not be compensable. For instance, an employee may sustain an injury at home and try to claim that it was occupation-related. Other examples may be injuries sustained by employees while traveling to and from work. Still others may include aggravated disease and old injury claims. The insurance company, while defending the claim, will also establish a reserve, often on a worst-case basis. This reserve will be maintained until the claim is resolved, often in a court. In the event that the claim is successfully defended, the insured may request the insurance company refile any and all data that included the disputed claim. Make a periodic check of past claims to determine if any were in dispute and if they were successfully defended. If so, your experience rating should be revised accordingly.

Once again, given the long lead time required to resolve complex cases, try to have the insurer agree that experience modifiers can be resolved after the current year if settlements warrant adjustments to reserved amounts on certain claims.

Duplication of Claims and Transposition of Numbers

Considering the billions of characters input into the experience rating system, some errors are bound to occur. For instance, a claim of $1,900 could be input as $9,100. A $5,000 claim could have an extra zero accidentally added, so that it becomes $50,000. Claims included in experience rating data should be carefully checked for such errors.

Other similar errors involve duplication of claims. For example, a claim might be shown open for $20,000 as of the last valuation date and subsequently be closed for $21,000. The closed amount of $21,000 could be included in the data provided by the insurer without the open reserve of $20,000 being deleted. This would erroneously inflate losses by $20,000.

There have been cases of employees who tried to file the same claim in more than one state. If insurance companies set up two separate files, they may end up showing reserves in two states where only one should be indicated.

When reviewing experience rating calculations, it is important to look for these types of errors by comparing the losses included in the calculation with those included in loss reports provided by the insurer.

Improper Limitation of Losses

Unfortunately, severe losses do occur. If an employee injury results in a quadriplegia, the ultimate loss cost and resulting reserves could range anywhere from $750,000 to $5 million. Obviously, if large, catastrophic losses were charged in their entirety to an insured, the experience modifier that would be developed could cause increases in premiums exorbitant enough to bankrupt the insured.

Therefore, experience rating plans allow individual losses to be limited to a certain amount per injured employee, while all multiple employee losses to more than one employee arising out of the same occurrence will be limited to a somewhat higher amount, usually twice the per employee limit. At the time of this writing, for instance, the per employee limitation in Wisconsin is $69,500 while the overall occurrence limitation is $139,000. In Maryland, the per employee limitation is $109,000 and the overall occurrence limitation is $218,000.

It is this loss limitation feature that causes loss frequency to affect modifiers more than loss severity. All small losses are included in their entirety, while only portions of large losses are included in the formula.

While there have been cases of individual losses that were not properly limited, errors occur more often when a number of employees are injured in the same accident. If proper input is not given to the rating bureau, these losses and loss reserves arising from one occurrence may not be grouped for application of the overall occurrence limitation. Therefore, if you know of instances in which several employees were injured in a single accident, the experience rating calculation should be examined to be certain they were all grouped together for the loss limitation instead of being included individually.

Summary

The errors described above should not be viewed as an indictment against the insurance industry. Mistakes can and do happen. While insurance companies and their bureaus should be expected to develop proper experience modifiers, it is also your responsibility to carefully monitor this area.

The experience rating process is complicated. Therefore, it may be advisable for you to use and retain insurance agents, brokers, and consultants who are thoroughly familiar with this process.

One of the services a professional agent/broker can and should provide is coordination and review of the experience rating process.

48. Recognize the Effect of Ownership Changes on Experience Modifiers

Ownership changes, including mergers, acquisitions, and spin-offs, and changes in the nature of your company's operations can have significant effects on how your company's experience modification factor is determined. However, since this is one of the most complex areas of the experience rating process, you should seek expert advice in these situations. The point, however, is to be alert to these types of circumstances.

In most instances, the past experience of a particular operation that has been sold will either be transferred to the new owner or retained by the previous owner (assuming the seller was not completely dissolved by the sale of the unit). An exception is made when a material change in ownership is accompanied by a change in the process and hazard of the operations *and* a change in the operations sufficient to result in a new classification code. If both of these conditions apply, the past experience of the operation will be excluded from the future experience of the buyer and seller, and the experience modifier of the buyer will also apply to the newly acquired entity.

When the conditions above do not exclude the prior loss experience of the entity sold, it is usually transferred to the buyer. If the new owner is not already experience rated, and if the purchase of the new entity qualifies it for experience rating, an experience modifier will be based on the experience of the acquired entity plus any applicable experience of the buyer.

The effective date of the new experience modifier will depend on the date the insurer and rating organization are notified of the change in ownership. If a written report is made within 90 days of the change, the experience modifier will be revised as of the date of the transfer of ownership. Otherwise, the modifier will be revised as of the next anniversary date following the earliest date either of the prior insurers was notified of a change. NCCI can provide a form (ERM 14—Request for Information) for filing information pertaining to a change in ownership.

If the seller is subject to experience rating based on its ownership in other entities, its experience modifier will be recalculated to exclude the loss experience of the entity sold. If the seller is disposing of only a part of its operations, and otherwise continues to operate its business, the experience of the disposed operations (prior to the date of sale) will continue to be included in its experience rating, *unless* the rating organization is furnished with appropriate information to allow it to transfer the data to the buyer.

Regardless of how you apply these or other specific rules relating to the combination of entities, such entities will not be combined unless you notify the governing boards and bureaus. These types of situations are addressed at length in the *Experience Rating Plan Manual,* published by NCCI.

It is impossible in this brief section to address all the fine details of ownership as it relates to experience rating. Given the complexity surrounding the interpretation and application of rules relating to ownership changes, there is an opportunity for meaningful savings or catastrophic additional premiums if your firm does not recognize the effects of ownership changes on its experience modifier. When your organization considers purchasing or selling a subsidiary, or merging with another firm, employing a knowledgeable person to perform a series of test ratings using various assumptions and make specific recommendations offers potential for premium reduction.

For further research and study

The *Experience Rating Plan Manual for Workers Compensation and Employers Liability Insurance* is available from NCCI in print and over the Internet: National Council on Compensation Insurance, 901 Peninsula Corporate Circle, Boca Raton, Florida 33487, (800) 622–4123, www.ncci.com.

Refer also to Chapter XI in *IRMI Workers Comp—A Complete Guide to Coverage, Laws, and Cost Containment*, published by IRMI, for a thorough discussion of the experience rating process. A less extensive treatment of the topic may be found in *IRMI Workers Compensation Insurance Guide*. Visit the Products and Services section of IRMI.com for more information on these publications.

7

PROPERTY INSURANCE

EVER SINCE THE FIRST HUT WAS BUILT FOR SHELTER, people have worried about the elements destroying their property. When the insurance industry began to develop in the late 1700s, the primary subject of insurance was property, such as cargo, homes, buildings, and factories. At first, such coverage was simple. It addressed the specific peril of fire. Over time, the market grew and coverages became broader. Windstorm, hail, collapse, theft, vandalism, and other unforeseen causes of loss became covered perils.

Property insurance is first-party coverage, as compared to liability insurance, which is described as third-party coverage. The insurance company, the second party, covers the policyholder, the first party, against damage. Under liability insurance, the insurance company is covering the insured against actions brought by an outside party, usually referred to as a third party. Generally, for a third-party policy to pay, there must be negligence involved on the part of the insured. Under first-party coverage, negligence is not an issue. If the property is damaged, and the damage was caused by an insured peril, the first-party policy pays. For most insureds, property insurance premiums are lower than liability and workers compensation premiums. However, improper coverage can result in financial catastrophes. Therefore, it is usually wise to buy as broad a policy as possible and, if in doubt, be prepared to overinsure, since any possible premium savings from reduced coverage may not warrant the adverse financial consequences that would arise from an uninsured or underinsured loss.

Today, there are two basic coverage forms: *named perils* and *"open perils,"* also called by its older moniker, "all risk." Named perils coverage is just what its name indicates: it covers damage caused by specifically named perils such as fire, lightning, hail, windstorm, vandalism, smoke, and explosion. For an insurer to pay a claim, the insured must prove that the damage was caused by a covered peril.

The broader and more generally desirable form is "all risk" or "open perils" coverage. This type of policy form covers all perils not specifically excluded by the policy. Under open perils coverage, the burden of proof shifts to the insurance company. To deny a claim, the insurer must prove that the peril that caused the loss is specifically excluded by the policy. Otherwise, the company must pay.

Property Insurance Rating

To develop a premium for a property insurance policy, a rate is multiplied by the limit of insurance divided by 100. It is common in the insurance industry to simplify this by speaking of multiplying the rate times the limit to arrive at the premium. In all jurisdictions except New Jersey, the District of Columbia, and Puerto Rico, Insurance Services Office, Inc. (ISO), publishes advisory prospective loss costs rather than advisory final rates. The difference is that prospective loss costs contemplate only expected losses and loss adjustment expenses, whereas advisory rates include loadings for insurer expenses and underwriting profit as well.

Commercial Lines Manual (CLM) users must obtain either individual insurer rates or instructions from the insurer on converting ISO loss costs to rates. Most insurers that use ISO *CLM* rating procedures for at least some of their policies supply manual holders with a loss cost multiplier (reflecting that insurer's expenses and desired underwriting profit) to use in converting ISO loss costs to final rates.

Many of ISO's member insurers elect to determine commercial property insurance premiums for some or all of the policies they write, in accordance with the ISO *CLM* advisory rating process. However, ISO member insurers are free to determine their own rating procedures (and some have elected to do so) for some or all of the policies they write. This discussion does not address individual insurer rating procedures, to the extent that they differ from ISO *CLM* advisory rating procedures.

ISO has established two methods of rating property insurance: class rating and specific rating. *Class rating* is used to determine premium for properties occupied by businesses that fall into certain "classes," provided that they meet specific eligibility requirements. Properties that do not qualify for class rating (in general, large or specially protected properties or properties that have high risk or very unusual occupancies) must be specifically rated. Class rating is rating directly from the *CLM,* from start to finish, using rates applicable to all properties meeting certain criteria. *Specific rating,* on the other hand, uses a rate applicable only to the property in question (a rate *specific* to that property) as the starting point of the rating process, which is then completed in accordance with *CLM* rules. Specifically rated properties are physically inspected by ISO personnel to enable them to arrive at a loss cost that reflects the unique characteristics of that property. This loss cost is referred to as the "published" loss cost—but it is published individually, not in the *CLM.*

As part of the rating process, regardless of whether class or specific rating is used, the following characteristics of the property are considered.

- Construction
- Occupancy
- Location

Construction

Rule 15.B of the *Commercial Lines Manual (CLM)* establishes six basic types of building construction to be used in categorizing property for ISO *CLM* rating purposes.

- *Frame*—Exterior walls of wood, brick veneer, stone veneer, wood ironclad, stucco on wood. (Code 1)
- *Joisted Masonry*—Exterior walls of masonry material (adobe, brick, concrete, gypsum block, hollow concrete block, stone, tile, or similar materials), with combustible floor and roof. (Code 2)
- *Noncombustible*—Exterior walls, floor, and supports made of metal, asbestos, gypsum, or other noncombustible materials. (Code 3)
- *Masonry Noncombustible*—Same as joisted masonry except that the floors and roof are of metal or other noncombustible materials. (Code 4)
- *Modified Fire Resistive*—Exterior walls, floors, and roof of masonry or fire-resistive material with a fire resistance rating of at least 1 hour, but less than 2 hours. (Code 5)

- *Fire Resistive*—Exterior walls, floors, and roof of masonry or fire-resistive materials with a fire resistance rating of at least 2 hours. (Code 6)

As a practical matter, buildings (and their contents) in the first three construction groups are often eligible for class rating, assuming that the occupancy qualifies as well. Those in the last three construction groups usually must be specifically rated, regardless of whether they would be eligible for class rating on the basis of occupancy alone.

Construction information can be obtained from a variety of sources, some of which are listed below.

- The insured or the building owner
- An appraisal report
- An insurer inspection report
- The declarations page of a property policy
- An ISO published rate on a specifically rated property

Occupancy

The occupancy of a building can drastically affect the rate. A concrete block building occupied by an explosives manufacturer will obviously have a higher rate for both building and contents than the same building occupied by a bottled water distributor. Furthermore, building occupancy can and often does change over time. This is particularly true of mercantile buildings leased to others. Consequently, it is important to make sure your occupancy information is up-to-date, particularly if the former occupant engaged in more hazardous operations.

Occupancy is a major determinant of eligibility for class rating; in some cases, it is the *only* determining factor. For example, restaurants are never eligible, no matter what type of building houses them. Apartments, on the other hand, are always eligible for class rating, regardless of building construction type.

The occupancy of a specifically rated property as it was last reported to ISO is part of the information supplied with the published loss cost.

Location

The location of the property to be insured is another vitally important factor in property insurance rating. Both class and specific rates are based in large part on the fire experience of the state, county, city, town, or township where the property is located, on the availability of the water supply, and on the size and type of fire department (paid versus volunteer). The location of the insured property also influences its susceptibility to other causes of loss, such as windstorm.

Public protection classes, established by ISO, categorize cities and towns according to the availability of water (e.g., fire hydrants and amount of water pressure) and the quality of fire protection (e.g., training of firefighters). They are graded from 1 (the best available protection) to 10 (no protection). Actually, classes 9 and 10 are both "unprotected" classes; that is, they indicate rural areas without adequate fire hydrants or fire departments.

Protection classes are particularly important in class rating. Lists of the protection classes assigned to each town or city in each state are published by ISO. Although they are technically published as components of a separate manual (the *Public Protection Classification Manual),* the protection class pages are commonly filed in the *CLM* with the state exception pages. Properties located outside the limits of towns and cities are usually rated as unprotected. Whether protection class 9 or 10 applies is determined by the distance from an available fire hydrant or fire department. The pages listing protection classes for the state in which the property is located should indicate the distances used to establish these classes. Published loss costs indicate the applicable protection class in the loss cost printout.

Similarly, ISO's building code effectiveness grading schedule (BCEGS) categorizes communities according to the adequacy of their building codes and the effectiveness of building code enforcement. Communities are graded from 1 (indicating exemplary commitment to building code enforcement) to 10. In states where all of the communities have been graded and the BCEGS system has been implemented, the BCEGS grade for the community where the property is located is used in developing the premium for windstorm and hail coverage for buildings constructed during or after the year in which the community was graded. Building code effectiveness grades for communities are published in ISO's *Public Protection Classification Manual.*

In some states, the class rating method may also entail the application of territorial multipliers to risks located in large cities. Territorial multipliers are used to reflect actual loss experience of the city.

Other Rating Considerations

In addition to the construction, occupancy, and location, some information about the type of insurance being provided also affects the rate charged.

- The limit of insurance provided for building and for personal property
- The amount of coinsurance applicable (usually 80, 90, or 100 percent)
- The applicable causes of loss form (basic, broad, or special)

Ways To Cut Costs

This chapter provides seven ways to cut property insurance costs.

49. Obtain Rate Deviations/Dividends

Throughout the years, insurance companies have thoroughly codified their approach to developing rates for different types of structures. For instance, there are higher rates for frame structures and lower rates for concrete structures. These rates are modified according to the type of business conducted by the occupants. For example, a brick manufacturing company presents a lower risk of fire than a fireworks factory.

In most states, rating bureaus have developed specific rates or loss costs for each individual commercial building. In developing policy premiums, insurance underwriters begin with these rates/loss costs and apply credits and debits to develop a final *manual premium.* Most states allow the insurer to discount these rates/loss costs up front through the use of "deviations," which can range from 10 percent during tight insurance markets to as much as 75 percent during soft markets.

50. Use Deductibles

As with other coverage lines, deductibles can substantially reduce property insurance premiums. Potential losses must be weighed against premium savings. Specific deductibles may be assumed per item or type of property, per location, or per occurrence.

Some buyers have assumed lower deductibles as a result of concern over an unexpectedly large number of occurrences in a given policy period. An alternative approach is to purchase aggregate deductible coverage for the year. For example, a policyholder may assume a $10,000 deductible subject to a maximum annual amount of $30,000. Under this plan, once the deductibles exceed $30,000, all additional amounts are paid by the insurance company (although sometimes a low, "maintenance" deductible applies to losses after the aggregate has been met). This facilitates budgeting since the worst-case scenario is known.

Deductibles may be very desirable if the premium credits allowed justify the additional risk assumed. A historical analysis of past losses, when weighed against the premiums quoted for various deductible amounts, is the most efficient manner for selecting an appropriate deductible level.

51. Invest in Fire and Loss Prevention

Steps taken to prevent fires will result in lower insurance premiums. A few suggestions are made below.

Fire Extinguishers

Most large fires begin as small fires that grow. Hand extinguishers have prevented many small fires from becoming major ones. As a result, one of the credits allowed is for hand extinguisher units if a proper number of such units are maintained by the policyholder.

The first step in determining the cost-effectiveness of adding extinguishers is to ask your insurance agent or adviser to obtain a copy of the manual rate work sheet. If no extinguisher credits are allowed, recalculate the rates with the appropriate credit and apply them to the insurable values. The difference in premium is the amount of first-year savings that can be compared to the additional cost of acquiring and maintaining the necessary extinguishers. In many instances, no additional units will be required. Upon installation of the required units, the governing bureau will promulgate a revised rate.

Sprinklers

Substantial premium savings are available to owners of medium- and large-sized properties if they install approved sprinklers. Determining the cost-benefit ratio involves two major steps. First, a major underwriter of highly protected risks such as a Factory Mutual affiliate or the Industrial Risk Insurers (IRI) should be asked to perform an engineering study to determine the type and size of the sprinkler system that will be required and the resulting estimated premium savings.

With these specifications in hand, you can approach two or three sprinkler installation firms for proposals. If the savings do not totally justify the cost, you might negotiate with the insurance company to determine whether it will reduce its requirements subject to minimums required by local governmental units.

Even if the direct savings do not totally justify the cost, consider the fact that very few sprinklered properties are ever destroyed by fire. It may be prudent to spend a reasonable sum today to avoid the heart-rending experience of being involved in a major property loss in the future. Also, while it is very costly to equip existing buildings with sprinklers, the expense is much lower in new structures. Sprinklers should be considered for your facilities even if not required by building codes.

Hood Systems for Restaurants and Painting Booths

While it may not be desirable to equip the entire premises with sprinklers, substantial credits are available for specialized sprinkler or fire control systems in especially hazardous areas. For instance, grease will build up in exhaust fans contained in hoods over restaurant cooking equipment. The fire exposure from the grease can be virtually eliminated with the installation of special hood systems.

Another example is painting booths. The paint spray may be highly flammable. Again, special hood systems substantially reduce the possibility of a fire starting and spreading.

Other special systems are available for other special exposures such as those presented by data processing facilities.

Alarm Systems

By giving early warning, alarms can substantially reduce losses resulting from the peril of fire as well as from burglary and robbery. Based on the exposure and location of the premises, a loud bell outside the building may be all that is needed. In other cases, a direct line to a central station with 24-hour monitoring may be required to obtain the maximum credit.

Again, the cost of such systems must be weighed against the premium savings and the availability of insurance, coupled with the financial consequences and inconvenience of a loss.

Insulate Columns of Steel Buildings

Generally, steel buildings do not burn. However, if the property inside burns even a short time, the metal supporting beams become so hot that they buckle and cause the building to collapse.

This collapse exposure can be substantially reduced by shielding the columns with fire-proof insulation during construction (or even sometime after the building has been completed). This usually inexpensive action may considerably reduce the fire rate.

Fire Doors

Usually the highest rated activity or highest rated construction materials are used to determine the insurance rates for contiguous structures unless the exposure is segregated. The most common method of segregating the exposure is to install fire doors that will contain fire to a specific area. The fire, in other words, is prevented from traveling to other parts of the premises. This allows different rates to be applied to different parts of the premises.

Fire Hydrants

Often, new buildings are located on the edge of the community and may not be near a fire hydrant. As a result, adequate water may not be available to fight a fire if one occurs. Consequentially, fire rates are surcharged.

As the community grows and new fire hydrants are installed, adequate water supplies become available. However, the fire rate surcharge may not be dropped unless the bureau is notified.

If a rate surcharge exists for a building, an effort should be made to encourage the city to install a fire hydrant nearby. Once the hydrant is in place, advise the bureau immediately.

Safe Storage of Volatile Materials

Many buildings will have a substantial surcharge added to the base rate if volatile or highly flammable materials are stored on premises. If such materials are stored, determine if there are any ways you can reduce or eliminate the exposure.

- Is storage of the materials absolutely necessary for efficient operation of your business? If not, determine whether a supplier can store such materials until they are needed.
- If storage of the materials on premises is desirable or necessary, can they be stored in an outbuilding? In that case, the surcharge would be applied only to that small structure and could be deleted from the much larger building.
- If there is continuous use of the material, can it be stored in a tank outside the building and simply pumped in as needed, with automatic shutoff valves? This method may also result in a reduced premium on the main building.
- If possible, a double-walled underground tank should be used, with monitors between the two walls. Or, better yet, an aboveground tank with a specially sealed concrete containment area around it is generally a safe method of storing volatile materials.

Again, the cost of these approaches must be weighed against potential premium savings and other positive factors affecting the business operation.

Fireproof Cabinets

Valuable papers, records, media, and accounts receivable are the heart of today's business. Industry statistics indicate that almost one-half of the businesses that lose their accounts receivable through fire or other perils never reopen.

While it is extremely important to carry proper coverage for this property, it is even better to avoid damage in the first place. Therefore, valuable papers, computer tapes, and accounts receivable records should be stored in fireproof cabinets, safes, or vaults. Substantial premium credits are then applied to the valuable papers, accounts receivable, and data processing insurance premiums.

Underwriters Laboratory-Approved UL–90 Roofing

In areas prone to severe windstorms, roof damage is a major concern for insurance companies. If a roof is installed or modified to meet the standards of a UL–90 roof (which means it is approved by Underwriters Laboratory), substantial credits are usually available. Basically, extra bolts keep the roof from taking off like a kite.

Review Fire Rating Schedule

There are numerous other credits that are available and debits that may be applied in determining property insurance rates. For instance, using metal shelving rather than wood can make a substantial difference. The departure of certain neighboring firms can also affect rates. For example, if a former neighbor was in the furniture refinishing business, its high exposure rate would have affected your rating. If the new neighbor is in ceramic tile sales, you should file for a lower rate.

Summary

You should review the rate schedules with your insurance agents or advisers to determine what credits might be available and what surcharges might be avoided. Remember, not only will the building rate be reduced, but so will rates for all other property coverages—such as contents and business interruption.

52. Obtain Duplicate Records Credit

For various reasons, duplicate records should be stored off premises. For instance, duplicate accounting records should be stored off premises if a firm's accounts receivable are used as collateral for a bank loan. If a loss occurs, information could easily be reproduced using the extra set of records.

Probably the best loss control device for use with accounts receivable and other valuable records is to make duplicate records and store them off site. The records should be updated frequently. The same approach is also applicable to computer data.

Generally, there is a credit of up to 50 percent for duplicate records.

53. Use the Business Interruption Reporting Form

Business interruption coverage is a form of disability protection for a commercial entity for use when its property is damaged. If an adequate limit of coverage is not in place at the time of a loss, substantial penalties may be imposed by the insurance company. However, business operations may fluctuate during the year, and limits may be higher than necessary during slow periods if the coverage limits are established during a peak period. Coverage only reimburses the insured for actual losses, so no "gain" would be experienced should a loss occur during a slow period.

To enable the insured to have appropriate coverage at all times without wasting premium dollars, the insurance industry has developed a reporting form endorsement. Under this approach, the insured sets a maximum limit such as 125 percent of the highest peak period. Actual business volume is reported each month, and the premium is adjusted to reflect the exact business activity for the previous 12 months. If you use a reporting form, be sure to complete the reports on a timely basis. Failure to do so will result in a substantial penalty at the time of a loss.

54. Obtain Coinsurance Credits

Probably 90 percent of all property losses are under $50,000. You could reason, then, that a $50,000 policy would cover the majority of losses. However, if all businesses only carried these low limits, the rates per $100 of covered limits would be substantially higher. In addition, there would be no coverage for the large, catastrophic losses that do occur.

Figure 7.1

Application of the Coinsurance Formula

The Formula

[Insurance Carried ÷ Insurance Required (100% of building value)]
x   Loss   =   Recovery

An Example

Insurance Carried:	$ 800,000
Insurance Required:	$1,000,000
Loss:	$ 100,000

[$800,000 ÷ $1,000,000] x $100,000 = $80,000

To collect enough premiums to cover small and large losses, insurance companies offer lower rates to firms that carry insurance "to value"; in other words, limits are 80, 90, or 100 percent of the actual exposure. The higher the percentage, usually referred to as the "coinsurance percentage," the lower the rate.

However, if the insured has "fudged" or simply fails to carry the proper limits, a coinsurance penalty will be imposed in the event of a loss.

To illustrate how a coinsurance penalty operates, assume that a building is worth $1 million and that you accept a rate based on a 100 percent coinsurance clause. However, you decide to carry only $800,000 of insurance. During the policy term, a $100,000 loss occurs. The claim payment will be determined by the formula indicated in Figure 7.1.

In the example in Figure 7.1, the coinsurance penalty is $20,000 ($100,000 loss less $80,000 recovery). Of course, the deductible would also be subtracted from the recovery before it is paid.

The recommended approach is to accept lower rates based on a specific coinsurance clause and then to maintain coverage at the stipulated percentage. It may be wise to select limits that are 5 percent more than the coinsurance clause. For instance, if 80 percent coinsurance is selected, then select a limit based on 85 percent of the insurable value.

In many cases, insurance companies will agree to endorse the policy to waive any coinsurance penalties if the initial values are documented as being similar to those required. This is called an *agreed amount* clause, and this endorsement should be obtained, if possible.

55. Report Proper Builders Risk Values

A builders risk policy covers new buildings and additions to existing buildings during the construction phase. Such a policy is also subject to a coinsurance clause, usually with a 100 percent value requirement.

The total cost associated with the building may not be the proper limit to select. Architectural fees are usually excluded from values used to select a limit. If the building is damaged by windstorm, for example, no additional design work will be required to reconstruct it. In addition, some items such as site preparation, parking lots, driveways, curbing, sidewalks, fencing, and light posts may not be covered by the policy; if not, such values should be excluded. If included, a much lower rate might be negotiated to apply to the specific values for these items.

In summary, only the value of covered work should be reported in developing the values on which builders risk insurance premiums will be based.

For further research and study

Commercial Property Insurance, published by IRMI, is a three-volume reference manual that is a definitive source of interpretations and alternative coverage recommendations for commercial property, inland marine, and crime insurance. It interprets not only the standard forms and endorsements but also analyzes many of the nonstandard forms widely used in the marketplace. Visit the Products and Services section of IRMI.com for more information on this publication.

# INSURANCE INDUSTRY RELATIONSHIPS

IN THE UNITED STATES, property and liability insurance is distributed by three types of systems: the direct writer system, the exclusive agency system, and the independent agency system. The direct writer and exclusive agency insurance companies market insurance through salaried salespeople or commissioned agents who sell only the insurance products of a particular company. Examples of direct writer and exclusive agency companies include Farmers Group, Liberty Mutual, Nationwide, and State Farm. The independent agency system insurance companies, on the other hand, depend on independent insurance agents and brokers to sell their products. These agents or brokers often represent many insurance companies. A few examples of the many independent agency system insurance companies are ACE, American International Group (AIG), Chubb, Crum & Forster, Hartford, St. Paul Companies, Safeco, Travelers, and Zurich. In a few instances, certain companies such as Liberty Mutual are represented by both exclusive and independent producers.

From the standpoint of the insurance buyer, each of these alternatives for marketing insurance offers both advantages and disadvantages. The principal advantages of the direct writer/exclusive agency system over the independent agency system are higher quality claims, loss prevention, rehabilitation, and similar services typically provided by these companies. Another key advantage of most direct writers is lower expense ratios, a fact that should ultimately be reflected in lower premiums. On the other hand, the sales representatives of direct writers and exclusive agency companies may not be as skilled and knowledgeable as independent agents and brokers. In addition, direct writers and exclusive agency companies' representatives can offer only the services and products that their employer provides. However, both segments are making improvements in their deficient areas, and, consequently, the advantages of one system over another in a particular area are diminishing.

Probably the most important advantage of using independent agents and brokers—as compared to direct writers and exclusive agents—is that agents and brokers can place insurance with any one company or a combination of many insurance companies with which they do business. An independent agency generally has contracts with the insurers it represents. Not being employees of the insurance company, some independent agents and brokers are more oriented toward representing the buyer of insurance than the insurance company. The insurance buyer should keep in mind, however, that an insurance agent is legally an agent of the insurance company and not of the insurance buyer.

An insurance buyer can have success using either the American agency system or the direct writer/exclusive agency system. The main point to remember is that the agent/broker or insurance company representative is the primary interface/supplier of your insurance protection, and it is therefore important to choose a representative that can best serve your interests.

Agent/Broker Compensation

The compensation paid to independent agents or brokers by the businesses that they insure can be in the form of commissions paid by the insurance company (and passed through as part of the premium), a fee paid directly by the insured business, or a combination of the two. Commissions vary from insurance company to insurance company, agent to agent, and region to region. They are, to some extent, a function of the size of an account, with larger ones generating lower commission percentages. In general, however, insurance companies will pay a commission of around 8 to 15 percent of the premium on commercial auto insurance, 10 to 15 percent on commercial fire insurance, 8 to 10 percent on commercial general liability, 10 to 15 percent on commercial package policies, and 3 to 10 percent on workers compensation. Risk managers of larger businesses may have the bargaining power to negotiate the commission percentage with their agent or broker. And sometimes an agent or broker will accept reduced commissions from the insurance company to compete on medium-sized accounts against other agents and brokers in a competitive bidding situation. If the agent or broker is receiving commission income from the insurance company rather than a fee from the insured, the insured should request an annual statement from the agent or broker regarding the income received from the insurer. This information should be helpful in evaluating the services provided by the agent or broker.

Additionally, agents/brokers can sometimes derive additional income known as contingent commissions. These are payable, usually on a preset, sliding scale, when the agent's book of business with an insurer generates especially favorable loss experience during a given year. Contingency commission plans have been highly criticized by the risk management community, and the future of this system is in question.

Business managers of medium-sized and large businesses may be able to negotiate with their agent or broker to operate on a fee basis. This could be a negotiated flat fee or a fee based on time and expense. Since income to the agent or broker computed in this manner is not a function of the insurance premium, possible disincentives to reducing premiums that are inherent in the commission system are eliminated. This approach can also smooth out the income of the agent/broker rather than having it subject to the cyclical nature of the insurance business. One problem in attempting to place agents/brokers on such a system, however, is that they are not accustomed to accounting for their time and expenses and frequently do not have the systems in place to do so properly.

Arranging Coverage and Determining Premiums

The process generally used to purchase insurance is illustrated in Figure 8.1. The insured asks an agent or broker to obtain a quotation. Underwriting data necessary to determine whether or not the risk is insurable is assembled by the insured and the agent. The agent may or may not then ask a *surplus lines broker* (a "wholesaler") to assist in approaching insurers. Surplus lines brokers are most often used for specialty coverages (professional liability, umbrella liability, aircraft insurance, and marine insurance, for example) or for insureds who are in very high-risk businesses (like chemical, pharmaceutical, or pollution cleanup). The independent agent and surplus lines broker are usually paid commissions that are included in the insurance premium.

Figure 8.1

Insurance Process—Distribution System

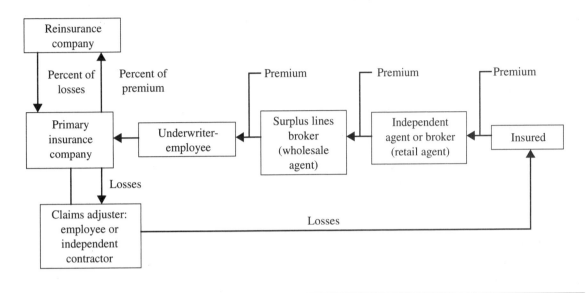

An *underwriter* at the insurance company reviews the underwriting data and determines whether the company wants to write the policy. In some cases, particularly in professional liability or other specialty lines, the underwriter will be an employee of a managing general agency (MGA) with authority from the insurer to underwrite on its behalf.

The underwriter who agrees to write the policy also decides how the premium will be determined. Rating technicians generally perform the actual mechanics based on the underwriter's instructions. Sometimes, particularly with large accounts, the local branch office underwriter must seek home office approval of a decision. Note that the underwriter does not become involved in paying claims. For this reason, all understandings related to the insurance coverage should be put in writing.

Often, the insurer wants to write a particular policy but does not want to bear the responsibility of paying all the losses. In such a situation, the insurer may arrange with one or more *reinsurers* to share a portion of the premium and of the insured losses. Usually the insured will not know whether or not its risks are reinsured or the identities of any reinsurers on the risk. The primary insurer is the only party to the insurance contract with the insured and bears all responsibility for insured losses, whether or not the reinsurer(s) pays. The claims process, also illustrated in Figure 8.1, is reviewed in Chapter 9.

Ways To Cut Costs

This chapter offers six ways to cut costs by understanding the working relationships in the insurance industry.

56.   Choose a Knowledgeable Agent or Broker

One of the most effective steps you can take to reduce business insurance costs is to choose an insurance agent or broker who can best serve your organization's needs. The individual(s) and the individual's firm represent your company to the insurance community, handle thousands or millions of dollars of its funds in the form of insurance premiums, provide consultative advice on how to protect the organization's continuing financial stability, and negotiate on behalf of the firm to recover from insurance companies after a loss has occurred. You should choose this individual and this firm as carefully as you would choose an accountant, attorney, or investment adviser.

Too often, agents and brokers are chosen because of social relationships rather than ability to do the job. This is particularly true in family-held businesses. In large businesses that have full-time professional risk managers, senior management should also be careful not to undermine the effectiveness of its risk management department as a result of social relationships with the agent/broker. Some agents/brokers will attempt to "go over the risk manager's head," and this can cost the organization considerable amounts of money if not properly handled by senior management. A similar problem occurs when the agent/broker is chosen because of a business relationship. For example, banks often succumb to an agent's offer to become a depositor in exchange for some or all of the "insurance pie." Care must be taken to assure that there is a proper trade-off of benefits. Only in very rare situations will an agent or broker chosen or retained solely because of family, social, or business relationships perform the quality services a particular organization deserves. Frequently, the agent/broker becomes complacent and fails to provide proper service.

A business that has grown rapidly over the years can actually outgrow the capability of its agent or broker. In this situation, the agent or broker was possibly well qualified in the early days of the firm. Over time, however, the business grew and the insurance industry changed dramatically. Agents and brokers must continually educate themselves and keep up to date on developments in the insurance industry as well as the industries in which their clients are engaged. A new agent or broker should be found if the organization outgrows the capability of its agent/broker or if the agent/broker fails to stay current with industry developments.

Many factors may be used to assist in the selection of an agent/broker. Some of the more important ones include industry expertise, experience, general insurance knowledge, access to insurance markets, and staff support.

Industry expertise of an agent/broker involves knowledge of your business and the industry in which it operates. This type of knowledge pays off in proper insurance coverages. It also ensures knowledge of and relationships with the insurance companies most interested in writing insurance for businesses in your industry. Insurers targeting your industry are most likely to give you the best terms and price. When interviewing an agent/broker, you can generally assume industry expertise if the agent/broker has a large book of business within the same industry.

Overall experience in insurance and risk management within your geographical area of operations may also be very important. Agents/brokers in this category are those who have been doing business within the geographical area for a long period of time and also have clients in the same industry.

Being of comparable size to the agent's/broker's other accounts is also usually beneficial. While there may be certain advantages to being the largest account written by an agency or brokerage firm, there is usually more to be gained from being one of a number of similar-size accounts. If your firm is much smaller than the agent's or broker's other accounts, you may not receive the attention you would with a different agent/broker.

General insurance knowledge of the agent/broker is extremely important. Although a substantial amount of experience is quite important, it should not be the only factor used to determine general insurance knowledge since the industry changes rapidly and some people simply have not kept up with the changes. To evaluate general insurance knowledge, find out whether the agent/broker attends industry seminars, participates in industry seminars as a speaker or lecturer, and/or has published articles for trade magazines. Participation on insurance committees of trade associations inside or outside the insurance industry is also a very good indicator of knowledge and capability. In addition, professional designations such as (in order of priority) Chartered Property Casualty Underwriter (CPCU), Certified Insurance Counselor (CIC), Accredited Adviser in Insurance (AAI), and Associate in Risk Management (ARM) attest to a general competency in the field of property and casualty insurance. While not as difficult to obtain, these programs resemble the Certified Public Accountant (CPA) designation in that they involve mastering in-depth, written examinations requiring considerable study and preparation.

Access to—and clout with—insurance markets is another important factor to consider when relying on an agent/broker instead of using direct writers, because this affects both the price and the coverage terms that can be negotiated. When talking with an agent/broker about the possibility of writing your firm's insurance, you should discuss the insurance marketplace. Determine how many insurance companies the agency does business with, the most predominant insurance companies used by the agency, and—if the firm's insurance involves any unusual insurance policies, such as professional liability insurance—the amount of experience the agent/broker has in the specialty coverage marketplace ("excess and surplus (E&S) lines insurance"). In particular, does the agent/broker have relationships with the insurers that focus on your industry?

Staff support available to the agent/broker, and the size of the agency/brokerage firm itself, affect service. Determine what support the individual primarily responsible for your account has in the areas of marketing (selling your risks to insurance companies), administration (accounting and billing), and account servicing (issuing certificates, reviewing audits and experience rating data, and checking insurance policies). Access to an assistant or a support staff to help with these functions will greatly increase the time the agent/broker has available for more creative work on the account.

57. Use a Limited Number of Agencies/Brokerages

For routine commercial accounts, a single agent/broker or a single direct writer should be used to provide all of the property and casualty insurance. (Firms should also consider working with that same agent/broker to provide employee benefits and health coverages since many agencies have excellent capabilities in these areas.) The use of a single representative substantially increases your influence with that agent/broker, avoids coordination problems that may arise when several firms are used, and makes your account more important to the agent/broker because of the volume of revenues that it provides.

Larger corporations sometimes use more than one firm to represent them in the insurance marketplace. Many corporate insurance buyers for large organizations will use two agents/brokers to maintain a certain level of constant competition on the account. When an organization has numerous complicated insurance needs, it also makes sense to use several brokers that have expertise in some of the complicated areas. For example, an organization with both national and international exposures might determine that it is in its best interest to use one agent/broker for the domestic insurance program and a separate one for the international program. Another logical split might be to use one agent/broker for all property coverages and another for all liability coverage.

It is important, however, to try to avoid using different agents to write coverages that need to carefully coordinate with each other. For this reason, for example, it is usually best to use the same agent to write your commercial auto, general liability, and umbrella liability insurance.

Never allow an agent's association or insurance placement committee to place your insurance. This process, which has most often been used by nonprofit and governmental entities, allows a number of agencies to place insurance and split the commission income. This will almost always result in a lack of competition, higher premiums, reduced service levels, and uncoordinated coverages.

In summary, very few, if any, companies can justify using more than four different firms to place their property and casualty insurance. Most organizations should use only one. When more than one agent or broker works on the account, the organization will experience the following costs and potential problems.

- Additional administrative time and effort in coordinating the activities of the agents
- Possible gaps in coverage from uncoordinated coverages in the various policies
- Possible loss of bargaining power with insurers because of reduced premium volume under control of each agent
- Possible lower service levels from agents because of reduced commissions as compared to what would be received if the entire account were controlled by a single agent

58. Use a Written Scope of Engagement

The agent/broker is paid a fairly substantial amount of money in the form of commissions or fees to service a business entity's insurance account. This often involves much behind-the-scenes work of which you may not even be aware. One of the most frequent causes of dissatisfaction is the feeling that the agent/broker is not providing the services that a firm needs. To ensure that your organization is getting its money's worth from its agent/broker, you can negotiate a written account service agreement with the agent/broker. Having a written agreement gives you a standard by which to measure the service levels of an agent/broker and, by the same token, provides the agent/broker with a means to justify income levels generated on the account.

Figure 8.2

Sample Agency Service Agreement

We feel it is important for the prospective insured to have an understanding of the services that will be provided by Cost Control Agency, Inc. The quotation on the insurance account is only a beginning. Cost Control Agency will perform the following services for Texas Manufacturers.

CURRENT POLICIES

1. **Policy Review.** Once the order has been received on a new account, it is very important that coverages be carefully checked to make sure you are delivered what has been proposed. In addition to checking coverages, the policy is completely rerated to make sure no errors were made.

2. **Comprehensive Checklist.** We prepare and provide you with a comprehensive insurance checklist for all your insurance exposures. If coverages have been proposed and not taken, we will ask you to initial the refusal so that there will be no confusion should an uninsured loss occur.

3. **Insurance Summary and Cost Comparison.** We will prepare a summary of all insurance policies written, with a brief description of coverage and premium that should be useful to obtain a quick review of your insurance program. Please understand, however, that this is only a brief summary and does not reflect all of the provisions of the policies.

4. **Claim Forms and Claim Kit.** We have prepared preprinted forms and a claims handling procedures manual that will explain the proper way to file a claim. Our office will work with you to make sure claims are handled properly and monitored on a timely basis. Cost Control Agency has a full-time claims staff to assist in settling claims.

RENEWALS

1. **Renewal Meeting.** We will conduct a renewal meeting and survey to determine your exposures for the coming year approximately 90 days prior to renewal. During this review we will discuss and request the following items from you.
   a. Updated vehicle schedule
   b. Updated equipment schedule
   c. Payroll classifications for workers compensation
   d. Estimates of receipts for the upcoming year
   e. List of current certificate holders
   f. Property values for building and contents currently insured
   g. List of named insureds
   h. List of additional insureds
   i. Uninsured motorist form for auto and umbrella
   j. Request for driver information

2. **Annual Report.** Within 2 weeks after our renewal meeting, we will prepare an annual report on such items as the following.
   a. Summary of agency service activities during the past year
   b. Brief review of major outstanding claims
   c. Summary of premium and loss experience
   d. Forecast of workers compensation and liability losses for the coming year
   e. Our views about the state of the insurance marketplace and how it might affect Texas Manufacturers
   f. Goals and objectives for the coming year

3. **Classifications.** We recommend a comprehensive review of all policy classifications for workers compensation, automobile, and general liability. The vehicle list will be carefully reviewed to make sure weights, usage, and garaging locations are correct. Of course, we will need your cooperation in performing this service.

4. **Certificates.** We recommend that certificate holders be provided new certificates 30 days prior to your renewal with copies to the insured. If the renewal process is prompt, this can be easily accomplished. You will be supplied with completed certificates that can be executed from your office when needed.

5. **Renewal Policies.** We endeavor to have renewal policies to our insureds prior to renewal. If this cannot be done for some reason, detailed binders will be prepared as a confirmation of coverage.
   Summary Checklist. We feel the renewal is more important than producing new business. We spend just as much time reviewing the renewal policies, preparing summaries and checklists as we did in the beginning. We try never to take our present insureds for granted.

continued

Figure 8.2 (cont.)

Sample Agency Service Agreement (cont.)

DAILY ACCOUNT SERVICE

Each principal agent has an account administrator to handle his or her accounts. The account administrator will handle the day-to-day activity on your behalf. We recommend that our account administrator visit your facilities and meet your personnel so that you can develop a good working relationship. Some of the areas in which we will provide service throughout the year are listed below.

1. **Audit.** The insurance audit is a very important function and should be coordinated by Cost Control Agency, so that a smooth and timely audit can be made. We will try to notify you within 30 days after your renewal as to the timing of the audit. We will discuss with you what records should be maintained so that you will not be overcharged in any area. Frequently, insureds are overcharged because of misclassification or the inappropriate application of a rating rule. Our involvement in the audit process should reduce the possibility of this happening to Texas Manufacturers. We insist on copies of the audit from our insurers and routinely review the audit for accuracy.

2. **Experience Rating.** We test rate your experience modification to ensure that no mistakes were made in the bureau calculation. We also recommend that your claims be reviewed to make certain that an old reserve that has had no activity is not being carried in your experience modification. We will attempt to have all the data used by the workers compensation bureau available for your review prior to its submission. We also recommend that experience rating data be developed for your automobile and general liability insurance. We will keep a record of your premium, broken down to base limits for bodily injury and property damage, along with losses for the general liability and automobile liability. We require this information to experience rate your account properly.

3. **Endorsements.** We have a special endorsement request form that we send to the company with a copy to our insureds. This form lets you know what coverage has been ordered and on what basis. You should review the form to make sure

that we have complied with your request. When endorsements are received, they are reviewed for their accuracy, and the premium is checked for correctness.

4. **Quarterly Loss Report.** Texas Manufacturers will be provided a list of all claims for the major lines of coverage on a quarterly basis.

5. **Quarterly Claims Meeting.** The staff will establish quarterly claims meetings with representatives of Texas Manufacturers. The purpose of these meetings will be to review open claims and discuss their disposition.

6. **Retrospective Premium Calculations.** Final retrospective premium calculations will be provided no later than 9 months after expiration of the applicable policy period. We will review these adjustments before sending them to you to reduce the possibility of mistakes.

7. **Location Visits.** The staff at Cost Control Agency, in conjunction with the insurance company, will visit plants on an as needed basis to evaluate unique loss exposures associated with your operations. Quarterly reviews are recommended.

8. **Communications.** We will communicate with you frequently to discuss any particular issues or concerns not previously addressed within the service agreement. We will be available on request to provide research assistance and consultation on risk management issues that may be of concern to you.

9. **Contract Documents.** We will review business contracts that you furnish us from a risk management and insurance perspective and provide you with our analysis. We suggest that whenever possible you let us see contracts before executing them in case an attempt to negotiate changes should be made. We make contract reviews only with the understanding that we are not attorneys and cannot give you a legal opinion. All contracts should also be carefully reviewed by qualified legal counsel.

ACCEPTED BY: Texas Manufacturers, Inc.

_____

Cost Control Agency, Inc.

The written scope of engagement and the agent's/broker's commissions or fees should be discussed, renegotiated, and revised annually. This approach will help you to get your money's worth.

Figure 8.2 provides a representative example of formalized agency service agreement that clearly enumerates the types of services that you might expect from a broker.

The scope of engagement provides a blueprint on which the appropriate compensation package can be developed. For this reason, the broker's compensation should also be discussed when the scope of engagement is agreed on.

Compensation plans vary; but they generally involve fees, commissions, or a combination of the two. These arrangements include commissions that are sometimes negotiated, flat fees, and time and expense billings.

Even if a straight commission arrangement is used, you should request to be advised regarding the amount of commission received by your agent. The commission may then be negotiated or, at the very least, you can assure that the agent is performing services commensurate with the level of income provided.

59. Maintain Communication

Tied into service levels of the agent/broker is formal communication between you and your insurance representative. To provide high-quality services, the agent/broker needs a substantial amount of information from you, not only at renewal time, but also at other times of the year. For example, changes in the business environment (such as acquisitions and new products produced) may necessitate adjustments in the insurance program.

To facilitate interaction between you and your agent/broker, consider holding an annual meeting prior to your insurance renewals. The timing of the meeting will vary somewhat with the size and complexity of your firm's insurance program, but it should generally take place between 90 and 120 days prior to renewal.

During the meeting, you should be prepared to provide the agent/broker with updated underwriting information (forecast annual sales, payrolls, number of vehicles for the next 12 months, information on any new properties that might be acquired, and planned changes in business activities). Your agent/broker should be prepared to inform you about the current status of the insurance marketplace, the planned approach to the insurance marketplace for the renewal of the account, and an expectation of premium levels for the next 12 months.

For all but the smallest commercial accounts, quarterly meetings should also be held with the agent/broker. The agenda for these meetings will vary with the activities and needs of the business and the agent/broker. Topics to be covered should include a review of open claims, updated information on your business activities, a review of renewal insurance policies when received from the insurance companies, a brief review of experience rating, annual audit, and—if applicable—retrospective rating calculations when received. The general status of the insurance marketplace should also be discussed to avoid surprises if there are any changes.

All too often, business managers meet with their agent/broker only when coerced into doing so by the agent/broker. To many, insurance is viewed as a necessary evil, and time spent discussing it is time wasted. Regularly scheduled meetings are extremely important, however, to ensure that the agent/broker is staying on track, that actions taken to deal with insurance marketplace changes are proactive rather than reactive, and that factors that may affect the firm's insurance costs are dealt with before it is too late.

60. Know Your Underwriter

Business managers of medium-sized and large commercial firms should meet and get to know the underwriter(s) for the major lines of insurance purchased by the business. In risk management and insurance, relationships can be very important when negotiating cost and coverage. You know your firm's operations and industry much better than your agent/broker does and are in a position to communicate information that will positively affect the underwriter's decision making.

Some agents/brokers will resist your attempts to develop a relationship with the underwriter. Usually, this is caused by an unfounded insecurity and desire of the agent/broker to avoid the development of relationships that will lessen your dependency. On the other hand, some underwriters truly have no desire to meet with their insureds, and forcing the issue in this situation can be counterproductive.

When a meeting is arranged, you, your agent/broker, and your business manager should discuss the meeting in advance and develop a strategy for it. Keep in mind that the agent/broker already knows the underwriter and can give valuable advice on how to best achieve your objectives.

61. Use Consultants

In the early-to-mid-1970s, a new type of professional insurance adviser emerged—the risk management and insurance consultant. Today, there are well over 100 risk management and insurance consulting firms in the United States. Typically, a risk management consulting firm employs a number of individuals with substantial experience in insurance and/or risk management, and it provides various services to insurance buyers for a fee. Organizations that cannot afford to hire a full-time risk manager can often save considerably more money than the consulting fee and, more important, can rest assured that a responsive insurance and risk management program is in place by retaining a consultant.

The services usually offered by these consultants include insurance policy coverage and cost reviews, review and feedback on overall corporate risk management programs, alternative risk financing plan feasibility studies (captive and self-insurance specifications, for example), assisting in bidding the insurance program, and conducting claim audits.

Since the risk management consulting industry is subject to virtually no regulation, you should be quite careful when choosing a consultant. First, determine whether the consultant sells insurance. Hiring an organization that sells insurance can create severe conflicts of interest and mitigate the positive effects of the consulting engagement. If a potential consultant also sells insurance, you should consider requiring an agreement that the consultant will not act as an agent or broker on behalf of your organization. Furthermore, you should resist all temptation to use that individual as an agent or broker for at least a 3- to 5-year period following the consulting engagement.

Other factors that affect the selection of a consultant are substantially similar to those that should be relied on in selecting an agent or broker. Verify that the consultant has meaningful experience and knowledge of insurance and risk management, especially in working for clients in your industry or a similar industry, and a good reputation for a quality work product. Obtain a number of references and telephone them to query the results of the consultant's work on their accounts.

Generally, the consultant's fee is based on the time involved in performing a consulting project. The larger firms use a number of individuals with specialized expertise relevant to the project. When hiring a consultant, be wary of organizations that use a highly experienced principal to sell consulting jobs and then rely on much less experienced staff to perform the work. Make sure you know exactly who will be doing the consulting work and evaluate his or her ability to perform it.

The Society of Risk Management Consultants (SRMC) is the leading professional organization in this field. Members must meet experience and ethical requirements and be independent of any organization engaged in the sale of insurance. Its membership list can be viewed online at www.srmcsociety.org.

Additionally, IRMI.com contains a Resource Directory that lists many consulting firms. Access is free at www.IRMI.com.

For further research and study

Construction Risk Management and *Guidelines for Insurance Specifications,* both published by IRMI, contain additional information on selecting and using agents, brokers, and consultants. Visit the Products and Services section of IRMI.com for more information about these publications.

9

CLAIMS

WHEN LOSSES OCCUR, insurers are expected to respond in a professional manner to rapidly settle the resulting claim or claims. Claims are the major cost component of insurance premiums and the reason businesses, nonprofit organizations, and governments purchase insurance. Depending on the line of insurance, claims costs generally represent between 50 and 90 percent of the premium dollar.

For all but the very smallest commercial insureds, insurance is simply a cost-stabilizing device. Most insureds will eventually pay all of their losses back to insurance companies in the form of premium dollars. This becomes most obvious in the liability lines (workers compensation, auto, and general liability) wherein experience rating, retrospective rating, and other loss-sensitive rating programs make the impact of claims on ultimate premiums quite obvious. However, this general rule is also true in other lines of insurance, such as property insurance.

The Importance of Claim Reserves

Workers compensation and liability insurance claims costs include not only the amount actually paid on claims but also an estimation of what will be paid on pending open claims (those claims that have not been closed through settlement or litigation). This estimate, which is made by the claims adjuster, is called a *case reserve*. The total amount of case reserves is included in *incurred losses* (paid claims and case reserves). Incurred losses are given to competing insurers quoting on the insured's account, used to calculate workers compensation experience rating modifiers, and used in calculating premiums under standard retrospective rating plans (as opposed to paid loss retrospective rating plans). Therefore, these estimated case reserves have a substantial effect on premiums, and any "overreserving" by the insurer will cause undeserved, often unrecoverable, premium increases. Premium costs can be controlled by monitoring and negotiating reserves.

Understanding Claim Reserves

The concept of claim reserves is simple and requires little explanation. Unfortunately, reserving practices are often poor and their rationale is not communicated by the insurer. Reserves seldom represent the actual value of a case and many adjusters are prone to frequent reserve changes. All this can leave you confused about the actual purpose of reserves.

Claim reserves are nothing more than the estimated cost to resolve a claim. An initial reserve should be applied to a case within a few days after the adjuster receives it and has had a chance to perform a preliminary investigation. A final reserve should be placed on a claim about 30 days after the adjuster has completed the claim investigation.

In theory, few reserve changes should occur once the 30-day reserve has been placed on the file. Frequent reserve changes are known as *stair stepping.* Stair stepping is generally viewed as a management weakness because it indicates a failure to fully grasp the significance of a claim and to adequately plot a resolution. However, that is not always the case.

More precisely, a case reserve is the total of several component reserves. An adjuster will establish individual reserves for medical payments, legal expenses, and *indemnity payments.* With workers compensation claims, indemnity payments include all benefits paid to the injured worker including weekly wage-loss benefits and permanent partial disability. With liability claims, indemnity is the amount the adjuster expects to pay out to the claimant. The claim reserve is the total of all these reserve components.

Claim reserves are usually reported to you on a claim report, which shows each case and the amount paid and reserved to date. Insurers will usually furnish a claim report at least quarterly and probably monthly for employers of significant size.

An adjuster should be able to provide an explanation for claim reserves. For instance, if an adjuster has established a $10,000 reserve for indemnity benefits, he or she should be able to explain the assumptions that support the reserve, such as the rate of compensation, the estimated number of weeks away from work, and the anticipated amount of a permanent disability award. If the adjuster cannot explain this, the reserve is probably not appropriate.

Reserves are important for a number of reasons beyond their importance in estimating losses. Reserves are an indicator that can be used to identify problem claims that deserve additional management attention. Claims that are underreserved do not draw the attention and management interest they should. It is also important that claims be accurately reserved so that an appropriate budget is established for the adjuster to resolve the claim.

Reserve Realities

As is often the case, the practical application of reserving often differs from the theoretical model. The most common problem is the stair stepping of reserves described above. Although the theory is that only two or three reserve changes should occur over the life of a claim, it is very common to see many more on "serious" claims.

Many "serious" workers compensation claims do not involve "serious" injuries. Rather, they result from other vocational factors. For instance, an employee may suffer a relatively minor back injury, but his return to work may be delayed by substance abuse problems, a lack of motivation, and a shortage of jobs in the community. An adjuster cannot calculate the impact of motivational factors and build it into a reserve at the time the injury is reported. The impact of such factors will be reflected as they delay the claim resolution. This often leads to several reserve changes before the file can be closed.

Another variation is that some insurers and third-party claim administrators now use software to estimate reserves rather than relying entirely on claims adjusters. Adjusters input details about the case into the program, such as the diagnosis and employee's age, and the system recommends a reserve. However, adjusters should still evaluate the system-generated reserve and determine that it makes sense for a particular claim.

The Claims Adjusting Process

When your firm suffers a loss, a claim is made to the insurance company. Except for very small claims, in which agents are sometimes given settlement authority by insurers, a claims adjuster is assigned to the case by the insurer. The adjuster may be an employee of the insurer, or the insurer may contract with an outside company to perform this service. Either way, the adjuster's primary allegiance is to the insurer.

As illustrated in Figure 9.1, the adjuster investigates the loss and compares the facts of the case to the terms of the insurance policy. If the adjuster determines that the policy does not cover the loss, the claim is denied. If the adjuster determines that the loss is covered, the adjuster will negotiate with the insured to settle a property claim or with the claimant to settle a liability or workers compensation claim. In the case of potentially severe liability or workers compensation claims, the adjuster may retain a law firm to investigate, defend, and/or settle.

The agent/broker will usually work with you to present the claim to your insurer. However, the agent or broker ordinarily cannot commit the insurer to a particular response. Likewise, the underwriter who negotiated the insurance policy does not normally become involved in the claims adjusting process.

Figure 9.1

Insurance Process—Claims

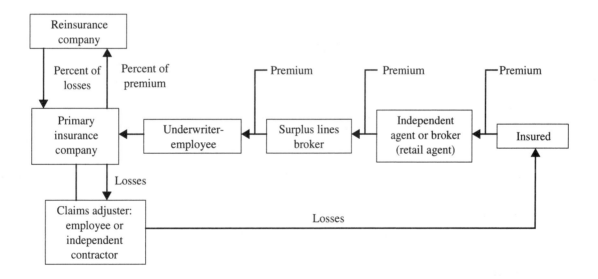

Because claim costs are such a large percentage of the insurance premium, they should be monitored, evaluated, and managed. In property insurance, claims recoveries are also negotiable with the insurer, and your goal when presenting your case to the insurance company is to maximize a recovery following a loss. Since paid claims in workers compensation and liability insurance will directly affect premium costs in the future, you should monitor the loss adjustment activity of the insurance company to ensure that only legitimate claims are paid, that unpaid claims are not being overreserved, and that claim costs are accurately recorded.

Another key point to recognize concerning claims administration is the close correlation between the quality of claims handling and adjuster file counts. This fact affects both insureds and self-insureds. On one hand, insurance companies have been cutting the size of their adjusting staffs in recent years. On the other, the claims administration business is extremely competitive, and firms sometimes slash prices to "buy business." The net effect is that whether you self-insure or purchase coverage from a commercial insurer, it is important to closely monitor the average file counts of the adjusters who handle your claims. This statistic is perhaps the single most important factor affecting the quality of the claims handling that your company will receive.

Ways To Cut Costs

This chapter presents seven ways to cut costs by monitoring claims activities.

62. Request Advance Payment of Property Claims

Insurance covering physical damage to property (buildings, contents, and inventory) will indemnify you for the costs incurred in repairing or replacing damaged or destroyed property. Usually, insurance companies wait until the property has been repaired or replaced and then reimburse the insured for the costs incurred. However, following a major loss you can ask the insurance company to provide an advance payment. Most reputable insurance companies provide an advance of 75 to 80 percent of the expected loss. These funds are then available for you to use in repairing or replacing the property, and the insured, rather than the insurer, will benefit from investment income on the funds during the period of restoration or repair.

63. Retain Public Adjusters for Large Property Losses

Public adjusters assist insureds in preparing proofs of loss and in negotiating with insurance company adjusters. Generally, the public adjuster's compensation will be based on a per diem fee or a percentage of the final loss recovery. A skilled public adjuster will almost always recoup far more from the insurer than is spent on the fees charged.

If your business suffers a large property loss, strongly consider retaining a reputable public adjuster to represent you in negotiations with the insurance company. This is particularly true if the loss involves a business interruption claim, the adjustment of which requires specialized expertise that public adjusters offer.

64. Have Periodic Meetings with Insurance Company Adjusters

Insurance company claims adjusters perform a critical, highly visible function and are an extremely overworked group of people. For example, a workers compensation adjuster may, at any one point in time, have responsibility for adjusting more than 200 open claims.

The insured that takes an interest in its claim services will frequently receive superior service, and, ultimately, lower claims costs. For this reason, it is wise to periodically (quarterly, semiannually, or annually) hold meetings at the insurance company with the administrator in charge of your claims. The status of your firm's largest open claims should be discussed during the meeting. This would include the amount reserved for such claims, actions that have been taken by the adjuster, future activity, and potential settlement strategies for difficult cases. In workers compensation, particularly, pay careful attention to reserves for open claims since they will be used in the experience rating process (see Chapter 6).

65. Obtain the Right To Approve Workers Compensation and Liability Claims Payments

Workers compensation, automobile, and general liability policies vest insurers with the right to dispose of claims as they see fit. In other words, insurance contracts do not require insurers to consult with you to determine whether to attempt to settle a claim or contest it. While in many cases the action taken by an insurance company is in both its and your best interests, there may be exceptions. Probably the most common problem area involves small, "nuisance" claims. Often, it costs the insurer less money to settle a minor (under $1,000), though questionable, claim than it does in attorney fees to fight it, and many insurers will pay these claims. When viewed on an individual claim basis, this approach appears to be logical. However, news travels fast within the plaintiff's bar, and an insurer or self-insured that adopts this philosophy will soon find itself inundated with small, nuisance claims. On the other hand, when you do not automatically pay these types of claims, the plaintiff's bar quickly loses interest in bringing such claims or suits against you, and the frequency will reduce dramatically over time.

While it is sometimes difficult to negotiate a policy provision requiring insurers to consult with you before settling with claimants, many will informally agree to do so in a side agreement. Seek an understanding with your insurer wherein your approval will be requested before any claim of more than a prespecified dollar amount ($5,000, for example) is settled. This is especially true in large deductible programs, in which the insurance company has an implied duty to communicate with the insured prior to settling claims, since the firm's money will be covering such settlements. You should also try to agree with the insurer concerning the procedure for handling small claims and then periodically spot-check such claims for compliance with this procedure.

66. Audit Claims Departments and Adjusting Firms

Medium-sized insureds, large insureds, and self-insureds should strongly consider arranging for periodic audits of workers compensation and liability claim files handled by the insurance company, independent claims administrator, or third-party administrator (TPA).

As a general rule, audits should be performed every 3 to 5 years, or more frequently in the event of specific problems or after a change of service providers. Conditions that may indicate the need for a claim audit are listed in Figure 9.2.

Figure 9.2

Problems Indicating the Need for a Claims Audit

- A rising percentage of litigated claims
- An abrupt, unexplained increase in the number of newly reported claims
- A higher-than-normal percentage of reopened claims
- A slowdown in the rate at which claims are being closed
- A lack of acceptable reporting by the adjusting firm or insurer (with respect to detail or timeliness)
- A larger-than-usual number of complaints from your company's operating managers, claimants, or regulators
- Unexplained increases or fluctuations in overall or individual case reserves, especially on claims that have been open more than 2 years
- A higher-than-normal number of late-reported claims

Claim audits involve the examination and evaluation of a representative yet manageable number of files. Usually, this encompasses 5 to 25 percent of all open cases, including all serious claims (those reserved for $50,000 or more, for example) in addition to a small percentage of closed cases. Figure 9.3 lists some specific areas that should be analyzed during a claims audit.

Risk management consulting firms, independent adjusting firms, and some insurance brokers offer claims auditing services. When choosing an auditor, be sure to look for a firm—and an individual within that firm—with experience in the types of claims that your organization most often experiences (such as workers compensation, general liability, auto liability, or medical malpractice). Also, be careful to avoid conflicts of interest. For example, an independent adjusting firm that has been trying to win your adjusting business would have an incentive to make your current firm look bad. In some cases, a broker who does not write your insurance would have a similar conflict. Be sure to explore these possible conflicts before hiring an auditor.

Figure 9.3

Areas Reviewed during Claims Audits

- Conformance with preagreed claim management procedures
- Prompt initial contacts with both claimants and internal operating personnel
- Compliance with periodic reporting requirements
- Timeliness, depth, and quality of investigation
- Accurate and thorough file documentation
- Properly determined coverage and liability
- Accurate and timely payments and no duplications or missed reimbursements
- Proper settlement levels and the accompanying degree of negotiating skills
- Management of physicians and attorneys in terms of both cost and work product quality
- Accurate and consistent reserving
- Reasonable adjuster and manager caseloads
- Adequate supervision on files
- Appropriate use of surveillance techniques

67. Maintain Loss Records

Many business managers make the mistake of not demanding periodic (monthly, quarterly, semiannually, or annually) loss reports from their workers compensation, auto, and general liability insurers. This information is invaluable in analyzing safety and risk control programs, in verifying the accuracy of experience rating and retrospective rating calculations, and in obtaining insurance quotations from competing insurance companies. The last use of this data, of course, is one reason why insurers are often reluctant to provide it to insureds. Obviously, it may also be used when negotiating premium costs with the current insurance company or a prospective insurer.

In addition to providing insurance loss data for the current policy year, the insurance company should be asked to provide updated, currently valued loss reports for each of the past 5 years on an annual basis. In other words, you should request 1996 loss data not only in 1996 but also in 1997, 1998, 1999, 2000, and 2001. The total dollars of losses will be different in each of these years as open claims are settled for either more or less than originally reserved in 1996. When negotiating with the current insurer or attempting to place coverage with another insurer, it will be important to have the most up-to-date information possible. When the market is "tight," it is even more important to have up-to-date loss information. In fact, some insurers will not even be interested in quoting your account without up-to-date loss information.

In addition, obtaining this information on an annual basis will allow you to review the reserving practices of your insurance company. If the total dollar losses for individual years continually decline as claims mature, this indicates that the insurance company is consistently overreserving open claims. Since experience rating formulas and some retrospective rating formulas include reserves on open claims in their calculations, this practice causes overpayment of premiums that might otherwise never be refunded to the insured. If such overreserving practices are discovered, it may be possible to negotiate lower case reserves that will reduce experience modifiers and/or increase retrospective rating returns.

68. Manage Litigation Costs Aggressively

Considering the high expenditures for legal services required by litigated claims, substantial sums can be saved by effectively managing the costs of lawyers' services. This applies particularly to firms that self-insure. But even if your company purchases coverage from an insurer, you should seek involvement in the selection and management of claims requiring the use of attorneys, because legal expenses will impact your experience modifier and, ultimately, premiums.

There are a number of techniques for managing legal fees associated with claims. They are noted and briefly discussed in Figure 9.4.

Figure 9.4

10 Steps to Managing Legal Costs

Adopt Written Billing Guidelines. By tailoring these guidelines to your company's specific requirements, you put law firms on notice that they will be held accountable for "fat" invoices. Savvy consumers of legal services can wield considerable clout in negotiating the cost of outside claims counsel.

Require Budgets. Request a litigation plan for each case with an estimate of the billable hours and total costs that will be required to conclude each case.

Negotiate Hourly Billing Rates and Billing Intervals. Discounts are especially achievable if a law firm handles a substantial amount of work for your company. By negotiating billing intervals, you can calibrate the timing of bills to your company's preferences and cash flow needs. Moreover, interim billing allows you to spot outrageous legal bills before their frequency becomes out of hand.

Negotiate Flat Fee Per Case Arrangements. Flat fees are usually preferable to hourly billing arrangements because they avoid situations in which "the meter runs." Although not suitable to all types of claims, "not to exceed" fees can be effective in certain instances.

Create a "Billing Alert" Threshold. This is a trigger point at which the attorney must notify you. You can define the trigger point in hours billed or total dollar amount billed. This method sends a clear signal to counsel that you are concerned with costs and encourages them to use their time effectively.

continued

Figure 9.4 (cont.)

10 Steps to Managing Legal Costs (cont.)

Control Reporting. Attorneys can expend significant amounts of billable hours writing full-captioned reports. Ask lawyers to distill written documentation and reporting to the essentials. Emphasize that you do not need lengthy reports of every case development except in certain narrowly defined categories involving serious claims.

Challenge Time Spent "Reviewing." Regular people read; lawyers "review," and they will bill you for it. Obtain a clear understanding of services for which you will and will not be charged.

Insist on Clear, Itemized Billings. Detailed information regarding the specific task performed and the time it took, in one-tenth-of-an-hour increments, should accompany all invoices. Your lawyer's bill should be as airtight as the receipt you get from the grocery.

Periodically Audit Legal Bills. If a significant number of your firm's claims are handled by a single law firm, legal bill audits are yet another effective approach to cost control and are perfectly justified in providing you with an accurate picture of the services you are receiving.

Carefully Monitor Expenses. Ancillary expenses associated with the legal function can also add substantially to your bill. Where possible, try to do photocopying in-house, since attorneys often charge as much as 25 cents per copy, an amount that can involve meaningful sums for cases requiring the copying of several thousand pages. It is also important to closely examine telephone charges, be selective in ordering medical records, require prior authorization on outside experts, place realistic limits on express mail charges, and set realistic meal guidelines when out-of-town travel is required on a case.

Source: *Litigation Management,* Kevin M. Quinley, International Risk Management Institute, Inc., Dallas, 1995.

For further research and study

Blueprint for Workers Compensation Cost Containment, IRMI Workers Comp, IRMI Workers Compensation Insurance Guide, and *Litigation Management,* all published by IRMI, can provide you with additional valuable ideas about how to manage and control claims costs. For more information on these titles, visit the Products and Services pages at www.IRMI.com.

10

RISK CONTROL

DEPENDING ON THE LINE OF INSURANCE COVERAGE involved and the size of your company, losses (and related claim expenses) often represent 50 percent or more of the premiums that your company pays. In view of this fact, the greatest areas for potential savings on your firm's insurance program lie in *preventing* losses from occurring and in *containing* the extent of losses after they occur. Efforts to control your company's losses could provide larger premium dollar savings than all of the cost control techniques presented in the other chapters in this book combined.

The term "risk control" (also often called "loss control") applies to both preloss and postloss activities. These approaches can decisively reduce your organization's cost of insurance and/or retained losses, as well as the often severe human costs that result from accidents and injuries.

Most of the material discussed in this chapter focuses on controlling workers compensation risks. In many instances, however, these techniques can also apply to other lines of coverage, particularly general liability and auto liability.

Ways To Cut Costs—Preloss

This section presents eight methods of cutting costs by preventing the occurrence of claims.

69. Obtain Senior Management Support for Risk Control

The foundation of every successful risk control program is obtaining the wholehearted support of a company's senior management team—especially the chief executive officer (CEO) or owner. Such support is critical because effective loss control requires that certain actions be taken within the organization that may either be unpopular or require significant operational changes requiring the assent of top management.

The most expeditious means of obtaining senior management's backing for loss control initiatives is to communicate the effect claim costs have on the organization's bottom line. It is important to recognize that in addition to the dollar amounts appearing on your company's loss reports, there are additional, "hidden" costs associated with claims. Lost managerial/ supervisory time, reduced morale, production delays, replacement worker training, property damage, and lower productivity when a worker returns are only a few of these costs that, according to industrial experts, can account for an additional two to four times the dollar amount indicated on a loss report. When perceived in this light, a $15,000 workers compensation claim may actually cost your company closer to $50,000.

Taking this example a step further, if your firm's net, pretax profit margin is 10 percent, approximately $500,000 of additional sales will be required to make up for the loss caused by this $15,000 workers compensation claim. Using this logic, but substituting your firm's real experience, during meetings with your company's executives will drive home the importance of preventing losses from happening and of containing them if they do occur. This is the critical first step in developing a successful risk control program for your company. It is only after winning the unconditional backing of top management that truly effective cost control measures can be accepted and implemented within your firm.

70. Allocate Costs on a Loss-Sensitive Basis

Regrettably, many companies apportion their workers compensation costs and insurance premiums for other coverage lines on the basis of factors bearing no relationship to the loss-causing activities of individual profit centers and operating locations. For example, many entities allocate annual workers compensation premiums (and/or self-insured losses) on such bases as gross sales, number of employees, or premium amounts noted on policy declarations pages for each location. Unfortunately, these approaches provide no motivation for the managers of individual profit centers to control costs. Alternatively, more positive incentive can be instilled by allocating premiums in proportion to actual incurred losses. If, for example, a given plant or location is responsible for 20 percent of your organization's workers compensation costs, it should pay 20 percent of the firm's annual workers compensation premium—regardless of other factors.

This is admittedly an oversimplification of the cost allocation process. Adjustments must be made to account for unusually large claims, administrative expenses, varying levels of internal deductibles, and a host of other factors. Nevertheless, efforts should be made wherever possible to avoid situations in which profit centers with unfavorable loss histories are being subsidized by those with effective cost containment track records.

Loss-sensitive premium allocations for all coverage lines involving controllable loss exposures are important because they ultimately send insurance costs directly to an individual profit center's bottom line. Since the bonus levels of operating managers are usually responsive to profitability, loss-sensitive allocation approaches can quickly gain operating management's support for loss control initiatives.

71. Involve Workers in the Safety and Risk Control Process

Just as both senior executives and operating managers need to focus their efforts on controlling losses, so too must rank-and-file employees. Research has shown that virtually all workers compensation losses result from either unsafe acts or hazardous conditions, with the majority caused by the former. It is therefore imperative that workers be allowed to play an integral role in any cost containment program.

The most common forum for obtaining employee input is via participation on plant safety committees. These groups should meet on a regular basis and include management, supervisory, and worker representatives. A detailed discussion of a safety committee's activities is beyond the scope of this discussion; however, they can be effective in lowering the frequency and severity of claims for two reasons.

- Safety committees promote the upward flow of communication. Workers have the closest encounters with accidents, so listening to workers is the best means of learning how to prevent accidents. Management theorist Peter Drucker summed it up best when he said, "Safety is, after all, a concern of people in the plant—and they know more about it than anyone else."

- Workers are more likely to be committed to safer practices if they are directly represented on safety committees. Since the recommendations they offer come at least in part from the rank and file, employees will find it easier to "buy into" the regulations and guidelines developed by a safety committee.

72. Motivate Safe Work Habits with Incentives

Motivating safe work habits among those who generate the bulk of a company's claims is another effective cost containment approach that you can apply. The most successful methods provide tangible rewards for claim-free work performance. Some examples of actual risk control motivation programs are provided in Figure 10.1.

Figure 10.1

Successful Risk Control Incentive Programs

- A California firm awards lottery tickets to every worker in each of its plants for every week during which a plant goes without a lost-time injury.
- A national workers compensation insurer conducts an annual safety drawing at each location that it insures (among those generating $500,000 or more in annual standard premium). The names of all workers who did not have a lost-time injury during the prior 12 months are placed in a raffle for a new car.
- A Wisconsin conglomerate conducts an annual corporatewide safety contest. Standings are based on Occupational Safety and Health Administration (OSHA) frequency and severity rates. Plants achieving the lowest scores in these two categories receive plaques, a visit by the CEO of the company, and $100 cash awards to each employee.
- An Ohio manufacturer gives each of its 400 production workers a $25 savings bond at the end of each month in which no lost-time injuries occur.

The programs in Figure 10.1 are not only effective in promoting safe work performance, they are also relatively inexpensive compared to the money they save. At first glance, the annual cost of the Ohio manufacturer's bond incentive program seems quite high (400 employees x 12 months x $18.75 = $90,000). However, the outlay is minimal when compared to the savings achieved by a claim-free year at a facility that formerly generated a $650,000 standard premium.

Incentive programs work well because they combine group and individual recognition, team effort, peer pressure, and direct monetary incentives to stimulate safer job performance.

73. Use Prehire Measures To Control Claims

Many claims can be avoided if certain preventive steps are taken before employees actually begin work. These measures fall into the following five major categories.

- Preemployment physicals
- Background screening
- Job placement testing
- Drug testing
- Orientation and education

Preemployment physicals provide a number of cost-saving benefits, although they are prohibited or limited by laws in certain states (and are impractical in other situations such as hiring day labor from union halls). They sometimes reveal preexisting health problems that preclude a hiring decision. In other instances, preemployment physicals can provide defenses against claims that are clearly not work-related. For example, a Michigan corporation had to pay an $85,000 workers compensation award to a man who suffered from a congenital heart abnormality that would have been easily detectable during a routine physical. However, his attorney argued successfully that the problem was caused by work-induced stress, an assertion that might have been refuted if a preemployment examination been conducted, documenting the congenital problem before the claim was made.

Employee background screening should include careful reference checking and verification of prior employment. In certain hazardous industries or in especially litigious jurisdictions, it is advisable to obtain index bureau reports so that a prospective employee's prior workers compensation claim history can be studied. Such information is valuable in screening out persons who exhibit a propensity toward initiating litigation against employers.

Preemployment investigation is especially important if your firm conducts motor vehicle operations. Companies should always obtain copies of the driving records of employees who will be doing significant amounts of driving. Awareness of prior accidents or violations can be instrumental in screening out potential employees who have a higher-than-average probability of becoming involved in claims.

Background checks can also uncover those situations in which second injury funds will contribute toward a claim payment. Specifically, when officials of a state second injury fund are advised of a preexisting impairment at the time of hiring, and a worker suffers an injury involving the original impairment, the fund will contribute toward the settlement.

Job placement testing can also prevent the occurrence of claims. These tests can reveal physical limitations (for example, the inability to lift certain amounts of weight) and therefore ensure that a person is not given a position that exceeds his or her physical capabilities. In certain environments, especially those involving chemicals and aerosols, individuals should be tested to reveal preexisting sensitivities. Screening of this kind can assist in preventing dermatitis claims and those resulting from allergic reactions to toxic substances used in the production process. Periodic monitoring of an employee's physical condition should also be conducted (hearing tests and chest X-rays, for example) once a person is on the job, to assure that adverse symptoms are not developing.

Employee drug testing is a controversial subject. However, an extremely good case can be made for drug testing workers whose jobs involve life-threatening dangers to themselves or third parties if performance is impaired by substance abuse (such as airline pilots, physicians, and heavy equipment operators). Construction industry studies demonstrating that approximately one-half of all lost-time accidents involve drug-impaired workers underscore the value of drug testing for employees involved in hazardous occupations.

It is generally considered advisable to have in place a company drug policy allowing employee screening, even if you do not intend to use it. Simply advising job applicants that they will be tested in the event of employment—and subject to termination if they test positively—will prevent the worst offenders from even applying. And having the policy in place will be very helpful if circumstances ever do compel you to screen employees.

Training and education for newly hired workers should also be a priority within your organization. Studies have shown that employees with less than 1 year of experience at a particular job are involved in a disproportionate number of industrial accidents. Therefore, it would appear that monies spent to orient new hires in both job functions and the hazards associated with them would contribute significantly to reducing losses.

74.   Communicate with Workers before Injuries

One of the cost drivers in the workers compensation system is the presence of attorneys representing employee-claimants. All other things being equal, the involvement of an attorney markedly increases the expenditure of dollars paid to settle and defend claims, but with questionable benefit to the injured employee—who must pay the lawyer a percentage of any settlement proceeds.

By effectively communicating with workers about the nature of workers' claims before the occurrence of an injury, however, the incidence of attorney involvement can be reduced. Unfortunately, many companies do not inform their employees about the availability of workers compensation insurance and how to make a claim. In view of this fact, it is not surprising that so many workers retain an attorney to guide them through the process of filing a workers compensation claim. In fact, many employees believe that hiring an attorney is required to even pursue such a claim!

Indeed, misunderstandings about the workers compensation system can result from a lack of information. Considering the increased likelihood of attorney involvement that such misunderstandings promote, the potential cost savings resulting from effective, preclaim communication with your company's workers is considerable.

75.   Investigate "Near-Miss" Incidents

The occurrence of an injury accident should not be a necessary prerequisite to conducting a safety investigation. Accident-producing conditions need to be identified and examined on a before-the-fact basis if a risk control program is to be truly effective.

Studies have shown that for every serious industrial accident, approximately 200 to 600 near-miss incidents also occur. For instance, the circumstances surrounding the following hypothetical, near-miss, noninjury events should be studied to ascertain their cause so that future accidents involving similar hazardous conditions or employee actions can be prevented.

Incident	Cause
A noninjury slip and fall	Excessive grease on a plant floor (poor housekeeping)
A metal chip flying from a grinding machine, narrowly missing a worker's eye	Worker not wearing safety goggles (lack of personal protective equipment)
A forklift swerving to avoid hitting a worker near an intersection in a plant	Defective warning buzzer not replaced (faulty maintenance)

In each of these situations, it was only by chance that serious injuries did not result. Any or all of these situations could have produced major claims. Such incidents are easily ignored and forgotten. However, near-misses of this type should be the subject of careful scrutiny because they result from the same types of conditions that produce serious injuries. As was noted earlier, "incidents" far outnumber major accidents. Thus, they provide a large number of case studies that can be examined in detail. The insights that result from thorough incident investigations can prevent future near-misses and, ultimately, significant injuries.

76. Commission an Independent Safety Program Audit

Independent evaluations of your company's operations can prove helpful in preventing accidents and claims. The advantages of outside safety evaluations include the following.

- *Objectivity.* Since they are not employees of the firm, risk control consultants bear no personal risk when they provide frank assessments that are critical of an entity's safety program or production practices.
- *Expertise.* Some risk control consultants specialize in certain industries and/or types of operations (such as mining, automotive, maritime, construction) and can therefore offer emerging, state-of-the art solutions to problems that might not be proposed internally.
- *Cost.* Although the hourly rates of top risk control consultants are steep (often as high as $250 per hour, with $1,200 daily minimum charges) their advice can provide both immediate and significant paybacks. These high but nonrecurring fees must also be assessed in comparison with the permanent and much higher cost of employing risk control staff personnel.
- *Convenience.* For firms that have operations spread across a variety of national and international locations, independent risk control consultants offer the advantage of proximity, which can be valuable in conserving corporate staff members' time and energy.

Independent safety audits are especially important for organizations that depend primarily on insurer-provided risk control services. Insurers have questionable incentive to control costs under most loss-sensitive programs, such as retrospective rating plans. (Retros are "cost plus" arrangements whereby insureds pay their own losses, within certain parameters, at least.) In addition, insurers have been on a cost-cutting initiative since the mid-1980s. Their efforts to reduce expenses have significantly lowered staffing levels and the quality of many insurers' risk control services has suffered as a result.

There are two major providers of safety audit services: independent engineering/consulting firms and insurance company staffs whose services are contracted to nonpolicyholders. Some agency and brokerage firms also offer risk control services on a fee basis. The American Society of Safety Engineers, 1800 East Oakton St., Des Plaines, Illinois, 60018–2187, (847) 699–2929, and the National Safety Council, 1121 Spring Lake Dr., Itaska, Illinois, 60143–3201, (630) 285–1121, are good sources for locating safety auditors.

The two most important factors to consider in identifying and evaluating such firms are industry-specific expertise and previous records of successful results. References should be questioned to ascertain the level of satisfaction provided by a consulting firm on their projects. Although cost cannot be ignored as a factor in the selection process, it should never be a primary criterion in choosing a safety auditor.

There is no generally accepted format for safety audits. Each will differ based on the kind of operation being evaluated as well as the unique exposures and problems confronted by your company. However, the major areas normally addressed in safety audits are listed in Figure 10.2.

Figure 10.2

Areas Typically Addressed in Safety Audits

- Individual job safety analyses (JSA)
- Assessment of employee/supervisor training programs
- An examination of safety committee activities
- A critique of record-keeping procedures
- An evaluation of accident investigation techniques
- An audit of compliance with OSHA requirements
- General and specific recommendations for improving the safety program and loss experience, including an assignment of individual responsibility for accomplishing such goals

---

In conducting a safety survey, the consultant usually inspects the premises when they are closed and will also observe workers and supervisors while they actually perform their individual jobs. The audit should include direct contact with all levels of a plant and/or company's hierarchy. It is essential that an all-encompassing picture of your firm's operations be obtained if an audit is to produce a set of truly effective risk control recommendations.

Ways To Cut Costs—Postloss

Of course, it is always preferable to prevent losses from occurring in the first place. Unfortunately, this will not always be possible. In the event of a claim, you must do everything possible to minimize the extent of the damage that results. The following three measures will go a long way in controlling the costs of injuries to employees and third parties.

77. Use Medical Bill Reviewers

Studies have shown that the medical cost component of workers compensation claims has risen at a much faster rate than the other elements (indemnity payments and allocated loss adjustment expense). Accordingly, you should focus your efforts on controlling this element of the exposure. One avenue is to contract with medical bill review services.

Physicians and hospital invoices frequently contain significant errors from a number of sources: charges for services not performed, excessive charges for services that were performed, and charges for services that need not have been performed. In the aggregate, such overcharges can add up to significant dollars. However, a person with specialized expertise is usually required to ascertain the exact nature and extent of improper or excessive charges. Medical bill audit services will review a client company's bills and then negotiate reductions directly with the hospital, physician, or clinic. Such firms typically employ registered nurses and charge a fee that is a percentage of the savings achieved. Thus, the use of medical bill audit services can typically produce a no-risk, "win-win" proposition for your company. If you self-insure workers compensation or even if you are on a retrospective or guaranteed cost program, you should request that your insurer contract for these services on all claims involving a certain threshold of medical expenses (say, $2,500).

78. Use Managed Care Arrangements

Managed care for workers compensation has become increasingly prevalent in recent years. Just as this approach has been successful in reducing the cost of employer-provided group health insurance coverage, it has been effective in cutting the medical cost component of workers compensation claims, without compromising the quality of treatment provided to injured workers. Typically, managed care arrangements for workers compensation entail a preferred provider approach, whereby employee injuries are treated through a single clinic. As a result of the volume of cases handled, your firm would receive an agreed-upon percentage discount for all services rendered. Another benefit of this approach is that since the medical provider would be treating all of your company's workers compensation cases, it would have less incentive to over-treat injuries. Thus, from both a cost-of-service and a quantity-of-service standpoint, you could achieve significant savings.

The laws of many states prohibit employers from requiring that an injured employee receive treatment from a certain provider. However, there is nothing wrong with *recommending* a specific provider to the employee. As another alternative, your firm can educate local physicians about the needs of injured workers. Such physicians can then direct their marketing efforts accordingly.

In the long run, education of workers as well as local medical providers will enhance cost control efforts.

79. Implement Visitation and Return-to-Work Programs

Studies have shown that the likelihood of a worker's disability becoming permanent increases the longer the person is out of work. A severely injured worker goes through various emotional phases, many of which involve questioning their self-worth and the company's loyalty to them. Accordingly, it is important to quickly show sympathy and empathy after a worker is seriously injured.

A visitation program combined with a return-to-work program can help to get an injured worker out of the house—away from televised lawyer advertising—and back on the job much faster. A visitation program merely involves periodic visits, follow-ups, and telephone calls by one or more parties at the company (a nurse or supervisor, for example). The purpose is to offer assistance and console the injured employee. Genuine concern of this kind can improve an employee's attitude, which will also speed the healing process.

Return-to-work programs involve "alternative" or so-called light-duty jobs for workers who are injured and unable to perform their regular jobs but are nevertheless capable of performing some type of lighter duties that involve less strenuous physical activity. A key benefit of such programs is that they have a positive effect on an employee's mental state, an important variable in promoting recovery from an injury.

Alternative work should not be "make-work." Rather, it should be designed to help workers feel productive, thereby speeding the healing process. Once a worker has faced the challenge of returning to work to perform alternative duties, he or she is eager to return to his or her regular position.

Supervisory personnel must also be encouraged to support return-to-work programs. Accordingly, incentive bonus and/or performance evaluations should consider the extent to which supervisors foster the implementation of this cost-saving approach.

Finally, ample support should be provided for workers when they return to work after an injury. For example, assisting in transportation arrangements and having supervisors personally follow up with a worker improve the worker's chances of making a smooth transition back to the work routine and reduce the possibility of a relapse to disability.

For further research and study

IRMI Workers Comp provides additional information on risk control techniques focused on workers compensation exposures. Visit the Products and Services section of IRMI.com for more information.

11

RISK FINANCING

INSURANCE IS A PROCESS by which the premiums of many pay for the losses of a few. This concept is especially applicable to personal lines insurance and insurance for small companies. However, as companies grow, insurance becomes more of an expense-smoothing mechanism. Over the long run, large insureds will reimburse their insurance companies for all but the most catastrophic losses, as well as expenses and profits. At the same time, insurance companies may retain the investment income generated by the cash flow.

There are three basic sources of potential profits available to an insurance company: underwriting income, investment income, and capital appreciation. *Underwriting income* is the difference between premiums earned and the sum of losses incurred and expenses. For many years, insurers have had underwriting losses rather than profits. The industry incurred a record $53.0 billion underwriting loss in 2001. *Investment income* is earned on funds held by insurers and includes dividends on common stock, interest from bonds, etc. Keep in mind that, while premiums to fund losses are paid at policy inception, losses are not paid until claims are eventually settled or adjudicated. Insurers invest the reserves to pay future claims and derive substantial income from these investments. Property-casualty insurers benefited from investment income of $37.1 billion in 2001. The third source of income, which has taken on a greater importance during the past few years, is *capital gains*. In 2001 this source added $6.9 billion to the insurance industry's bottom line.[1] As a result of the poor performance in all of these areas the industry experienced its first ever after tax loss in 2001. Without investment income and capital gains, the industry as a whole would have lost money in most other years as well. In negotiating insurance, particularly for the larger insured, these three sources of income must be understood and taken into account.

Importance of Insurance Cash Flow

As mentioned above, there are often significant time lags between acts that may lead to legal liability and the settlement or payment of the resulting claims. These time lags are caused by the following.

- Delays by plaintiffs in reporting and filing claims
- Delays in settlement from the slowness of the legal process
- Delays in cash payments after settlement (particularly from claims that result in periodic payments in the workers compensation area)

---

[1]*Insurer Financial Results: 2001.* Insurance Services Office, Inc., 2002.

The party that holds these funds, whether the insurer or insured, benefits from their income-generating capability. In the early days of insurance and risk management, insurers demanded that annual premiums be paid at policy inception and thus enjoyed all of the cash flow benefits. In the 1970s and 1980s, however, insurance buyers became more concerned with cash flow and which party held the funds until paid; as a result, insurers began sharing it.

Now there are various ways insureds can participate in the investment income earning ability of unpaid claims reserves. These plans are available from insurers and may be simple, such as an agreement to pay premiums monthly instead of at policy inception, or they may be quite complex—as will be shown when compensating balance plans are discussed.

There are also risk financing plans in which insurers do not play a dominant role. The most common of these plans are captive insurers, self-insurance, and group self-insured trusts or pools.

Rating Plans

The basis of any "cash flow" risk financing plan purchased from an insurance company is the rating plan used. Virtually all cash flow programs are variations of guaranteed cost rating or retrospective rating. Until the mid-1950s, the most common approach to financing risk was through a *guaranteed cost insurance* program. Under this approach, the insured pays a predetermined premium that stays the same regardless of the losses covered by the policy. In effect, the insurance company takes all risks of loss when this type of insurance is purchased. As premiums began to increase in the United States, particularly in the workers compensation area, a demand grew for cost-plus programs that would allow the insured to share some risk with the insurance company. While large insureds were able to negotiate these types of plans from Lloyd's of London and a few insurance companies in the United States, such plans were not available to the average American business. To meet this need, the U.S. insurance industry developed a formal cost-plus program, called *retrospective rating.*

As with a guaranteed cost rating plan, a premium is developed at the inception of the retrospective rating policy period. However, this premium is only provisional and is subject to a cost-plus calculation that will reflect actual loss experience. Approximately 6 months after the end of the policy period, the insurance company will look back and compare the actual premiums earned to the losses incurred (paid and reserved claims) and recalculate the premium. Subject to an agreed-upon minimum, the insured will receive a return premium if losses are lower than expected. If losses exceed original expectations, additional premiums will be paid by the insured subject to the maximum. Figure 11.1 contains a brief glossary of retrospective rating terms and an illustration of the retrospective rating formula. Unfortunately, retrospective rating plans are often perceived as very complicated and, in some cases, punitive. However, this is a fairly simple cost-plus plan and should be viewed as a positive management tool for midsized to larger corporations that wish to control their insurance costs through positive actions.

Generally, retrospective rating plans can be written on 1- or 3-year terms. They are most often used with workers compensation insurance, but general liability and automobile exposures are sometimes included, too. Other lines—such as burglary, plate glass, and other casualty exposures—can also be included. A general rule of thumb is that a business should be paying at least $500,000 in subject premium (the premium that would be subject to the plan) for a retrospective rating plan to become a viable option.

Figure 11.1

Retrospective Rating Formula and Terms

(BPF x Standard Premium) + (LCF x Losses) + (Excess Loss Premium) x Tax Multiplier = Indicated Retro Premium

Basic Premium Factor (BPF). A percentage factor that, when multiplied by the standard premium (premium derived from manual rates), will provide a charge (the basic premium) for insurer profit, contingencies, and expenses (except loss adjustment expenses). This is the "plus" part of the "cost-plus" formula.

Loss Conversion Factor (LCF). A percentage factor that, when added to 1.00 and then multiplied by the dollar value of losses, will provide a charge for both the losses and the loss adjustment expenses. Most of the "cost" part of the retrospective premium charge comes from this calculation.

Excess Loss Premium. Charge for limiting individual losses to a specified level to reduce the effect of unusually large losses on the final premium. The excess loss premium is calculated by this formula: Standard Premium x Excess Loss Premium Factor x LCF.

Tax Multiplier. Reimburses the insurer for premium taxes paid to the state(s).

Indicated Retro Premium. Amount of premium, subject to the minimum and maximum premium, that the insured must pay. The minimum premium is the lowest premium that will be charged, even if the formula results in a lower indicated retro premium. Likewise, the maximum premium is the highest premium that may be charged, even if the formula results in a higher indicated retro premium.

In the mid-1990s, changes in state workers compensation laws allowed insurers to introduce a new type of cost-plus plan: large deductible workers compensation programs. With this approach, the insured pays a guaranteed cost premium for coverage with a relatively high deductible ($10,000 or more, for example). Since the insured periodically reimburses the insurer for the deductibles paid on its behalf, it operates very much like a retrospectively rated plan. However, high deductible programs have an advantage over retrospective rating plans in some states because state premium taxes and residual market charges—which are passed on to the insured—are lower than those associated with a retrospectively rated program.

Before purchasing a retrospective or large deductible rating plan, you would be wise to consult an experienced insurance adviser or agent.

Ways To Cut Costs

This chapter gives seven ways to cut retrospective rating plan costs or capture cash flow.

80. Carefully Select Retrospective Minimum and Maximum Factors

To develop the net costs (insurer overhead and profit) of a retrospective rating plan, the standard premium is multiplied by a basic premium factor to develop a *basic premium*. The basic premium includes such items as insurance company expenses, agent's commission, insurer profit, and an "insurance charge." The insurance charge compensates the insurer for risk that the insured will have losses that cause the indicated retrospective rating premium to exceed the maximum premium. As a result, the higher the maximum premium assumed by the insured, the lower the insurance charge. Similarly, the minimum premium amount also affects the insurance charge. For instance, the higher the minimum premium, the higher the likelihood that losses will fall below those that would produce the minimum premium and that the minimum premium will have to be paid by the insured. Thus, the minimum premium guarantees a certain level of premium income to the insurer. Therefore, the lower the minimum, the higher the insurance charge.

At some time, there is a point of diminishing returns. In fact, the insurance charge actually disappears and any additional increases in the maximum or minimum will not depress the basic factor any further.

A reasonable set of factors for a 1-year plan is usually a 50 percent minimum and a 120 percent maximum. Many insureds will ask for a basic factor based on these minimums and maximums. A question along the following lines should then be asked, "Assuming a 50 percent minimum, at what maximum level will the insurance charge disappear?" If the answer is 1.40 (or, a possible penalty of 40 percent), the buyer should try to avoid assuming a maximum factor above 1.40 since no compensation will be received for assuming additional risk.

Some insureds are so attracted to the possibility of a very low minimum premium that they select it even though it would be virtually impossible for their organization to benefit from it. In other words, the amount spent by the insured on loss and claims control efforts to attain such a low minimum would not be offset by the payment of very low losses. Past loss experience should be considered when choosing a minimum premium. It is often a better deal to increase the minimum and lower the basic premium charge.

A 3-year term plan is sometimes used to reduce the insurance charge. Under this approach, 3 years' premiums and losses are used in the calculation instead of 1 year's. As a result, an insured could conceivably have excellent experience for 2 years and 11 months and expect a large retrospective return only to have a series of severe losses occur during the 36th month, eliminating all of the returns for the past periods as well as creating an additional premium. The 2 or 3 percentage points' reduction in the basic factor may not warrant this large exposure. If you choose a 3-year plan, assume a higher minimum and lower maximum than you would under a 1-year plan. The higher minimum will recognize the fact that the law of averages will better operate under a 3-year plan while the lower maximum will reduce the possibility of your paying significant additional premiums.

81. Negotiate the Agent's Commission Outside the Rating Plan

As discussed in Chapter 8 on page 92, insurance buyers for midsized and large organizations are now negotiating commissions with agents. Besides allowing for tailored services for fees paid, this may also reduce certain overhead, tax, and reinsurance charges. Many overhead and reinsurance charges are determined as a percentage of premiums. A general rule is that these overhead charges will run 30 to 35 percent of premiums.

For instance, assume that retrospectively rated workers compensation premiums will be $500,000 and the commission rate will be 5 percent, resulting in a commission of $25,000. Rather than paying $500,000 directly to the insurance company, an alternative might be to pay $475,000 to the insurance company and $25,000 to the agent. Since the insurer will not be paying the agent's commission, the basic factor would be reduced by 5 percentage points. The net effect would be a basic premium factor and premium tax rate applied to a lower premium ($475,000 versus $500,000). In this example, the resulting savings would be approximately $1,000 to $1,500.

Few insurers will allow the full credits as applied in the above example because they try to determine the dollars needed and back into the basic premium factor. In other words, they might reduce the basic premium factor by 2.5 to 3.0 percent instead of the full 5 percent paid to the agent. Even this more conservative approach avoids paying premium taxes on the agent's commission and may, therefore, be worthwhile.

If this approach is also applied to auto liability and general liability premiums, another 25 percent might be saved on the firm's umbrella premiums. This is because umbrella premiums are normally based on the underlying auto and general liability premiums.

82. Negotiate Other Retrospective Rating Factors

Other retrospective rating factors may be modified through negotiated factors or dividends. The remaining factors that might be negotiated are loss limitation factors, loss conversion factors, and tax multipliers.

Loss Limitation Factors

To avoid a situation in which one major catastrophic loss adversely affects the entire retrospective program, a *loss limit* can be purchased that limits a particular loss to an agreed amount. For agreeing to limit this loss, the insurance company charges a premium. While most states have guidelines for what the charges should be, the insurance company may charge more or less based on its perception of the risk or its cost of reinsurance. As a result, this is often a key point of negotiation.

Loss Conversion Factors

The *loss conversion factor* is charged by the insurance company for the adjustment of claims by its own staff and, in the case of workers compensation, outside legal counsel. Insurance companies will sometimes agree to reduce the loss conversion factor by 2 to 3 percentage points, as there is a hidden profit factor included in this charge. (Reducing it will probably raise the basic premium.)

Tax Multipliers

The *tax multiplier* is supposed to reflect the amount of premium taxes paid to the state by the insurance company. However, insurance companies have methods of managing their state taxes to reduce them. Some insurance companies will pass along these state premium tax savings to insureds; this may be another important point of negotiation.

83. Explore a "Paid Loss" Retrospective Rating Plan

Under the retrospective rating plans discussed above, adjustments are made based on losses as valued 6 months after the end of the policy period and at 12-month intervals thereafter until all claims are closed. These "losses" include not only the amounts actually paid to claimants but also estimates of the amounts that will be paid in settlement of open claims. These estimated losses are called *loss reserves*. Well-managed insurers have a tendency to reserve conservatively hoping that claims will close out lower than anticipated. However, this is not always the case. In any event, retrospective rating plans are adjusted annually—with settlements made between the insured and the insurance company on any additional or return premiums. It may take as many as 10 years for all of a given year's claims to be settled and paid. In the case of severe injuries under workers compensation, payments could go on for 40 or 50 years.

The timing difference between the date on which premiums are paid and the dates on which losses are actually paid is significant and usually results in substantial cash flow to the insurance company. Larger insureds, particularly those who pay more than $1 million in premiums, have often successfully negotiated to share in the investment income on loss reserves. Perhaps the most common approach has been the *paid loss retro*. Rather than paying in premiums as earned, the insured simply reimburses the insurance company for its estimated expenses as well as actual paid losses during the first year. The balance of the loss fund is then paid to the insurance company over a period of time as the insurance company disburses such funds, thereby leaving the cash flow with the insured.

Under a paid loss retrospective rating arrangement, the insurance company assumes a much larger-than-normal financial risk in that it is responsible for the claims but has not collected the entire premium from the insured. As a result, the insurance company will usually require the insured to sign a premium note that is collateralized by a clean letter of credit or a special type of surety bond.

Many of these arrangements terminate after 5 years and the insured will make a balloon payment, equal to any unpaid reserves, to the insurance company to "close out" that year's retro. While this plan leaves a substantial amount of cash with the insured until paid out in claims, some insurance companies will increase some of the retrospective rating factors to recoup their loss of the investment income. The increased rating factors can drive up the costs enough to eliminate the advantages of retaining the cash flow.

Paid loss retrospective rating plans are obviously a competitive tool and will be more available during soft markets than in tight ones. Also, the larger the premiums paid by an insured, the stronger the insured's negotiating position.

Care should be taken in structuring these plans from a federal tax standpoint. The Internal Revenue Service (IRS) is taking the position that deferred premiums are not deductible business expenses until actually paid to the insurer. You should seek appropriate counsel when considering a paid loss retrospective rating plan.

84. Consider Other Cash Flow Programs

Other commonly used cash flow programs include negotiated deposits, deferred premiums, compensating balance plans, interest on reserves, and workers compensation deductible programs.

Negotiated Deposits

Many premiums, particularly those for workers compensation and general liability, are paid on a monthly or quarterly basis. Rather than accepting the creditworthiness of the insured, virtually all insurance companies require deposits to cover the period involved (the month or the quarter). For example, assume that premiums will be $10,000 per month. Most insurance companies will require a deposit of 20 to 25 percent of the annual premium, in this case $24,000 to $30,000. Typically, interest is not paid on these deposits, and the insured thereby suffers a loss of investment income. Some insureds have been successful in negotiating arrangements with a very low deposit premium ($500, for example), using a clean letter of credit or appropriate surety bond as collateral for the additional amount owed to the insurer. If the insured can earn more on the invested money than the letter of credit or surety bond costs, the organization will realize a net savings.

Deferred Premiums

Many insureds have also been successful in negotiating a depressed premium payment arrangement. With this mechanism, the insured makes a low monthly payment during the policy period and a balloon payment at the end to make up the difference. If, in the example in the previous paragraph, a $120,000 annual premium were involved, only $5,000 might be paid each month with the other $5,000 deferred until the end of the policy period. About 90 days after the end of the policy period, a balloon payment of $60,000 (12 monthly payments at $5,000 each) would be made. Generally, there is no required collateral such as surety bonds or letters of credit.

Compensating Balance Plans

Many businesses negotiate annual lines of credit with their banks. In return, they may be required to maintain certain cash balances in non-interest-bearing accounts to support the line of credit. For example, the bank might require a compensating balance equal to 10 percent of the overall line of credit as well as 10 percent of the average outstanding loan balance.

Assume that the insured has negotiated a $2 million line of credit and expects to have a $1 million average loan balance during the year. Based on a requirement of 10 percent of these two amounts, the insured will be required to maintain a compensating balance of $300,000. Arrangements could be made for the insurance company to collect the premium and deposit it in a non-interest-bearing account at the insured's bank to maintain a bank balance of $300,000. Even though the deposits are under the insurance company's name, the bank agrees to allow these deposits to satisfy the insured's compensating balance requirement. The insured can thus avoid tying up $300,000 in cash, which could be used to reduce the average loan balance from $1 million to $700,000, and can thereby attain an interest savings that is somewhat higher than the short-term investment rate.

This approach is complex and difficult to negotiate because bankers usually do not understand insurance and insurance underwriters often do not understand banking arrangements. For insureds with high compensating balance requirements, however, the results may justify the effort.

Interest on Reserves

Perhaps the simplest way for insureds to benefit from the cash flow on reserves is the interest on reserves concept. It might be better described as a "now account" in the insurance arena. Just as a bank keeps a record of all deposits and disbursements, the insurance company would do the same for premiums and losses and would pay interest on the balance of funds held. To simplify administration, most insurance companies use ending or beginning balances rather than the daily balances typically used by banks. The insurance company applies a mutually agreed-upon interest rate to the funds being held and remits the investment income, often as a "dividend," to the insured at a predetermined interval.

Interest on reserves avoids the complications, the financial risk to the insurance company, and the expense of letters of credit and/or surety bonds necessary with the paid loss retro. The interest on reserves concept might be particularly attractive to the insured that must collateralize with the actual funds the letter of credit used with a paid loss retro.

Some risk managers have described this approach as "cash value" casualty insurance. It is a simple method of sharing in the investment income otherwise enjoyed solely by the insurance company.

Workers Compensation Deductible Programs

The advent of deductible plans for workers compensation insurance has become evident in recent years. Prior to the late 1980s, such coverage was written almost exclusively on a first-dollar basis. Now, programs with deductibles from as low as $100 to $250,000 or more are available in various states. The cost-saving effects of such plans are threefold: (1) they allow insureds to capture cash flow given the relatively long payout periods associated with workers compensation claims, (2) they promote greater internal motivation for controlling losses since the organization—rather than an insurer—will be paying a sizeable proportion of most claims, and (3) they reduce the "frictional cost" component that is built into insurance premiums because a deductible will eliminate the involvement of an insurer on many claims.

A detailed discussion of workers compensation deductible plans is provided in Chapter 5.

85. Examine the Self-Insurance/Captive Option

When the insurance market tightens and becomes less competitive, insurance companies increase rates and decrease availability of cash flow alternatives. In addition, some types of insurance simply become unavailable during tight markets. This causes some insureds to consider and implement self-insurance programs or captive insurance companies.

Great confusion arises over the term noninsurance versus the term self-insurance. *Noninsurance* is the assumption of risk without formalized management (such as record-keeping and reserving). An example would be an auto garage that does not insure against theft of its hand tools, nor does it set up a reserve for such loss and carefully account for losses during a fiscal period. On the other hand, *self-insurance* is the formal assumption of risks and the accounting of results. Specific accounts or funds are set aside to fund the risks, and losses that do occur are charged against those accounts or funds. Not only does this process allow the business organization to proactively manage the risks involved, it also facilitates a return to the regular insurance market if that approach becomes desirable in the future.

Self-insurance is used when losses occur with enough frequency to make them predictable. It can be applied to an exposure in its entirety or to only a portion of the exposure. For example, a portion of an organization's annual workers compensation losses may be predictable. This is often called "working layer" or "burning layer" and is the layer that the organization would self-insure. Potentially catastrophic losses should not be self-insured.

The exposure most often self-insured is physical damage to personal property such as automobiles and equipment. Many companies with large numbers of employees self-insure all or part of the workers compensation and/or group health risks. As respects liability insurance, even the largest organizations must buy insurance at some level. Therefore, many will self-insure some first-dollar amount determined according to their ability to pay (such as $25,000, $250,000, or $2,500,000) and purchase *excess liability* insurance above that amount.

Excess insurance coverage may be purchased to protect against large, catastrophic losses. In addition, *aggregate stop loss* coverage may be purchased to limit the amount assumed when an unexpectedly large number of losses occurs.

Advantages and Disadvantages of Self-Insurance and Captives

The advantages of self-insurance are numerous. They include greater financial rewards to insureds who control losses, potential cost reduction, increased cash flow, and more control over claims.

Disadvantages of self-insurance include delays in federal tax deductions until losses are actually paid, increased administrative costs, and the loss of a buffer between the employer and employee in self-insured workers compensation claims (the employee can blame the employer for denying a workers compensation claim instead of blaming the insurer). Another drawback to self-insuring workers compensation involves the problems that may be encountered when firms doing work for others (say, contractors) need to comply with contract requirements. Providing proof that the firm is a qualified self-insurer might not satisfy such requirements. Finally, the need to qualify as a self-insurer under a variety of state laws for firms with multistate operations is another obstacle that must often be overcome.

A natural extension to self-insurance is the formation of a *captive insurance* company. A captive is an insurance company that insures only the risks of its parent or affiliates. Advantages of captives include more control over reinsurance placements, flexibility in arranging services such as claims and engineering, and formal handling of risk for which insurance is not available in the marketplace. Disadvantages include additional administrative costs and IRS scrutiny.

Any business paying more than $750,000 in workers compensation or primary liability insurance should carefully review self-insurance, and any company paying more than $2.5 million should review the wholly owned captive approach.

86. Consider Alternative Risk Financing Facilities

While medium-to-large-sized business organizations have developed and used the self-insurance and captive concepts, small-to-medium-sized businesses also want the benefits of those options. Individually, small firms do not generate sufficient premium volume or spread of risk to self-insure or justify the overhead required to a form a captive insurer. However, when a number of small companies band together, these roadblocks can be overcome, thus opening the possibility of forming or participating in various alternative risk financing facilities to reduce the cost of coverage.

Many states made group self-insurance and group captives possible by passing legislation enabling qualified groups of employers to join together in self-insured trusts for workers compensation insurance, often called "workers compensation pools." Where legislative support to allow pools was not available, associations and other groups formed group captives.

Association/group plans have met with varying degrees of success. Common problems have involved lack of adequate reinsurance, inadequate capital, and poor management. However, group programs can work if the participants view them as a long-term approach to meeting their insurance needs and are willing to commit the appropriate time, capital, and resources to the project.

Group Captives

The tight markets experienced from 1976 to 1978 and 1984 to 1987 spawned numerous group and industry captives, and it appears that the current hard market (of 2002) is going to see a similar spurt in group captive formations. Reasons for forming a group captive, rather than each organization funding its own risks, include the following.

- Increased accuracy of statistical forecasts because of the volume of data (the law of large numbers)
- Better purchasing power in regard to reinsurance and services

- Reduced overhead because fixed costs can be spread over more units
- Greater risk retention capabilities (financial muscle)
- The degree of risk transfer and distribution may make premiums deductible for tax purposes

Problems commonly associated with group captives include the following.

- Improperly reserved losses, since captive owners have a tendency to be overly optimistic
- Underestimated development, start-up, and maintenance expenses
- Involvement of too many middlemen
- Use of inexperienced management
- Frequent heavy broker and insurance company resistance

The growth of group-owned captives, especially offshore captives, has been fueled by tax issues. Once membership exceeds 15, there is probably sufficient "spread of risk" to meet IRS guidelines and make premiums deductible business expenses.

Self-Insured Trusts, Pools, and Risk Retention Groups

The 1986 Risk Retention Act facilitates the formation of group captives by reducing the amount of state regulation faced by groups that qualify. Under the Act, two or more businesses are permitted to join together and pool any type of liability risks. In other words, automobile liability, general liability, umbrella liability, directors and officers liability, professional liability, and other liability exposures could be covered by a *risk retention group.* Workers compensation, on the other hand, may not be covered in a risk retention group.

To start such an operation, a group must form an insurance company that is licensed in a specific state. Of course, some states require lower initial capitalization and impose fewer regulatory constraints than others, making them more favorable domiciles. Favorable domiciles currently include the states of Colorado, Delaware, Hawaii, Tennessee, and Vermont. The Act then requires the risk retention group to file a business plan in all other states in which it will operate; however, it gives insurance commissioners very little authority to regulate risk retention groups that are not domiciled in their state.

Perhaps equally as important, the Act also authorizes the establishment of *purchasing groups* that really do not assume any risk. They merely use the group's buying power to purchase insurance more economically on behalf of group members. In the past, associations have established "safety groups"; however, many states and insurance companies did not recognize these as legal organizations. The new legitimacy conferred on purchasing groups by the 1986 Act has affected the entire marketing system of commercial insurance in the United States.

Overall, the 1986 Risk Retention Act has been the most significant piece of insurance legislation enacted in this country during the last 50 years, and it has injected additional competition into the insurance arena. A group or an association that forms an insurance purchasing group is also well positioned to convert it into a risk retention group if the insurance industry fails to respond to the purchasing group's needs and/or if the insurance market experiences a sudden hardening.

Figure 11.2

Questions To Ask about Alternative Risk Financing Facilities

The following are a few of the important questions that should be answered before a firm participates in any type of group insurance or self-insurance scheme.

- Who are the sponsors and what is their experience in managing such facilities?
- What financial and time commitments are sponsors prepared to devote to the facility?
- Do the insureds share the same goals and objectives for the facility? (For example, do they plan to develop into a large-scale facility that competes with traditional insurers *or* do they view it simply as a vehicle for obtaining broad, cost-effective coverage and quality services for a small group of insureds?)
- Are the insureds relatively homogeneous in terms of industry group and financial size?
- How will initial formation expenses be allocated to participants?
- What is the minimum required participation time, if any?
- How and to what extent is the facility capitalized?
- Are there any limitations and restrictions on the sale of the facility's stock by sponsors?
- Are there provisions for withdrawal of participants and the entry of new participants?
- How financially secure and experienced are the reinsurers?
- At what levels (both per claim and aggregate) will reinsurance be purchased?
- Given its current reinsurance program, how well could the facility handle multiple shock losses and what would happen if it became financially incapable of handling adverse loss experience?

- What, if any, risk control efforts does the facility require of participants, both initially and after joining?
- Are formal policies and procedures in place for determining the distribution of profits, assessment of premiums, an acceptable premium-to-surplus ratio, allocation of operating expenses, and establishment of reserves for losses?
- Are policyholders assessable, and to what extent?
- Are financial statements audited by an independent certified public accountant (CPA) firm?
- Are loss reserves reviewed by an independent, Fellow, or Associate of the Casualty Actuarial Society?
- Who provides the claims adjusting and loss control services, and how are these entities compensated?
- Is the coverage provided by the proposed policy form reasonable or is it overly broad compared to traditional market forms?
- Does the facility plan to work with the traditional insurance industry or compete against it?
- How is the facility viewed by the traditional insurance marketplace and what reaction to participation, if any, is expected from insurers?
- Are there any possible antitrust problems that may arise from the particular group joining to form the facility?

Source: *Risk Financing*, International Risk Management Institute, Inc., Dallas. Copyright 2002.

Risks of Group Programs

While group self-insurance/pooling programs offer small and medium-sized organizations opportunities to enjoy the benefits of self-insurance, they also present new risks to their members. Since they are not significantly regulated and usually are not heavily capitalized, there may be a substantial risk of insolvency. There may also be substantial penalties for early withdrawal from these programs. Figure 11.2 lists some of the more important points you should consider before joining a group/association captive, self-insurance trust, pool, or risk retention group.

Summary

This chapter applies primarily to medium- and large-sized businesses. However, some of these points also apply to small firms, particularly the points pertaining to risk retention groups and insurance purchasing groups.

For insureds who wish to assume reasonable risks for profit, the assumption of insurable risk and the resulting savings provide an outstanding opportunity to reduce operating costs.

For further research and study

Additional information concerning captives, risk retention groups, retrospective rating, and other approaches to funding property and liability loss exposures can be found in *Risk Financing*, a detailed, two-volume reference manual published by IRMI. *Captives and the Management of Risk* is an IRMI book focusing solely on the use of captive insurers. *Captive Insurance Company Reports* is a monthly newsletter from IRMI that helps owners and managers of captives maximize the benefits they receive from them. Visit the Products and Services section of IRMI.com for more information on these publications.

12

SAVING WITH COMPETITIVE PROPOSALS

INSURANCE BIDDING IS A TECHNIQUE widely used for selecting an agent/broker or arranging an insurance program. The most common goals to achieve in bidding an insurance program are the following.

- Reduce premium costs
- Obtain broader coverages
- Select a new agent/broker or insurer

In a buyers' market, the competitive proposal process may provide all of these benefits. In a tight insurance market, it may take competitive proposals to even procure insurance for the organization, or bidding may be necessary because the current insurance company decides to severely restrict coverage or substantially raise premiums.

To Shop or Not To Shop

You should bid your insurance program only when you have reason to be displeased with or concerned about your relationship with your current agent/broker or insurer. This may occur because service levels fall below acceptable levels, the firm has turnover at key positions on its staff, the insurer's financial position deteriorates, premiums are expected to increase substantially, coverages are expected to be cut back, or any number of other causes.

It is generally not a good idea to bid your program to simply keep your current agent/broker and insurer "honest"—unless you are truly willing to make a change. If you bid the program, be prepared to change to the winning agent/broker or insurer.

Figure 12.1 depicts a decision tree that can be used to determine whether your organization should stay with its current insurance program, change insurers only, or solicit competitive proposals on its insurance program. This tree illustrates a logical, progressive decision process.

Bidding Methods

There are a number of insurance bidding methods. The one selected depends largely on the method to be used for selecting an agent/broker. Basically, you must decide if a single producer will be chosen to approach the insurance companies or if several producers will be allowed to approach them. In either case, some preselection of producers will be needed

Figure 12.1

Shopping an Insurance Program: The Decision Process

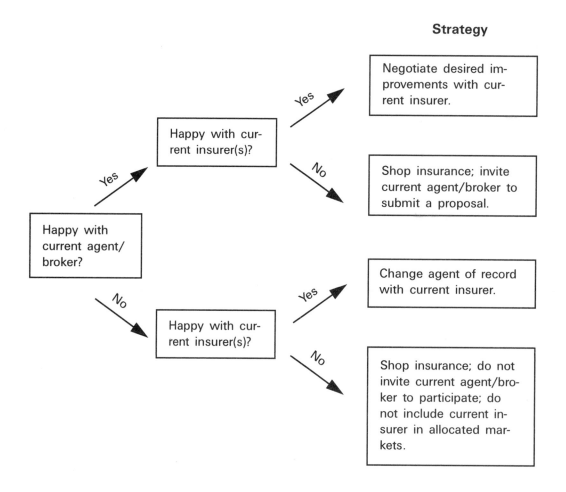

unless there is a decision to remain with the current agent/broker. Requesting several agents/brokers and/or direct writers to quote on an account has many advantages, including the following.

- More insurers will usually be approached and evaluated.
- Competition between producers will encourage participants to be effective, creative, and conscientious in preparing their proposals.

The disadvantages of using several producers/direct writers, rather than selecting a single source for quotations, include the following.

- Greater time commitment
- Potential market disruption

- Inability to market specialty and excess lines with primary coverages
- Combinations of insurers restricted by market allocations
- Use of a hired consultant may be required, since it is usually not good practice to allow one of the brokers to prepare specifications. Otherwise, management will have to take an active role in doing so.

The following are advantages of appointing a single producer to market the insurance.

- No market disruption
- Increased flexibility to explore combinations of insurers to underwrite the program
- Reduced time commitment for the insured
- Specialty and excess lines can usually be marketed simultaneously with primary coverages.
- The broker can be responsible for preparing specifications, subject to management review.

The following are disadvantages of appointing a single producer to market the insurance.

- Fewer markets are approached.
- Benefits of competition among brokers are lost.

If a decision is made to consider agents/brokers or direct writers in addition to, or instead of, the current producer, some preselection is necessary. A number of producers and direct writers should be approached and asked to provide data regarding their qualifications for properly servicing your organization's insurance needs. This information should address the following: number of years in business, number of employees, number of similar types of accounts, and résumés for the account executive and the assistant who will be working on the organization's insurance program. This process can involve as many insurance agents/brokers and/or direct writers as you desire. Once the information is received and an initial review is performed, consider inviting each agent/broker to come in for an interview to discuss your firm's overall needs, the manner in which the agent/broker might handle the account, and the agent's or broker's qualifications. Based on this information, all but four or five agents/brokers and/or direct writers are eliminated from consideration. Two or three agents/brokers and two or three direct writers can then be used, or only one agent/broker can be chosen.

At this point, either a conceptual proposal or a competitive proposal can be requested. A *conceptual proposal* involves a specific explanation of how the agent/broker or direct writer would design the program. The proposal might include a list of the insurance companies to be approached, an outline of recommended insurance coverages, modifications to standard policies that could probably be negotiated, an explanation of how the producer would be compensated, and a discussion of the services that would be provided to your organization. In a review of the conceptual proposals, such strengths as innovation, thoroughness, knowledge of exposures common in your industry, service capabilities, and communications ability of the producer should be evident.

Although practices vary, the conceptual proposal is generally utilized when there is a desire to select only a single producer to prepare specifications and approach the insurance marketplace. In any case, the field should be further pared down—following the conceptual proposals—to one, two, or perhaps three agents/brokers and/or direct writers. If a single organization is chosen, it is then asked to arrange the recommended program. If the list is narrowed to two or three organizations, they should be asked to provide competitive proposals.

Competitive proposals are used when more than one producer and/or direct writer are to be invited to bid on the organization's insurance or when a single producer is to obtain proposals from several insurance companies. This process involves preparing written insurance specifications that contain underwriting data and an outline of the desired insurance coverages for use by the producers or direct writers in preparing their proposals. If a single agent/broker has been selected to market the program, the producer can prepare the specifications and approach the markets chosen to quote on your account. If, however, several producers/direct writers will quote on the account, insurance specifications should be prepared by a party that will not be competing for your business. When several producers are involved, it is normally best to avoid conflicts of interest by allowing one of them to prepare specifications; however, their input and advice could be solicited. If you do not have the experience to prepare the specifications, you might consider hiring a consultant to help.

Ways To Cut Costs

Five ways to increase the effectiveness of, and cost savings associated with, competitive bidding are presented in this chapter.

87. Don't Bid Too Frequently

Many organizations, particularly public entities, make the mistake of bidding their insurance too frequently. An organization that bids its insurance too frequently will quickly earn the reputation of being a "shopper," resulting in a diminishing amount of competition each time the insurance is bid. Eventually, all agents/brokers and insurers in the community will lose interest in the organization's account. This causes difficulties in finding insurance at all and, when it is available, it is at higher costs than are necessary.

While it is difficult to generalize about frequency, most risk management and insurance professionals would agree that, barring very unusual circumstances, the program should not be shopped more than every 3 years. Beyond this maximum frequency, opinions will vary as to the "ideal" frequency. A 4-to-8-year cycle is generally not so frequent as to jeopardize your reputation in the market or undermine your long-term goal of reducing your company's total cost of risk. However, as long as you are satisfied with your program, you should first try to negotiate with your current insurer for improvements rather than engage in a competitive process. And, as mentioned above, don't bid your program unless you will be willing to move it to the successful bidder.

88.   Allocate Insurers to the Agents/Brokers

When you allow several agents/brokers to bid competitively on your insurance program, it is important to maintain a certain amount of control over the bidding process. One key area to oversee is insurance markets selection to maintain a level playing field for all agents/brokers. When no control is exercised, a number of agents/brokers may approach some of the same insurance companies to obtain proposals for your account. Each underwriter, immediately recognizing that the insurance is being bid, will be forced to work only with the first agent/ broker (to whom the proposal will be given) to ask for a quote, to provide all agents/brokers with the same proposal, or to decline to bid on the account at all. Knowing this, many agents will immediately contact every insurer possible to "lock up" the marketplace, which will mean decreased competition for your account.

To avoid this scenario, ask the agents/brokers who will be bidding on your account for a list of the insurance companies they want to use. The list should be prepared in order of priority and should indicate the premium volume that the agent/broker has with each insurer. In allocating insurers, try to give every agent/broker either its first or second choice, as many agents/brokers have lead markets with which they have considerable influence. If a national or large regional broker is being used, request the premium volume for that branch office only rather than for all of the brokerage's offices combined. When these lists are received, eliminate duplicates by using the order of priority and the premium volume indication as criteria. In eliminating duplications, it is important to not split a company group between two or more agents. Keep in mind that many large insurance company groups (such as Hartford Insurance Group, U.S. Insurance Group, CIGNA, The St. Paul Companies, and American International Group) provide coverage through several different insurers. These sister companies will not bid against each other.

Advise all agents/brokers of the markets they may use and inform them that they will be disqualified from the bidding process if they approach any others. Additional markets may be requested by agents/brokers during the bidding process, and the agent/broker should be allowed to use them as long as they have not been allocated to a competing firm.

The use of market allocation will avoid the confusion in the marketplace that would result if several agents/brokers solicited proposals from the same insurance companies; it will also cause the agents/brokers to approach a large spread of insurance companies that might be interested in the account. The process is important and should be required of all bidders.

89.   Allow Adequate Time To Secure Proposals

It can take a substantial amount of time to properly prepare a proposal for an insurance program. The amount of time required will depend on the size and complexity of your account, the time of year in which the program will become effective, and the number of proposals that you will receive. However, it will take between 3 and 5 months for most commercial accounts. In general, allow 30 to 60 days to preselect producers and prepare specifications, 30 to 90 days for the underwriters to produce quotations, and 30 days to evaluate the proposals and place coverage.

Figure 12.2

Timetable for Conducting a Competitive Proposal Process

Task	Time Requirement
Obtain current loss data.	Allow 6 months (this really should be done on an ongoing basis).
Obtain preliminary information from potential agents and brokers.	Perform this task 4–6 months before anniversary date. Allow respondents at least 4 weeks if a conceptual proposal is involved.
Develop all necessary underwriting data.	Complete this task at least 4 months before anniversary date.
Finalize specifications.	Complete this task 3 months before anniversary date.
Preselect agents, brokers, direct writers.	Complete 3 months before anniversary date.
Assign markets.	Complete at least 3 months before anniversary date.
Marketing by agents, brokers, direct writers.	Begin task 3 months before anniversary date.
Receive proposals.	Allow adequate time to review the quotations—at least 45 days, preferably 60.
Analyze proposals.	Allow 30 or more days depending on above.
Award the bid.	Complete no later than 2 weeks before anniversary in case last-minute problems arise.
Market excess and specialty coverage.	Begin as soon as account is awarded.
Receive renewal binders.	Schedule before anniversary date.
Compare policies against the specifications.	Perform as soon as policies are received.

Although it is impossible to state the "right" amount of time needed to conduct the competitive bidding process, experience has shown that the longer a firm waits to begin, the less money it will save. The following table estimates the cost of waiting to begin a competitive program.

Days Prior to Renewal	Savings
90 to 120	20 percent
60 to 90	10 percent
30 to 60	7 percent
0 to 30	5 percent

Figure 12.2 provides a more detailed sequence of events involved in the bidding process, along with suggested time periods that should be allowed for the various tasks to be performed.

90.   Provide Adequate Information

Probably the most common mistake made when obtaining competitive insurance proposals is failing to provide adequate data to the underwriters. Some insureds make the mistake of simply presenting copies of the current insurance policies to the various agents/brokers and direct writers who will be bidding on the account. This approach has the following major disadvantages.

- Any coverage deficiencies or mistakes made by the current agent or company may be repeated in the new program.
- Important underwriting and rating data will not be up to date.
- The loss history of the firm is not disclosed.
- The potential for obtaining broader and better coverages will be reduced if the producers are told to simply duplicate the current program.
- The agent/broker may be biased by the current rates.

To avoid these mistakes, prepare written insurance specifications. The results will be well worth the time and effort. The overriding consideration when designing insurance specifications is to achieve a total interchange of necessary underwriting information in a formal, yet easy-to-work-with, manner.

The information included in specifications should consist of the company's operational and management history, plans for the future, coverage required and coverage desired, loss exposures, past loss history and details of major losses (those over $50,000, for example), and information regarding the organization's loss control and safety program. Figure 12.3 outlines the possible contents of a set of specifications. If you want information on what to include in insurance specifications, consider purchasing the IRMI *Guidelines for Insurance Specifications*. It provides a model set of specifications (in Word files) that can be tailored to your organization's individual needs.

In summary, the following data is of key importance to underwriters and should always be provided when an insurance program is bid competitively: at least 5 years of current loss information, details on large losses, exposure base information (updated payrolls, sales, and property values), and information regarding the organization's safety and loss control program.

Figure 12.3

Insurance Specifications Outline

Preface. Set forth procedures to be followed, such as requirements for presentation, deadlines for proposal submission, who to contact for additional information, whether specimen forms should be included in the proposal, and any additional requests (such as 5-year history of solvency ratings of quoting insurers), etc.

Description of the Firm. Include types and locations of operations; products manufactured; services performed, even if only occasionally; description of management; financial information, including recent financial statements (particularly if sophisticated risk financing programs are being considered).

Comprehensive Coverage Requests. For each line, specify minimum limits, desired coverage extensions, acceptable levels of retention, and preferred rating programs.

Service Requests. This could include claims administration, loss control services, etc.

Detailed Underwriting Information. Depending on the lines of coverage being bid, underwriters will want the following types of information.

- Schedule of current values of owned equipment, vehicles, and real property
- Classification codes
- Number of employees in each classification
- Number of employees at each location
- Experience modification factors
- Breakdown of revenues and payroll
- Description of loss control program

Five-Year Loss Summaries in Each Line of Coverage. Make sure you use currently valued loss data.

Detailed Loss Information for Large or Unusual Losses.

Description of the Current Risk Management Program. Types, limits, and expiration dates of policies in force; rating plans, deductibles, self-insured retentions (SIRs), or other retentions.

91. Don't Bid "Excess and Surplus Lines" Coverages Among Agents

Certain types of insurance policies are written by such a limited number of insurance companies that it is a severe mistake to try to competitively bid them among a number of agents/brokers.

Usually these types of policies are the ones obtained in the excess and surplus (E&S) lines insurance marketplace. In general, the E&S marketplace consists of insurance companies that write unregulated lines of specialized insurance. For example, Lloyd's of London operates in this marketplace. Typically, the types of insurance policies that fit into the category—and that should not be competitively bid among a number of agents/brokers—include errors and omissions, malpractice, and professional liability insurance.

In addition, organizations seeking high dollar limits (over $5 million, for example) of umbrella liability insurance should not attempt to obtain competitive proposals from more than one agent for the entire amount of coverage that they will need. When obtaining competitive proposals from several agents, request no more than $5 million in umbrella liability insurance.

In situations where professional liability or high limits of umbrella liability insurance will be needed, it is suggested that the agent or broker who is awarded the other portions of the account be requested to obtain competitive proposals from several insurance companies. Therefore, even if one agent or broker is used for these lines of insurance, that agent/broker can canvass the market and present several proposals from various insurance companies from which you may select.

For further research and study

Guidelines for Insurance Specifications, published by International Risk Management Institute, Inc., provides a model set of specifications for all major coverage lines, in both Word files and hard copy formats. The specifications, which can be tailored to your organization's individual needs and circumstances, are an invaluable aid in preparing competitive proposals.

13

GENERAL RECOMMENDATIONS

TODAY, MANY ORGANIZATIONS PAY MORE for insurance premiums than for income taxes. For this reason, the insurance cost center should be managed proactively like the income tax cost center. To manage an insurance program, you do not necessarily have to be an expert on insurance and risk management. You do need enough knowledge to ask the right questions and demand effective services. This knowledge can be obtained by reading industry technical publications and attending seminars.

Insurance Cycles

The property and casualty insurance industry is cyclical in nature. Figure 13.1 presents a 20-year summary of premium, losses, and net pretax financial results of the industry. Until 1981, the higher underwriting losses were offset by even higher investment income. Rocketing stock prices enhanced the investment earnings of insurance companies in 1982 and added to operating results in 1983. As can be seen, insurance industry underwriting losses were mounting during the early 1980s while investment income growth was slowing.

In 1984 and 1985, the bottom fell out; the worst operating results until that point in the industry's history were produced in 1985. Insurance companies drastically increased rates and premiums during 1985 and 1986. The industry began recovering in 1986 and insurance companies engaged in strong price competition with each other.

An expanding U.S. economy and the soaring stock market fueled this intense competition in the commercial lines marketplace throughout the 1990s. While insurers were making substantial gains with their investment portfolios, underwriting losses began to mount. However, investment income was so strong that even a record underwriting loss in 1992, from Hurricane Andrew, couldn't squelch the competition. Insurance rates declined throughout the decade.

Things changed in 2000. That year the stock market reversed its course and began a steep decline. Underwriting losses, however, continued to mount and the $32.3 billion loss in 2000 was second only to the record losses of 1992. As a result, the insurance market began firming in the fourth quarter of that year. Continuing declines in the stock market, reductions in interest rates, and escalating underwriting losses caused the insurance market to become progressively harder all year long. By the end of August, businesses were receiving premium increases as high as 50 percent, along with increases in their retentions, when they renewed.

On September 11, 2001, everyone's worst nightmare occurred. While the final insured losses won't be known for years, they are estimated to be around $45 billion for insurers worldwide with U.S. insurers responsible for an estimated $25 billion of that number. The U.S. economy was in a recession, and the stock market continued its downward spiral. The final straw—

Figure 13.1

U.S. Property and Casualty Insurance Industry Results
(in Billions)

	Written Premiums	Under-writing Gain (Loss) +	Invest-ment Income =	Operat-ing Income (Loss) -	Federal Income Taxes (Credit) +	Realized Capital Gains (Losses) =	Net Income after Taxes
1981	**95.7**	**(6.3)**	**13.2**	**6.9**	**0.4**	**(2.4)**	**4.1**
1982	99.4	(9.9)	15.1	5.2	(0.3)	3.5	9.0
1983	**109.3**	**(13.3)**	**16.0**	**2.7**	**(0.8)**	**3.5**	**7.0**
1984	118.6	(21.7)	17.7	(4.0)	(1.6)	0.2	(2.2)
1985	**144.9**	**(25.0)**	**19.5**	**(5.5)**	**(1.9)**	**10.7**	**7.1**
1986	175.3	(16.1)	21.9	5.8	(0.6)	8.9	15.3
1987	**193.7**	**(9.9)**	**23.9**	**14.0**	**2.8**	**.3**	**11.5**
1988	202.3	(11.5)	27.7	16.2	3.6	5.4	18.0
1989	**208.8**	**(19.6)**	**31.2**	**11.6**	**2.6**	**12.9**	**21.9**
1990	218.1	(21.2)	32.9	11.2	3.3	2.9	10.8
1991	**223.2**	**(19.8)**	**34.2**	**13.8**	**4.4**	**4.8**	**14.2**
1992	227.8	(36.0)	33.7	(2.5)	1.5	9.9	5.8
1993	**241.7**	**(17.8)**	**32.6**	**14.6**	**5.1**	**9.8**	**19.3**
1994[1]	250.7	(22.2)	33.7	11.6	2.4	1.7	10.9
1995[1]	**259.8**	**(17.7)**	**36.8**	**19.5**	**4.9**	**6.0**	**20.6**
1996	268.7	(16.7)	38.0	20.8	5.6	9.2	24.4
1997	**276.6**	**(5.8)**	**41.5***	**35.5***	**9.5***	**10.8**	**36.8***
1998	281.6	(16.8)	39.9	23.4	10.6	18.0	30.8
1999	**286.9**	**(23.1)**	**38.9**	**14.4**	**5.6**	**13.0**	**21.9**
2000	301.0	(32.3)	40.6	8.8	5.5	17.0	20.3
2001	**324.0**	**(53.0)**	**37.9**	**(15.2)**	**(.4)**	**6.9**	**(7.9)**

NOTE: Figures may not balance because of rounding.

*When ISO adjusted the 1997 data for $2.3 billion in nonrecurring special dividends received by two insurers, income equaled $39.2 billion, operating income equaled $33.2 billion, federal income taxes equaled $9.0 billion, and net income after taxes equaled $35.0 billion.

Sources: Insurance Services Office, Inc., A.M. Best Co., Inc.

the one that broke the camel's back—landed in December with the collapse of Enron. In addition to roiling the stock market, this debacle will result in hundreds of millions of dollars in directors and officers liability, fiduciary liability, professional liability, and surety bond losses for the industry.

The result of this horribly "perfect storm" was the first-ever net after-tax loss ($7.9 billion) for the U.S. property and casualty insurance industry in history. The underwriting loss in 2001 ($52.9 billion) is nearly 50 percent greater than the previous record of $36.0 billion set in 1992. With this loss, the industry's net worth (i.e., statutory surplus) fell below $300 billion for the first time since 1996.

Now, we're well into 2002, and it is truly a seller's insurance market, or, in insurance parlance, a "hard market." Premiums and retentions are being increased dramatically, which forces the insured to explore alternative markets for coverage. As a result, agents, brokers, and underwriters are feeling overworked as they struggle to deal with substantially increased workloads. Insurance buyers are frustrated because they are being forced to pay substantially higher premiums, often for greatly reduced limits and/or coverage terms. Many will explore alternative market options in the hope of controlling costs now and escaping the cyclical nature of the market in the future. This hard market very well may last for a few years, particularly if the industry experiences any significant catastrophe losses.

This discussion should show you that while insurance industry cycles are not totally predictable, changes can be anticipated. By proactively managing your insurance and risk management program, you can place your firm in a position to anticipate these changes and take advantage of trends toward a "soft" (buyer's) insurance market. This can protect your organization from drastic upswings as the market begins to harden. Proactive management of an insurance and risk management program can be achieved by expending some time and effort to learn the basics of risk management and insurance and follow insurance industry developments.

Ways To Cut Costs

This concluding chapter reviews 10 general techniques for cutting the premiums on all your insurance policies. These techniques apply to several of the insurance policies you purchase or can be used for your entire risk management program.

92. Consolidate Effective Dates

One trick insurance agents may use to retain clients is to apply a different renewal date to every insurance policy. If the various insurance policies (such as automobile, general liability, and property) expire in different months of the year, it is virtually impossible to obtain competitive insurance proposals on the entire program from other agents or companies. It also makes it difficult to simply move the entire program to another agent with an "agent's letter of record." Furthermore, using different renewal dates for the primary (auto and general liability, for example) policies and the umbrella liability policy can cause gaps in insurance coverage. (See Appendix A for a detailed illustration of this concept.)

For this reason, it is advisable to arrange your insurance program with a common renewal date. Larger organizations may prefer two or three anniversary dates, to spread out over a period of time the work involved with renewals. For example, a large organization may use one date for all of its liability policies and another for all of its property insurance policies. Some organizations might even use a third common renewal date for all specialty and professional liability insurance policies. In addition to making it easier to competitively bid the insurance program, the use of one, two, or three common policy anniversary dates will allow you to consolidate the gathering of renewal and underwriting information for the insurance companies.

It is strongly recommended that you avoid using January 1 or July 1 as the anniversary date for any of your insurance policies. January 1 concludes the busiest period of the year for the insurance industry. (There are probably more insurance policy renewals effective on January 1 than on any other day of the year.) In addition, many insurance companies renew their reinsurance treaties on January 1 and have difficulty committing themselves in advance of that date since they often do not know the terms of their reinsurance. July 1 is also a busy time of the year for insurance companies because, again, many reinsurance treaties renew on that date. In a year that the marketplace is changing, insurance companies will be reluctant to quote terms far in advance of these reinsurance treaty renewals since they are not certain of their own costs for providing insurance.

For all but the largest firms, it is probably advisable to arrange the insurance program so that the policies renew in March, April, or early May. These months fall between the January 1 and July 1 busy periods of the insurance industry and avoid the summer vacation season. Except for the smallest organizations, the months September through December should probably be avoided because in "hard" insurance markets, insurers' capacity (the ability to write insurance or high limits of insurance) is often used up during the earlier months of the year and may not be available in the fall and early winter. However, smaller insureds will not generally be affected by capacity shortfalls unless they are for some reason purchasing very high limits (limits of over $50 million, for example) of umbrella liability insurance or need a specialized professional liability policy (such as accountants, attorneys, and hospitals).

93. Maximize Purchasing Power with One Insurer

One touted advantage of the independent agency system over the exclusive agent or direct writing insurance distribution system is that the independent agent has the ability to place your organization's insurance with more than one insurance company. Frequently, this approach can be used to maximize coverage and reduce costs. However, it is also possible to spread an insurance program too thin by using too many insurance companies for the various coverages. When this is done, the organization may not be considered an important account to any of the insurance companies that insure its risks. While this mistake happens most frequently when an organization uses numerous insurance agents, it can also happen when there is only one agent or broker.

Make sure that your organization is an important account to at least one of its insurance companies by placing enough policies (premiums) with that company to become an important account. By strengthening your position with the insurance company, you put yourself in a better position to negotiate on any claims for which an insurance policy's coverage is questionable. In the long run, this negotiating power in the claims area may be even more important than the ability to negotiate lower insurance premiums.

When thinking about this tactic of maximizing purchasing power with one insurer by giving that company a meaningful amount of your premium volume, do not overlook the substantial premium dollars being spent on employee benefits (such as group health and accident) programs. Some insurance buyers have quite successfully used their group employee benefits programs as carrots to help obtain liability insurance that was otherwise unavailable in the marketplace or available only at an inordinate cost.

94. Buy Package Policies

This book has treated each line of insurance (automobile, general liability, and property, for example) as a separate insurance policy. However, the insurance industry has developed some package policies that combine these various coverages into a single insurance policy for use by medium-sized and smaller insureds. For example, the extremely popular Business Owners Policy (BOP) package allows an insurance company to write general liability, property, and crime insurance in one policy. Many insurers have even developed customized versions of this policy for insureds in certain industries they target. Insurance companies typically give a "package discount" in recognition of the reduced administrative costs of issuing a single policy rather than three separate ones. These discounts vary, but they generally range between 7 and 35 percent of the total premium.

95. Consider Multiyear, Noncancellable Policies

During relatively soft markets, you should examine the possibility of arranging coverage on a multiyear, noncancellable basis. For example, some insurers will write 3-year policies. Doing so will have the effect of "locking in" favorable premium rates for an extended period of time. During very competitive market cycles, underwriters may be agreeable to offering such policies, especially for existing insureds with favorable loss histories, whose accounts they are anxious to retain. Multiyear programs of this type can be written to encompass all major lines of coverage, such as workers compensation, commercial general liability, business auto, and property insurance.

In hard markets, on the other hand, you may be better off with 1-year policy terms.

96. Prepare or Verify Premium Audits

When workers compensation insurance (and sometimes general liability and automobile insurance) is first written, the actual exposure base for the year (payroll, sales, or number of vehicles) must be estimated. The actual earned premium for these policies is then usually determined after policy expiration based on the actual exposure based on a premium audit performed by the insurer; given the magnitude of these premiums, the year-end premium audit should be approached with the same degree of concern as the federal income tax return.

In most cases, it is worthwhile to be as cooperative as possible with these auditors and avoid adversarial confrontations. There are a number of ways your organization can work with the premium auditor to make sure that the information received is appropriate. You may even want to prepare the audit yourself to be certain it is done properly.

Prepare It Yourself

At the beginning of the policy period, or a relationship with a new insurance company, a sample of the audit department's work sheets may be obtained. At the end of the year, you or your company's accounting department can develop the ratable payrolls, using this work sheet format. The insurance company's audit department will make an appointment. At the time of the appointment, you simply furnish the prepared work sheet, along with the records from which the information was compiled. The auditor can then check the work sheet, and you can discuss any changes that are to be made before the auditor leaves your premises. If necessary, your insurance agent or consultant can be invited to any meetings involving disputed classifications or procedures. However, the auditor will usually accept the statistics that you compile.

Verify the Auditor's Work

If the premium audit is not prepared internally, as suggested above, ask the premium auditor to provide copies of the handwritten work sheets used in performing the audit before leaving your office. A typed audit and premium invoice or return premium will be mailed at a later date.

When the typed audit is received, you can check it against the handwritten work sheet for transposition errors. It should also be ascertained that the correct experience modifier (if applicable) has been used and that all mathematics involved in determining the premium are correct. Finally, all rates utilized in determining the premium should be checked against the original insurance policy; any discrepancy should be explained by the insurance agent or broker.

The calculations in the premium audit can easily contain mistakes made by the insurance company, and these mistakes can increase your organization's premium expense considerably. If the above suggestions are followed, the premium audit can usually be checked in a short period of time.

97. Defer Premiums

You may be able to negotiate payment of premiums on a monthly or quarterly basis rather than paying a lump sum at the beginning of the policy period. In fact, many insurers offer this payment schedule without charging interest on the deferred amount. In turn, this allows your organization to retain and invest or otherwise use the deferred premium until it is due.

If the insurance company will not finance the premiums, consider the specialty premium finance companies that charge interest at a rate slightly higher than prime. Since these notes are secured by the unearned premium of the policy being financed, the rates may be lower than your firm's normal borrowing rate and, in any case, will allow you to hold your company's normal credit resources in reserve.

98. Develop a Comprehensive Insurance Database

The importance of accumulating risk management and insurance data cannot be overemphasized. Indeed, it is probably best compared to the importance of maintaining proper income tax documentation. You can use risk management and insurance information to negotiate with insurance companies, evaluate loss control programs, analyze appropriate deductible or retention levels, and audit the cost components of your firm's insurance or risk management program. This data is also crucial when obtaining competitive bids. An accurate and current risk management and insurance database will save your organization considerable sums of money over the long run. In fact, this information is so important that some companies spend substantial sums of money to set up and maintain computerized risk management information systems (RMIS).

The minimum standards for a risk management and insurance database, whether computerized or not, are the following.

- Premium audit statements for the past 5 years for each line of insurance audited
- Retrospective rating adjustment statements for the past 5 years for each applicable line
- Currently valued loss reports for each of the past 5 years for each line of insurance
- Copies of insurance policies including all endorsements
- Experience rating work sheets for the past 5 years for each experience rated line
- Current property schedule
- Current vehicle schedule
- Current equipment schedule
- Copies of important lease agreements, construction contracts, and other business contracts

For organizations of any size, loss information is very important. If you do not maintain your own computerized database (or contract with a service provider for one), be sure to at minimum require them from your insurer. In doing so, keep in mind that claims develop over time. For this reason, you should obtain a current loss report annually, covering the last 5 policy years. Do not allow your insurer to provide only the current year's losses in its reports.

Even without a sophisticated risk management information system, it is not difficult to track the development of claims. In fact, it is relatively easy to simply record the paid, reserved, and total incurred amounts for your company's workers compensation losses on a monthly basis. Performing this task over several years will help to create a good feel for the way in which claims develop over time within your firm. Ultimately, the exercise can put you in a stronger position when negotiating with an insurance company because this data allows you to more accurately forecast future losses—the key element involved in the pricing of insurance coverage.

99. Prepare Early for Renewals

The importance of timing and of allowing adequate time to obtain competitive proposals was emphasized in the previous chapter. Even when you have no intention of changing insurance companies, it is just as important to prepare early for renewals. Accumulate all of the important underwriting data that the insurance agent and underwriter will need well in advance (90 to 120 days) of the renewal date. The insurance agent/broker should be pressured to provide the renewal quotation 2 to 3 weeks prior to the renewal date. This will allow time to negotiate with the underwriter regarding any unacceptable aspects of the renewal quote or even to obtain alternative quotes from other insurers if the renewal quote is unacceptable.

As a word of caution, however, an underwriter's quotation should not be "shopped" in the marketplace. Insurance buyers who do this will quickly establish a poor reputation in the underwriting community that will eventually cost them more than they gain from the activity. Never tell one underwriter the price quoted by another underwriter that has to be beat.

In a tight marketplace, some underwriters withhold renewal quotations until the last minute. These underwriters are attempting to avoid having their renewal quotations shopped or to avoid providing you with the opportunity to obtain an alternative quotation should the renewal quotation be unacceptable. While pressure should be placed on the insurance agent/broker to obtain the renewal quotation well in advance of the renewal date, it should be recognized that failure to do so may not be the agent's or broker's fault.

100. Hire a Risk Manager

Medium-sized and large organizations should consider the possibility of hiring a full-time risk manager. Such an individual has knowledge of the insurance industry and the risk management process and can implement a cost-effective program. Particularly for medium-sized firms, it is often difficult to decide whether or not the expenses of hiring a full-time individual to administer a risk management program would be cost-justified. One risk management commentator, David Warren, has suggested using 10 percent of the sum of the insurance premiums and self-insured losses as a guideline for establishing the budget of a risk management department; in other words, 10 percent of the total cash flows within the department.

This same guideline might be used to determine when to hire a risk manager. If the costs of hiring a risk manager and establishing the department are equal to or less than 10 percent of the sum of insurance premiums and losses, it would probably be worthwhile to hire a risk manager. The theory underlying this rule of thumb is that a risk manager with specialized knowledge and expertise should be able to save the organization at least 10 percent more than an individual who does not have this specialized knowledge and expertise.

101. Implement Contractual Risk Transfer Programs

The effective use of hold harmless clauses and insurance requirements in business contracts (such as leases and construction agreements) can reduce or eliminate the need for certain types of insurance and/or reduce insurance premiums. Losses that the organization would otherwise have to pay can be transferred to other parties in these contracts. In addition, these other parties can be required to purchase insurance to pay any losses experienced by your organization. For example, a firm that is leasing office space in a building might require the landlord to assume responsibility for purchasing insurance on that building and waive the rights of its insurer to subrogate against (sue) the organization even if an employee of your firm was liable in starting the fire.

If your company employs independent contractors, contractually require those contractors to purchase liability insurance and workers compensation insurance. Otherwise, your firm could be held legally liable to third parties for injuries or damage to their property caused by the independent contractor or even be liable to pay workers compensation benefits to injured employees of independent contractors. Because of this, your organization's liability and workers compensation insurance company may charge extra premium for this additional loss exposure if your company does not require these insurance coverages from independent contractors. Be sure to procure certificates of insurance from independent contractors showing that such insurance coverage is in place.

It is beyond the scope of this book to provide an in-depth discussion of the many uses of and pitfalls involved with contractual transfer of risk. However, you should be aware that others will attempt to pass their risks on to you in business contracts. You can reduce costs and control premiums by being cautious in accepting their risks and attempting to pass your risks to others. This is an area in which active participation from a knowledgeable attorney, risk manager, and a professional insurance agent or broker can be quite useful.

For further research and study

Contractual Risk Transfer is a two-volume reference manual, published by IRMI, which addresses the effective use of hold harmless clauses and insurance requirements in business contracts. The manual shows ways to lessen or eliminate the need for certain types of insurance and discusses means of reducing insurance premiums via contractual transfer of risk. *Construction Risk Management* provides many risk management and insurance strategies and tactics for construction companies. Visit the Products and Services section of IRMI.com for more information on these publications.

Appendix A

A DOZEN IMPORTANT COVERAGE CONSIDERATIONS

ALTHOUGH THIS BOOK CONCENTRATES ON WAYS TO CONTROL property and casualty insurance costs, you should not fall into the trap of focusing solely on premiums while ignoring coverage. After all, the reason you buy insurance is to make sure that your organization is not financially impaired by unexpected losses. This appendix discusses a few of the more important coverage issues that you should address.

Coordinate Liability Policies

An organization's automobile liability, employers liability, general liability, and umbrella liability insurance policies must be arranged to coordinate with each other to avoid coverage gaps and overlaps. Not only must these insurance policies be reviewed individually, but consideration must be given to how they may interrelate to each other on a single loss event. Too many agents, brokers, and insurance managers fail to consider the possibility of a liability loss "falling through the cracks."

Coordinate Automobile and General Liability

An area in which disputes may arise with insurers is the distinction between an automobile-related claim and one that should be covered by the general liability policy. While the insurance industry has made attempts to clarify the distinction within policy contracts, there is still room for disputes when a liability loss involves the loading or unloading of a vehicle. In this situation, the automobile insurance company may claim that it is a general liability loss and the general liability insurer may claim that it is an automobile liability loss. Frequently, the insured is left with no coverage (or a poorly coordinated defense) and ends up paying legal fees trying to get one of the two insurers to cover the claim. It is strongly recommended, then, that the same insurer be used for both the automobile and the general liability insurance.

A problem can arise even if the same insurer writes both the automobile and general liability insurance or when the two policies have different limits of liability or deductibles. In these situations, the insurance company has an incentive to push the loss into whichever policy has the lower limits of liability. In most situations, this will not be a problem, but organizations with a heavy auto exposure should probably consider using the same limits of liability for both types of insurance.

Coordinate Coverage Triggers

Coverage triggers are another way that policies must be coordinated. Mixing coverage triggers in a layered liability program can result in gaps in coverage where one policy will cover liability losses but the one below or above it does not. When you purchase claims-made policies, try to coordinate the various provisions affecting the claims-made trigger. Generally, it is also preferable to use the most liberal policy forms in the lower layers of coverage, relegating the ones that provide you with the fewest safeguards to the upper layers that are less likely to be needed far into the future.

Coordinate Primary and Umbrella Coverage

The primary (general liability, auto liability, and employers liability) insurance policies must also coordinate with the umbrella liability program that provides the excess limits for catastrophic losses. To the extent possible, the umbrella should provide at least the same coverage (have the same exclusions, conditions, etc.) as the underlying policies. Of course, it is best for the umbrella to provide even broader coverage. However, areas in which umbrella policies are frequently more restrictive than primary policies include the following.

- Coverage for pollution
- Coverage for damage to the work of an insured contractor
- Coverage for liability arising from aircraft and watercraft
- Coverage for certain contractually assumed liabilities

There can also be other areas in which the excess or umbrella liability program is more restrictive than the underlying coverage. But generally, anytime the underlying coverage is enhanced by a policy endorsement, it may be necessary to add a similar endorsement to the umbrella liability policy.

An equally important area in which the primary and umbrella/excess liability policies must be coordinated is the limits of liability provision. Since an umbrella policy should begin providing coverage once the primary policy exhausts its limits, it is important for the "Schedule of Underlying Limits" in the umbrella policy to accurately reflect the actual underlying limits purchased. For example, if the underlying limits are actually lower than those reflected in the umbrella policy schedule, the umbrella insurer will argue that it is not required to pay until the insured has made up the difference between the limits shown in the umbrella's schedule and the actual limits purchased. It is amazing how often mistakes are made in this area.

Another, less obvious, way that underlying policy limits can be lower than those required by the umbrella occurs when different inception dates are used for the primary and umbrella liability policies. Most umbrella policies require that the full aggregate limits of the primary policies be in force as of the inception date of the umbrella. If the primary insurance has an inception date earlier than that of the umbrella, any claims paid by the primary insurer prior to the inception date of the umbrella reduce the primary policy's aggregate limits, causing a violation of this umbrella policy warranty. The resulting coverage gap is easily avoided by simply using the same inception and expiration dates for the primary liability insurance and the umbrella liability policy. This is another widely violated guideline.

Beware of Joint Venture Liability

Joint ventures are becoming a common way of doing business. They are frequently used by two or more manufacturers, contractors, real estate developers, or other business entities to combine their property, labor, skill, experience, or time, or some combination thereof, for a single undertaking. Whenever an organization enters into a joint venture, a new, distinct legal entity is formed. However, its liability exposures are not usually confined to the joint venture; the joint venturers usually have joint and several liability for the entity's actions. Unless appropriate steps are taken to insure this legal entity, the organization becomes exposed to potential uninsured liability losses.

The organization's liability insurance policies will not typically provide automatic coverage for liability arising out of past or current joint ventures unless specific modifications are made to the policy or the joint venture is scheduled in the policy as an "insured." It is usually preferable to arrange a separate insurance program to cover liability arising from the operations, products, and/or services of an active, ongoing joint venture, including the joint venture partners as insureds in the policies. Sometimes, however, one organization will simply endorse the joint venture and the partner(s) as insureds in its insurance program to provide coverage; this is most common when the other partner supplies only capital and remains relatively silent in the operations and management of the joint venture.

Recognize that there is a legal liability loss exposure arising from the products and completed operations of past, dissolved joint ventures. This is the area in which uninsured liability losses are most likely to arise since former legal entities are often forgotten. In addition, specific liability insurance policies are not purchased for these dissolved legal entities. Make sure that any such loss exposure faced by the organization is covered by your liability insurance program, and this will usually require special modifications to your insurance policies. One noninsurance technique for addressing such exposures is to create limited liability companies, which can also reduce the potential for financial loss under these circumstances.

Schedule All Insureds, Comply with Additional Insured Requirements

Another basic area not to overlook is inclusion of all related entities as insureds in the various insurance policies. It is not uncommon for one or more subsidiaries or related organizations to be omitted from the schedule of insureds. One method of avoiding such an omission is to negotiate an omnibus named insured clause with the insurance company. In general, this endorsement would stipulate that all entities in which the primary named insured owns a majority interest are automatically included as insureds in the insurance policies. If such an omnibus clause is not obtainable, take great care to review the schedule of insureds to ascertain that none have inadvertently been omitted.

Don't Overlook Additional Insured Requirements

A similar problem can arise in regard to the inclusion of "additional insureds" on liability policies. It has become common practice for one party to a contract to require the other party to include it as an "additional insured" on the other party's insurance policies. For example, owners of construction projects will frequently require the general contractor to name the owner as an additional insured in the contractor's general liability policy. Without specific modifications of the policy to provide automatic coverage in these situations, this can be achieved only by adding an endorsement to the policy specifically naming the additional insured. Frequently, contractors and others forget to request this endorsement, which could result in a breach of contract claim against the party that was supposed to take the action. Your liability policy will not cover this breach of contract, which will result in an uninsured loss.

For this reason, it is important to have a procedure in place to assure it occurs. Alternatively, you can ask your insurer to attach a "blanket" or "automatic" additional insured endorsement to your policy. This endorsement will automatically add any party with whom you contractually agree to add to your policy.

Report Acquisitions

Usually, liability insurance policies provide 60 or 90 days of automatic coverage for newly acquired or newly created organizations owned by the insured. The insured must report the acquisition or formation of a new company to the insurance company during this period and arrange for coverage after it has elapsed.

Consider the Implications in Advance

Many organizations make the mistake of not considering in advance the risk management implications of a merger, acquisition, or newly formed organization. After the fact, they often learn they have assumed uninsurable liability exposures or operations that are extremely costly to insure. Whenever possible, have the risk manager, agent, or broker make an analysis of the risk management implications of the deal before it is executed.

In recent years, innovative new insurance coverages have been introduced to cover the representations and warranties included in merger and acquisition agreements. These insurance products can dramatically improve the viability of an otherwise too-risky or too-costly deal. Involving knowledgeable risk and insurance experts early in the transaction can help bring these options into play.

Promptly Report Potential Claims

Virtually all insurance policies contain a requirement to report "as soon as practicable" accidents or occurrences that may result in a claim(s). Failure to promptly notify the insurance company of known events that present the potential for liability claims can result in denied coverage for claims eventually made in conjunction with the incident. Prompt reporting of accidents provides the insurance company with an opportunity to investigate the situation and receive statements from witnesses while memories are fresh. This puts the insurer in a better position to defend any claims that are eventually made. In the area of property insurance, insurance companies usually prefer to be advised of the loss and provided the opportunity to investigate prior to the commencement of major cleanup or repair operations. This enables them to also make an early determination of whether or not the loss event is covered by the insurance policy.

Establish an incident reporting system whereby all accidents and events that may lead to insurance claims are promptly reported to whomever has responsibility for the risk management and insurance program. It is also recommended that an attempt be made to secure an endorsement to your liability insurance policies clarifying that the knowledge of an employee or agent of the insured does not constitute knowledge of the insured that a loss event has occurred for the purpose of reporting the accident. Knowledge would be recognized only when the individual is a corporate officer. This clarification will help avoid the potential for coverage denials based on late reporting when an employee knew about the accident but did not report it to management; therefore, there was no notification to the insurance company.

Extend Notice of Cancellation

Most insurance policies require the insurer to provide the insured with either 10 or 30 days' notice of its intent to cancel coverage. Insurance policies impose no notification requirement on the insurer of its intent to not renew a policy or to substantially change a policy when it is renewed. (A few states do require insurers to provide such notice under certain circumstances.) For most commercial accounts, 30 days is an inadequate amount of time to remarket most insurance policies, and it is virtually impossible to do in 10 days. To avoid this situation, request that the cancellation provision be modified to require the insurer to provide at least 60 days' notice of its intent to cancel, and some companies will even agree to provide 90 days' notice.

In addition, the cancellation provision should be modified to address the issues of nonrenewal and material policy changes. An insurance company should be required to provide the same amount of previous notice (60 or 90 days, for example) of its intent to not renew coverage or to make a material change (such as including additional exclusions or requiring substantially higher deductibles) when the policy is renewed. This type of policy modification is usually relatively easy to obtain in a soft, buyer's market and provides the insured protection when the market changes to a tight, seller's market. While more difficult to obtain in a tight market, it is often available in a tight market to medium-sized and larger commercial accounts.

Buy Adequate Policy Limits

A basic area of insurance management that deserves more attention than many firms give it is the selection of policy limits. More uninsured losses probably are caused by improper selection of limits than by any other mistake.

Liability Limits

One way of controlling insurance costs in a tight marketplace is to reduce the limits of liability applicable to the liability insurance policies you purchase. To the extent that the organization buys higher limits than it needs in a soft marketplace because of reduced premium costs, it is appropriate to reduce the limits applicable to the umbrella/excess liability policies it purchases in a tight market. However, your overriding concern should be to protect the organization from catastrophic losses that, though they occur infrequently, can substantially impair the financial position of the firm. You should always keep in mind that it is better to assume risk at the lower levels through deductibles or self-insured retentions than in the high limits areas.

All businesses need at least $1 million of coverage, and most professionals agree that the absolute minimum liability insurance virtually any business organization should purchase is $5 million. Of course, many organizations will need even higher limits. Cost-cutting point number 36 in Chapter 4 contains additional guidelines on how to select an appropriate limit of liability.

Report Adequate Property Values

You should also devote time and effort to making certain that the property values used for insurance purposes are adequate. Many insurance policies include a *coinsurance provision* that requires an insured to maintain insurance greater than or equal to a specified percent of the property's value (generally between 80 and 100 percent); failing to do so causes the insured to become a coinsurer with the insurance company and receive a reduced payment in the event of a loss. The purpose of a coinsurance clause is to promote "insurance to value" by penalizing the insured if proper values are not purchased. The following formula determines the amount of the loss the insurer will pay.

$$[\text{Valued insured} \div \text{Value required}] \times \text{loss} = \text{recovery}$$

The value required is determined by the value of the property *at the time of the loss,* multiplied by the applicable coinsurance percentage. For example, assume a business owns a building that has an insurable value of $250,000 and insures it with a policy that contains an 80 percent coinsurance clause. The business would be required to insure the building for at least $200,000 ($250,000 x .80) to avoid a coinsurance penalty. If the business purchases only $150,000 coverage and sustains a $50,000 loss during the policy period, the recovery is limited to $37,500, less any deductible. The formula would be applied as follows.

$$[\$150,000 \div \$200,000] \times \$50,000 = \$37,500$$

Maintaining insurance to value is very important. Property should be appraised periodically to ensure that the amount of insurance maintained is adequate. Another technique for avoiding coinsurance penalties is to purchase insurance on an *agreed amount* basis. Under this approach, property values for insurance purposes are determined and submitted to the insurance company. The insurance company reviews these property values and agrees that they will be adequate for insurance purposes. In essence, the insurance company will waive the right to apply a coinsurance penalty at the time of a loss even if these values turn out to be less than the stipulated percentage.

As a word of caution, agreed amount endorsements are generally on an annual basis even when attached to a policy with a 3-year term. Therefore, the property values usually must be reviewed and the agreed amount endorsement renewed annually. When 3-year term policies are purchased, this is sometimes overlooked, which could result in a coinsurance penalty if a loss occurred in the second or third year.

Review Property Valuation Clauses

Under standard property insurance policies, the business is reimbursed for property losses on an *actual cash value* (ACV) basis. Valuation on an ACV basis is defined as the cost to replace the property with materials of like kind and quality, less an amount determined for physical depreciation. This valuation clause does not correspond to book value because book value is based on the original purchase price rather than the "cost to replace the property." Book value, then, should not be used for insurance purposes because substantial underinsurance would usually result (since book value is based on original purchase price rather than current value).

Coverage can also be purchased on a *replacement cost* basis instead of the ACV valuation. When replacement cost coverage is indicated on the policy's declaration page, the organization will be reimbursed for the cost to replace the property with no deduction for physical depreciation. Replacement cost coverage can be effected for little or no charge; however, the insurable value for the property will be greater and therefore the policy's premium will be somewhat greater. Even when replacement cost coverage is purchased, the policy will only pay actual cash value if the property is not repaired or replaced. Therefore, organizations that would replace a building or premises following its destruction by fire or other peril should insure it on a replacement cost basis. On the other hand, if the building would not be replaced, actual cash value insurance should be purchased.

Buy "All Risk" Property Insurance

For property insurance coverage on buildings, contents, inventory, etc., there are several standard policy forms that may be purchased to insure against different perils.

Named Perils Coverage

The *basic form* provides for direct loss caused by the specifically listed perils of fire, lightning, explosion, windstorm, hail, smoke, aircraft, vehicles, riot, civil commotion, vandalism, sprinkler leakage, sinkhole collapse, and volcanic action. The *broad form* expands the perils covered to also include glass breakage; falling objects; weight of ice, sleet, or snow; water damage; and limited collapse coverage. The third option, the *special form,* covers all risks of physical loss unless the loss-causing peril is specifically excluded from coverage.

All Risk Coverage

The special form property policy provides broader coverage than either the basic or broad form policies. In essence, this form provides what has historically been called *"all risk"* or "open perils" property insurance coverage. Typically, all risk insurance provides broader insurance protection than *named peril* insurance such as that provided by the basic and broad form policies. In addition, all risk insurance places a higher burden of proof on the insurer to deny a claim than does named perils insurance. Under an all risk policy, an insurer must demonstrate that a loss falls within the policy's exclusions to deny a claim. With a named perils policy, on the other hand, it is up to the insured to prove that a loss falls within the insured perils of the policy. For these reasons, all risk coverage is generally preferred over named perils coverage.

Don't Overlook "Time Element" Exposures

Property insurance policies cover only direct loss to insured property caused by insured perils. However, damage to insured property may also lead to a type of indirect loss, usually referred to as a *time element* loss—one that results from a covered peril but is not caused directly by it. Time element losses include such losses as business interruption, extra expense, rental value, and leasehold interest. Obtaining proper coverage for indirect losses is very important since, in many cases, these losses can far exceed the direct physical loss to property. In fact, studies of businesses that failed following a fire or other catastrophe indicate lack of business interruption coverage is a primary cause of their failures.

Business Interruption Insurance

The most common of the indirect loss coverages is called *"business interruption"* or *"business income"* insurance. This coverage is designed to reimburse the insured who suffers a direct property loss for any loss of earnings that results during the period required to restore the property to its normal operating condition. For example, a manufacturer would suffer a severe loss of sales after a major fire at its warehouse destroyed inventory that would have been sold. For business interruption insurance to reimburse the insured for loss of earnings, the physical damage must be caused by a covered peril. If this is the case and an interruption of business occurs, the insurance company will pay for both lost net profit and expenses that continue even though operations have ceased (such as salaries of executive officers, insurance premiums, lease or rental expenses, taxes, etc.). Coverage is limited to the length of time required, with the exercise of due diligence, to repair, rebuild, or replace the part of the property that has been damaged or destroyed. Moreover, there are some types of business interruption policies that provide coverage up to the period in which a business returns to its preloss volume of sales.

Extra Expense Insurance

Some types of organizations have no need for business interruption insurance because their operations can or must be continued even though their premises are damaged or destroyed. For example, hospitals, banks, and newspapers would generally have to continue operations at all costs to avoid losing customers and to fulfill what they perceive as their moral commitments to their customers and communities. To help pay for the extra costs associated with continuing operations at a temporary location, *extra expense insurance* is available. Extra expense insurance covers the necessary extra expenses required to continue normal operations following damage or loss by covered perils to insured property. It will, for example, reimburse the insured for the costs associated with paying overtime to employees, advertising the new location, renting necessary equipment, renting a facility, and so forth.

Leasehold Interest and Rental Income

If an organization is leasing property (office space, for example) under a long-term contract, it is possible that the current lease agreement calls for a rental payment that is significantly less than the cost of renting comparable property in the current market. Since many leases call for the termination of the agreement if the property becomes untenantable because of a fire or other peril, the occurrence of such a peril and the subsequent cancellation of the lease could cause an indirect loss to the organization equivalent to the additional cost of renting comparable space. *Leasehold interest* insurance is available to insure against the additional cost of renting comparable space under these circumstances.

Likewise, if the organization leases space to others, a loss of rental income would occur if the property were damaged to the point that lease provisions call for termination of the lease. *Rental value* insurance is available to reimburse the organization for this type of income loss.

Consider Directors and Officers, Fiduciary, and Employment Practices Liability Insurance

In addition to standard property and liability exposures, your company also faces the threat of claims from what are sometimes referred to as "executive liability" exposures. These claims can be covered by three types of insurance: directors and officers (D&O) liability, fiduciary liability, and employment practices liability insurance.

Directors and Officers Liability Insurance

Directors and officers liability insurance is a form of errors and omissions coverage for persons who serve as officers of corporations and/or sit on corporate boards. The following allegations most frequently give rise to claims against directors and officers: wrongful termination, misstatement of financial conditions, inadequate/inaccurate financial reporting or disclosure, antitrust allegations, mismanagement of funds, and conflicts of interest. In recent years, the majority of claim dollars paid out by insurers have been the result of so-called securities litigation. Such claims are most often triggered by a corporation's restatement of its earnings and a subsequent drop in the price of the corporation's stock price.

Although they are generally less susceptible (given the lack of a securities claim exposure), the directors and officers of nonprofit corporations and privately held companies are also confronted with the possibility of D&O claims. Despite the absence of stockholders—the most likely plaintiffs in D&O litigation—such firms should not consider themselves immune to claims against their directors and officers. Current/former employees, customers, competitors, and government agencies are also potential plaintiffs.

Each year, the Tillinghast-Towers Perrin Company, a prominent international consulting firm, conducts a survey pertaining to D&O claims and coverage. The 2001 survey revealed that the average cost of shareholders claims was $17.18 million and the average cost of claims by employees was $245,000. Defense costs for shareholder and employee claims were $1.05 million and $105,000, respectively.

D&O policies actually consist of two separate parts: (1) *corporate reimbursement coverage,* which reimburses your company for the loss it sustains when it must indemnify directors and officers, as required under your corporation's bylaws or state law, and (2) *directors and officers liability coverage,* which covers the personal liability of directors and officers when, according to corporate bylaws or state law, your company is not required to indemnify them for their acts.

There are a number of other key limitations and exclusions built into D&O policies of which you should also be aware.

- D&O policies are written on a claims-made basis, meaning that for coverage to apply, the policy must have been in force at the time a claim is actually made against the insured directors and officers. This is in contrast to the more familiar occurrence policy form that requires only that the loss took place during the policy period—regardless of when the actual claim is made against an insured. The effect of such a provision is that coverage gaps can result when the insurance is temporarily discontinued. Gaps can also occur when a policy is written by a new insurer who may restrict coverage for acts that took place during the policy period of a prior insurer.
- The expenditure of defense costs reduces the policy's limit of coverage. This is in contrast to commercial general liability (CGL), auto, and many other types of liability policies under which defense is paid in addition to the limit of liability.
- There is no coverage for illegal, intentional, or fraudulent acts. The insurer will, however, provide defense coverage if such allegations are made against a company's directors and officers—provided the allegations are ultimately proven to be groundless. Moreover, if certain directors or officers are found innocent of wrongdoing—while others are not—the policy will pay defense costs for the innocent directors/officers.
- There are substantial per claim retentions, which can easily exceed $1 million, especially for large corporations
- Bodily injury and property damage claims are excluded by D&O policies, because this is a general liability exposure.

Despite the coverage limitations built into the policies, you should at least obtain a quotation for D&O coverage, so that the decision to purchase or not purchase it can be an informed one. Nevertheless, given today's highly litigious environment, it will be very difficult to attract talented, qualified board members without having D&O protection in place.

Fiduciary Liability Insurance

Fiduciary liability insurance covers claims against persons serving as trustees or administrators of employee benefit plans. Fiduciaries are personally liable for losses sustained by a breach of their discretionary duties. However, by law, corporations are not permitted to indemnify fiduciaries for such losses, hence the need for some form of insurance protection.

Although its passage did not mandate the purchase of fiduciary liability insurance, the Employee Retirement Income Security Act (ERISA) of 1974 promulgated specific standards for fiduciary conduct, which in turn created a definite liability exposure to persons serving in such capacities. Examples of the types of allegations that would be covered by a fiduciary liability policy include losses caused by failure to diversify assets of a pension plan, failure to select a financially solvent health insurer under an employer-paid health insurance program, and failure to supervise an investment manager under a 401(K) plan. Firms that offer company stock as a 401(K) plan investment option have an especially significant fiduciary liability exposure.

Fiduciary liability insurance is often confused with employee benefit liability coverage. In contrast to fiduciary liability coverage, employee benefit liability insurance is designed to address nondiscretionary, administrative errors and omissions associated with employee benefit plan management (such as failure to enroll an employee in a 401(K) program, inaccurately advising an employee about the amount of the monthly benefit payable under a pension plan, and designating the wrong beneficiary under a group life insurance policy). Employee benefits liability coverage is available as an endorsement to a CGL policy. However, since the vast majority of fiduciary liability policy forms also afford employee benefit liability protection, it is preferable to secure employee benefit liability coverage by purchasing a fiduciary liability policy that also picks up the employee benefits liability exposure.

According to the Tillinghast-Towers Perrin Company fiduciary liability survey conducted in 2000, the average payout to claimants was $1.9 million. This compares to an average payout of $875,000 in the 1993 study. Average defense costs were $124,000 in the 2000 study.

Recognize also that, like D&O policies, fiduciary liability insurance precludes coverage for intentional or criminal dishonesty, although defense coverage for allegations of intentional acts is provided. Moreover, the policies do not cover exposures arising from managing workers compensation, unemployment, social security, disability, or similar plans of a federally or state-mandated nature. Finally, the policies typically exclude coverage for losses as a result of the bankruptcy of a bank or broker. Thus, if your company sponsors a benefit plan that goes bankrupt because of the insolvency of a bank or broker, a fiduciary policy would not cover such a loss.

Despite the foregoing limitations inherent in fiduciary liability insurance, strongly consider purchasing a policy, preferably one that also covers the employee benefits liability exposure.

Like D&O insurance, it may be difficult to find persons willing to serve as trustees of benefit plans in the absence of such coverage.

Employment Practices Liability Insurance

A marked increase in the number of claims arising from the employment process has become evident in recent years. A combination of heightened awareness concerning workplace injustices, liberal federal employment-related legislation, significant downsizing and corporate staff cuts, and the increased presence of women and minorities in the workplace have produced a number of multimillion-dollar settlements and verdicts, in addition to an increase in routine claims involving the workplace.

In response to these trends, employment practices liability insurance was developed to cover corporations and individuals for claims arising from wrongful termination, discrimination, sexual harassment, and miscellaneous employment-related allegations (breach of employment contracts, wrongful discipline, employment-related defamation, and wrongful evaluation, to name a few).

Recognize that even if claims under employment practices liability policies are for allegations that are ultimately proven false or groundless with no payment ever made to a claimant, the costs of defending against such allegations are nonetheless significant.

A key difference between employment practices liability insurance and D&O coverage is that the insureds under the former are not solely restricted to directors and officers; in fact, the policies also cover your corporation if a lawsuit is filed against it, in addition to specific individuals.

Key restrictions built into the policies include the following.

- Payment of defense costs reduces policy limits
- The forms are written on a claims-made basis
- The policies sometimes impose a 5 to 10 percent coinsurance penalty on amounts payable (which also includes defense costs)
- Exclusions for intentional acts or injuries

One less expensive alternative to buying employment practices liability insurance is to have your firm's D&O policy endorsed to cover this exposure. Despite the relative cost-efficiency of such an approach, however, it is not without certain drawbacks, including potential dilution of D&O limits in the event of a claim. Another disadvantage is that coverage under some D&O endorsements will apply only to directors and officers but not to the corporation itself. Finally, certain perils normally covered by employment practices liability policies, such as constructive discharge and deprivation of a career opportunity, may not be covered by an endorsement to a D&O policy.

Premiums for employment practices liability insurance are relatively high. Much of the increase can be attributed to rising employment-related claim levels in recent years. For example, in January 2001, the Jury Verdict Research Institute (Horsham, PA) reported that the median national jury verdict for employment cases rose 44 percent in just 1 year, from $151,000 in 1999 to $218,000 in 2000. Thus, some organizations have taken the position that rather than buying a policy, a more cost-effective means of addressing this exposure is to develop and implement significant claim prevention and control efforts. Toward that end, you should make sure that your organization has a well-written and strongly enforced anti-discrimination policy conforming to Equal Employment Opportunity Commission (EEOC) guidelines. It is also necessary to develop a policy addressing sexual harassment and enforce it strongly. Your organization should take great care in the hiring process, being certain to conduct periodic performance evaluations, provide notification of and the opportunity to remedy unacceptable performance, and avoid statements at the time of hire or in employee handbooks that promise permanent employment. A formal grievance procedure should be in place so that employees can freely report, without fear of retaliation, any behavior or conduct they feel constitutes grounds for an employment practices claim. One final, cost-effective option is to purchase a policy with a relatively high deductible, such as $25,000 or $50,000. This approach conserves premium while affording coverage for infrequent but severe claims.

Regardless of whether your company decides to purchase employment practices liability insurance, you should first implement the loss control measures discussed above.

Evaluate Environmental Liability Exposures and Coverage

The need to purchase coverage for your organization's environmental and pollution liability exposures arises from two sources: environmental laws and company-specific operations.

There are numerous federal environmental laws in effect, most notably the Comprehensive Environmental Response Compensation and Liability Act (CERCLA, also known as "Superfund"), the Resource Conservation and Recovery Act (RCRA), the Clean Water Act (CWA), the Clean Air Act (CAA), and the Toxic Substance Control Act (TSCA). These and myriad other federal, state, and local regulations could create a multitude of liabilities for your organization.

Regarding your operations, the entities most susceptible to pollution liability claims are those that own and operate hazardous waste facilities, landfills, surface impoundments, and underground storage tanks. However, there are many other types of organizations that, while not directly involved in environmentally oriented businesses, could also be held liable for violating environmental laws, simply because they contract with other parties to dispose of their hazardous wastes. Such businesses could include, but are not limited to, manufacturers, contractors, hospitals, and automotive repair operations.

Given the complexity of and expertise required to properly assess the extent of your organization's exposure to pollution liability claims, coupled with the maze of environmental laws that could apply to your firm's operations, you may want to consider hiring an outside engineering firm to conduct an environmental audit.

Insurance Coverage

The standard CGL policy excludes coverage for both sudden/accidental pollution (except, in general, for incidents that occur from products-completed operations) as well as for gradual pollution.

There are, however, means of extending the breadth of pollution coverage available under the basic CGL form. Coverage for your company's pollution exposure can be obtained by purchasing what is known as environmental impairment liability (EIL) coverage. This term encompasses a broad range of pollution liability products that will be discussed in the following paragraphs.

Pollution legal liability (PLL) insurance covers off-site third-party bodily injury and property damage liability including third-party cleanup costs. The PLL policy is most suitable for firms with operations that present a threat of contamination to surrounding properties from any materials considered to be pollutants under the CGL policy. The coverage responds to both sudden and nonsudden pollution that migrates off-site and causes injury or damage if the pollution emanates from a site specifically scheduled in the policy. PLL insurance does not cover cleanup of the insured's site but may be endorsed to cover bodily injury to visitors at the site. Also excluded are liabilities associated with the use of nonowned disposal sites, although underwriters have been willing to add this coverage by endorsement for specific sites. A thorough environmental engineering survey of potential properties ensures that liabilities resulting from known environmental damages are excluded from coverage.

There are other specialized pollution liability coverages including the following.

- Environmental remediation coverage, which is designed to cover the cost of unknown contamination when a property is sold. These policies cover remedial cleanup if required within 5 years of the sale of such property.
- Hospital pollution liability, which covers claims from medical wastes that are removed from and disposed of off hospital premises, because hospitals have ultimate responsibility for losses caused by such waste, even if handled and stored by an outside contractor.
- Engineers and contractors pollution liability, which, unlike EIL coverage, is not site-specific. Policies of this type are needed because engineering and contracting firms conduct their operations at a variety of locations.
- Nonowned disposal site liability covers businesses for which hazardous wastes are hauled and deposited with others and seek to cover their potential liability.
- Coverage for transport of hazardous cargo. Under the Motor Carrier Act, trucking firms are required to demonstrate financial responsibility for spills and cleanup, which can be achieved by means of such coverage.
- Underground storage tanks. Given the high exposures to claims, coupled with an abundance of regulations applying to underground storage tanks, it is advisable for owners/operators of such tanks to secure liability coverage, if possible.

Finally, last-resort consideration might be given to periodic reorganization of the corporate structure of your firm, to further insulate it from future liability associated with pollution exposures.

For further research and study

Extensive treatments of directors and officers, fiduciary, and employment practices liability exposures and coverage can be found in *Professional Liability Insurance,* a three-volume reference set published by IRMI. *D&O MAPS,* another IRMI reference, analyses the coverage provided under every available D&O liability policy. *EPLiC,* a quarterly IRMI journal, offers tools and strategies to help you reduce exposures to employment-related claims and buy the broadest, most cost-effective employment practices liability insurance coverage possible.

For a detailed analysis of additional insured requirements and related issues, refer to *Contractual Risk Transfer* or *The Additional Insured Book,* which are also published by IRMI.

The following IRMI publications are also excellent references.

- *IRMI Insurance Checklists* provides forms to use in analyzing insurance policies.
- Refer to *Commercial Liability Insurance* for additional material on pollution liability coverage.
- There is an analysis of contractors pollution liability coverage in *Construction Risk Management.*
- For comprehensive discussions of property, automobile liability, and general/umbrella liability exposures and coverages, refer to *Commercial Property Insurance, Commercial Automobile Insurance,* and *Commercial Liability Insurance.*
- Less comprehensive discussions of these topics are provided in *IRMI Commercial Auto Insurance Guide, IRMI CGL and Umbrella Liability Guide,* and *IRMI Workers Compensation Insurance Guide.*

Visit the Products and Services section of www.IRMI.com for more information about these publications.

Appendix B

EVALUATING INSURER SOLVENCY

THE CHEAPEST INSURANCE POLICY IS NO BARGAIN if the insurer cannot, or will not, pay a loss you have sustained. Unfortunately, an insurer's ability to pay its claims is often overlooked when selecting insurance programs. When considering purchasing coverage from a particular insurer, it is important to carefully evaluate the current financial position of that insurer to avoid unpaid claims, potential interruption of coverage, inability to recover unearned premiums, and the inconvenience of state guaranty funds. This appendix reviews several approaches that you can use to examine an insurer's financial integrity.

One goal of all risk financing decisions is to ensure that sufficient financial resources are available in the event of a loss so the impact on the firm's financial condition is within an acceptable level. When an insurance contract is purchased for this purpose, the risk manager relies on the insurer's ability to pay claims. The insurer's solvency is critical to the risk manager's program. While the insolvency rate in the property-casualty insurance industry is relatively low, solvency problems are most likely to arise when a policyholder needs to rely on its insurers the most—after a loss. For example, the losses caused by Hurricane Andrew and other storms in 1992 contributed to the insolvencies of 63 property-casualty insurers.[1] Many studies show that the property-casualty industry is quite unprepared to handle the financial impact of a similar storm in a heavily populated region.

Today, there is a heightened awareness of solvency issues. The ultimate responsibility for who can be held liable for an insurance company's insolvency is unclear. Brokers and agents in particular exercise extreme caution in this area. Most of the larger brokerage firms even go so far as to ask their clients to sign off on any insurers that do not satisfy their minimum financial security ratings or company size requirements. Regardless of the ultimate responsibility, everyone involved incurs costs when an insurer undergoes liquidation. This is true even when an insured has not suffered a loss at the time of the insolvency and is able to purchase replacement coverage immediately. This section will describe in some detail the costs of insolvency and how to identify financially impaired insurers, and give you reliable sources of information regarding insurer insolvency.

Costs of Insurer Insolvency

Having an insurer become insolvent increases the total cost of risk for a firm. The degree to which any one party suffers a particular type of cost following an insurer liquidation will be circumstance-specific, yet practically everyone involved with the insurer will be

---

[1]"Financing Catastrophe Risk: Capital Market Solutions," Insurance Services Office, Inc., January 1999. http://www.iso.com/docs/stud013.htm.

affected in some way. The potential costs associated with an insolvency are enumerated in Figure B.1 and described in more detail below.

Figure B.1

Costs of Insolvency

- Personnel time
- Duplication of premiums
- Unplanned retention

- Disruptions in cash flow
- Premium increases
- E&O claims

Personnel Time

Search costs will materialize for all risk management and insurance professionals in the form of personnel time required to find replacement coverage. Brokers and agents must identify affected clients and assist in their transition to a new insurer. In the more extreme case where the insolvency results in a loss of confidence in the current agent or broker, risk managers must search for a replacement. Claims must be filed promptly against all applicable guaranty funds and with the liquidator of the insurer's assets. Finally, risk managers and their agents and brokers should try to identify gaps in coverage arising out of the insolvency and take appropriate actions to cover these exposures.

Duplication of Premiums

Insurance premiums are generally paid in advance. When an insurer cancels a policy, policyholders are entitled to a pro rata refund of unearned premiums. Liquidations and most guaranty funds recognize unearned premiums as a debt owed to policyholders, but in reality the insured may wait years for a partial refund. Therefore, premiums paid for replacement coverage are redundant in the sense that the insured has now paid twice for the same protection.

Premiums on replacement coverage may reflect changes in the general insurance marketplace. If the market has hardened, premiums may be higher; likewise, if the market has softened, they may be lower. In the former case, the insured bears not only a *duplication* of premium but an *extra* cost associated with the loss of a favorable contract as well.

Unplanned Retention

Of all the headaches firms face following the bankruptcy of an insurer, the most worrisome is likely to be the potential loss of or gaps in coverage that might occur as a consequence. Losses that contain a time element, such as business interruption and extra expense coverages, are particularly vulnerable when the loss is already "in progress."

Property insurance policies can generally be replaced promptly and without gaps in coverage periods. Liability insurance is a different story. An injury arising out of an insured's negligence may not be brought to the insured's attention for years after the injury occurred. Since most liability policies are written on an occurrence basis, the insolvency of an insurer that provided coverage to an insured at any time in the past could have serious ramifications in the present or future.

All state guaranty funds contain statutory limits and other provisions that limit firms' collections. And, depending on the degree to which an insurer's liabilities exceeded its assets at the time of liquidation, claims filed in a liquidation proceeding may be paid at a short rate (such as 70 cents on the dollar). Therefore, claims that exceed guaranty fund statutory limits will almost certainly result in some amount of unplanned retention. (Figure B.2 provides a summary of statutory limits in each state.) Additionally, claims made against the insurer's estate after the filing deadline are not granted the priority over "general creditors" that policyholder liabilities are otherwise afforded. Consequently, the probability of receiving any substantial reimbursement for incurred but not reported (IBNR) claims is slim to none.

State Guaranty Associations

State guaranty or security associations have been established as mechanisms for reimbursing policyholders and third-party claimants of insolvent admitted insurers. However, relying solely on these guaranty funds for protection against insurer insolvency is not recommended for several reasons.

- Reimbursement amounts payable by the guaranty fund are generally subject to a deductible and a maximum limit of liability as shown in Figure B.2.
- Many guaranty funds make no allowance for the return of unearned premiums.
- Long delays in payments are frequent, mainly because of litigation between the state regulators and the owners/managers of the insolvent company.
- Guaranty funds are not applicable to nonadmitted insurers, surplus lines companies, life and health insurers, and fidelity insurers (although separate insolvency funds may exist in some states for some of these types of insurers).
- Guaranty funds are not designed to accommodate the insolvency of a major insurance company or multiple insolvencies among medium-sized insurance companies.

In short, while state guaranty funds may provide some protection, it is a mistake to rely solely on them without making some effort to choose fiscally responsible insurance companies.

Guaranty Fund Statutory Limits and Surety Coverage

State	Maximum Per Claim[1]	Surety Covered	State	Maximum Per Claim[1]	Surety Covered
AL	$150,000	No	NJ	$ 300,000[6]	No
AK	$500,000	No	NM	$ 100,000	No
AZ	$100,000	No	NY	$1,000,000[7]	Yes
AR	$300,000	Yes	NC	$ 300,000	No
CA	$500,000	No	ND	$ 300,000	No
CO	$100,000	No	OH	$ 300,000	No
CT	$300,000	No	OK	$ 150,000	No
DE	$300,000	No	OR	$ 300,000	No
DC	$300,000	No	PA	$ 300,000	No
FL	$300,000	No	PR	$ 150,000	Yes
GA	$100,000	No	RI	$ 300,000	No
HI	$300,000	No	SC	$ 300,000	No
ID	$300,000	No	SD	$ 300,000	No
IL	$300,000	No	TN	$ 100,000	No
IN	$100,000[2]	No	TX	$ 300,000	No
IA	$300,000	No	UT	$ 300,000	No
KS	$300,000	Yes	VT	$ 300,000	No
KY	$100,000	Yes	VA	$ 300,000	No
LA	$150,000[3]	No	WA	$ 300,000	No
ME	$300,000	Yes	WV	$ 300,000	No
MD	$300,000[4]	Yes	WI	$ 300,000	No
MA	$300,000	No	WY	$ 150,000	No
MI	0.05% of Aggregate Premiums[5]	Yes			
MN	$300,000	Yes			
MS	$300,000	No			
MO	$ 300,000	No			
MT	$ 300,000	No			
NE	$ 300,000	No			
NV	$ 300,000	No			
NH	$ 300,000	No			

[1]Most associations have a provision that workers compensation claims are covered in full.

[2]$300,000/occurrence maximum

[3]$300,000/occurrence maximum

[4]$1,000,000/bond maximum

[5]Maximum claim is 0.05% of aggregate premiums written by member insurers in the preceding calendar years.

[6]$75,000/auto claim

[7]$5,000,000/policy maximum for exposures located out of state

Sources: *1993 Summary of Property and Casualty Insurance Guaranty Association Acts of the Various States & U.S. Territories,* National Conference of Insurance Guaranty Funds, October 1993; *Best's Key Rating Guide—Property-Casualty,* 1998 edition, Oldwick, NJ: A.M. Best Co., Inc., June 27, 1998.

Disruptions in Cash Flow

Most insureds will see a negative impact on cash flow when an insurer folds. Unearned premium refunds from canceled policies may not materialize for years, if ever, while premiums on replacement policies usually are due immediately. Claims against the insurer's estate or a guaranty fund will have to be absorbed internally in the short run to minimize disruptions in operations. Paying these losses up front will require either higher-than-anticipated cash outlays or increased borrowing, either of which imposes a cash flow "cost" on the insured.

Premium Increases

In each of the 50 states, the District of Columbia, and Puerto Rico, solvent insurers are assessed a proportional share of the policyholder liabilities of an insolvent insurer that wrote business in that state (or territory). These "guaranty funds" are a form of policyholder "insurance," yet their existence does not relieve policyholders of insolvency costs for two reasons. First, losses that exceed statutory limits on guaranty fund claims are retained by the insured. Second, insurers are allowed to recover guaranty fund assessments through future rate increases, which ultimately transfers the cost back to insureds.

Errors and Omissions Claims

Insurance representatives may face errors and omissions (E&O) claims for placing coverage with an insurer that subsequently declares bankruptcy. The success of E&O claims of this nature will be a function of numerous factors, such as the degree to which the insured relied on a representative's judgment and whether the representative exercised reasonable care in evaluating the financial stability of the insurer prior to placing the coverage. Even if E&O claims fail because of lack of evidence of negligence, the mere existence of claims eats personnel time and could create negative press that results in a loss of business.

Identifying Financially Troubled Insurers

Insolvency, for the most part, is not a disease that picks its victims randomly. While some industry insiders contend that industry troubles are the result of external forces, most insolvencies to date can be traced to some combination of underwriting, accounting, investment, and managerial practices. However, the extent of external forces' contributions to future insolvencies may be more substantial.

Numerous sources of consolidated information concerning an insurance company's financial status are available. Analyzing and rating insurance companies is big business, and these services can be purchased on a per-insurer basis or for the industry as a whole. Qualitative as well as quantitative factors should be considered in evaluating an insurer's overall financial condition. This section will discuss the leading causes of insolvency and warning signs that an insurer may be headed for trouble. It also provides an overview of some of the rating organizations and the products and services they offer.

Contributing Factors

The study of failed insurance companies reveals a set of common factors that are widely believed to have contributed to the ultimate insolvencies of the firms. Inadequate pricing (and/or inadequate loss reserves), rapid growth, asset misevaluation, catastrophes, and mismanagement (including fraud) are included in this set. By monitoring these proven indicators and other qualitative data and by taking appropriate precautions, risk management and insurance professionals can reduce their exposure to insolvency risk.

Figure B.3 lists some warning signs that an insurer's financial condition is deteriorating. Remember that not every company experiencing financial difficulty will exhibit every sign, nor will every company exhibiting these signs be experiencing financial difficulty. These indicators are simply "red lights" that should prompt a risk manager, agent, or broker to look further into the company's financial condition. Subscribing to the adage that "an ounce of prevention is worth a pound of cure," any abnormalities in these areas should be explained to the contractor's or broker's satisfaction before buying or placing coverage.

Figure B.3

Warning Signs of Financial Instability

1. Unusual growth in premiums written, relative to surplus

2. Downward trend in ratings or several key financial indicators over a 2–5 year period

3. Below-average ratings in the most recent year by two or more of the top rating agencies

4. Premiums that are "too good to be true"

5. Excessive delays in settling even the simplest of claims

6. A large number of complaints filed against the company with the state insurance department

7. An unusually high rate of management turnover

Items 1–3 of Figure B.3 are discussed in the text of this section, and the reader is referred there for further discussion. Items 4–6 may be indications that the firm is experiencing cash flow problems and is taking desperation measures to generate cash inflow by slashing premiums or to reduce cash outflow by delaying and denying claims. Item 7 may indicate that "insiders" who are aware of the impending failure are jumping ship rather than facing the inevitable or asking for help in minimizing the damages.

As stated in the introduction to this section, most property-casualty insurer insolvencies are the result of poor underwriting, investment, accounting, and managerial practices. Discussion of the causes of insolvencies can most easily be broken down into these four areas.

Underwriting Practices

Risk managers should be alert to dangerous underwriting practices of insurers. In particular, they should give consideration to prices that seem too low, a heavy concentration of property exposures in one geographical area, and excessive growth in premiums written.

Underpricing. Despite the fact that the general public seems to believe insurance is overpriced, many insolvencies can be traced to inadequate pricing for insurance coverages. Underpricing can be intentional or unintentional. When it is intentional, underpricing and underreserving for losses feed off one another, creating a downward spiral in operating results that will eventually ruin a company. Common reasons for underpricing of insurance include competition, expansion into unfamiliar lines of business, ex post facto expansion of legal liabilities, and desperate attempts to "save" a company experiencing financial difficulties and cash flow shortages.

As in other highly competitive industries, the fastest way for an aggressive insurance company to increase its market share is to lower its price. Because the pricing of many commercial policies relies heavily on the judgment of the underwriter, the temptation to lower prices as a means of "winning" business is particularly strong in insurance, where ultimate losses and payout patterns are uncertain and variable. Price competition is most fierce during soft markets and periods of high interest rates. High interest rates may tempt insurers to engage in "cash flow underwriting," which sacrifices underwriting results for the promise of higher investment income.

Gross underpricing may also be an *indicator* (versus, or in addition to, a direct *cause*) of financial trouble. Companies that are, for whatever reason, on the brink of failure often make last-ditch efforts to survive. Undercutting other insurers' prices is a common short-term cash flow generating tactic. For this reason, and because bankruptcy costs can be significant for insureds, policyholders should be leery of any premium quotes that are far below industry norms. Desperation tactics are counterproductive, as they generally only manage to increase the gap between assets and liabilities, which makes survival through reorganization less likely and lowers the eventual liquidation payout ratios.

Underpricing can also be the result of factors beyond insurers' control. By expanding interpretations of contractual provisions and legal doctrines, courts can impose liability on insurers for losses the policies were not intended to cover, which were consequently excluded from the premium determination. By definition, therefore, these policies were inadequately priced.

To illustrate the potential impact of court-imposed liabilities, projected insurer costs for environmental claims range from a low-end estimate of $25 billion in one study to a high-end estimate of $608 billion in another. A large percentage of the costs arises from gradual pollution claims that insurers did not contemplate sufficiently in their pricing or intended to exclude altogether. At the time of the studies, the combined statutory surplus of the entire property-casualty industry was approximately $191 billion. However, the cost of the environmental claims will not fall evenly across the industry. It is estimated that the combined surplus of the 35 insurers expected to bear the greatest cleanup costs was $85 billion.[2] Obviously, if the higher loss estimates are accurate, the sums that insurers might have to pay clearly exceed their expectations.

Geographic Concentration. Major natural disasters, including earthquakes, hurricanes, and tornadoes, inevitably raise concern over the financial stability of the property-casualty insurance industry. At the time of a study conducted for the Natural Disaster Coalition in 1995, it was estimated that hurricanes that strike certain areas could cause more than $75 billion in insured property losses.[3] This figure was validated in 1999 by research conducted by Arkwright Mutual Insurance Company, which pegged the figure at $50 billion to $100 billion.[4] The 1995 study estimated that a magnitude 8.5 earthquake in the New Madrid Fault Zone in the central United States could cause insured property losses of $115 billion or more. While the probabilities are low, few argue that such an event would never happen.

Despite events such as Hurricane Andrew in 1992, the Northridge Earthquake in 1994, and the severe hailstorms across the Midwest in 1998, no major national property-casualty insurer has declared bankruptcy in recent history. However, numerous small insurers with heavy geographical concentrations were unable to meet their liabilities arising from these disasters. This is not to say that small insurers are, by definition, high-risk. It merely points out that many of them are unable to achieve an adequate spread of risks over which to distribute the cost of catastrophic losses. Competition likely prevents these insurers from charging a price that accurately reflects their higher exposure, which leads back to the issue of underpricing.

Insureds holding policies or evaluating bids on new policies that are issued by small regional insurers should examine their insurers' exposure to catastrophic loss. For example, a heavy concentration of property risks in California or on the East Coast will indicate a greater vulnerability to catastrophic loss than a concentration of liability risks in either of those same areas. Additionally, an insurer's business mix is an important consideration, as the majority of the losses associated with most natural disasters are in personal lines of coverage.

Abnormal Growth. In most industries, rapid growth is viewed as a positive occurrence. Because of the way in which property-casualty insurers are required to report revenues and expenses, abnormal growth can have a detrimental effect—from an accounting standpoint—on a firm's financial condition because of what is known as "surplus drain." See "Accounting Practices" later in this section for further discussion of the impact of unusual growth on an insurer's balance sheet.

---

[2]"Superfund and the Insurance Issues Surrounding Abandoned Hazardous Waste Sites," Insurance Services Office, Inc., December 1995. http://www.iso.com/docs/stud003.htm.

[3]"Financing Catastrophe Risk: Capital Market Solutions," Insurance Services Office, Inc., January 1999. http://www.iso.com/docs/stud013.htm.

[4]"Arkwright Research Shows United States Faces Potential Hurricane Damage of $50 Billion to $100 Billion," *Business Wire,* January 11, 1999.

Investment Practices

A series of major life insurance company insolvencies in the early 1990s led to national attention and concern over the status of the entire insurance industry. However, most of the insolvencies were the result of investment practices vastly different from those of property-casualty insurers. For example, real estate, mortgage loans, and collateral loans, which were at the root of several bankruptcies, constitute a small percentage of property-casualty (P-C) insurers' investments, as they do not provide the liquidity P-C insurers need. In addition, regulations limit the percentage of their assets that can be invested in low-grade (junk) bonds, which were the cause of another large life insurer's failure.

Nevertheless, the quality of an insurer's investments is an important consideration in measuring its financial condition. Unfortunately, the riskiness of an insurer's portfolio is not obvious from a casual glance at the balance sheet, and most risk managers, brokers, and agents have neither the time nor the staff that would be required to investigate the individual components of every potential insurer's asset portfolio. Fortunately, other firms specialize in analyzing and evaluating not only the quality of the assets but also liquidity, capitalization, and other important solvency considerations. Information on rating agencies and other evaluation services is provided later in this section.

Accounting Practices

Insurance companies are required to follow statutory accounting rules for financial reporting that differ substantially from generally accepted accounting principles (GAAPs) in some areas. The goals of statutory accounting have been to provide an accurate reflection of an insurer's ability to meet its policyholder liabilities and to provide early signs of any problems in doing so.[5] However, some statutory accounting rules may lead to an appearance of financial stability when an insurer is in fact at or near the point of bankruptcy.

As previously stated in the "Underwriting Practices" section, high rates of growth can actually have a negative short-term impact on an insurer's solvency. Statutory accounting requirements create a mismatching of revenues and expenses, which in turn causes a drain on policyholder surplus. It literally is possible for an insurer to "grow" right into bankruptcy.

The problem arises out of a statutory accounting requirement that revenues (premiums) be recognized as income only as they are earned, while production and underwriting expenses are recognized immediately. Unearned premiums are carried as a liability on insurers' balance sheets. The difference between earned premiums and acquisition expenses is charged against surplus, so selling an insurance policy actually has a negative impact on surplus. Surplus drain is magnified when losses begin to develop and loss reserves are established. Since loss reserves represent a liability, a simultaneous increase in assets or decrease in net worth (policyholder surplus) is required to maintain the balance of the balance sheet. Asset values are not affected by loss development, so policyholder surplus receives the charge.

---

[5]For an in-depth discussion of statutory accounting principles, see *Property-Liability Insurance Accounting and Finance,* second edition, Malvern, PA: American Institute for Property and Liability Underwriters, 1983.

If an insurer has adequate capital to absorb the charges against surplus that a growth spurt necessarily causes, earned premiums will eventually replenish surplus, since the offsetting expenses have already been recognized. Firms with inadequate capital will quickly realize that they have taken on more liabilities than they can meet. (This further explains the higher rate of insolvency among small firms. Many of them simply do not have the surplus to sustain them during a period of rapid growth.) This is not merely an accounting or "paper" problem, as excessive growth in premiums written is cited in almost all relevant studies as a primary cause of insolvencies. An insolvent firm may have the cash needed to pay losses (since premiums are collected in advance), but because unearned premiums technically still belong to policyholders and are a legitimate financial obligation, using all of its assets to pay losses would be "robbing Peter to pay Paul."

Because of the counterproductive impact of excessive growth and its potential to cause a rapid deterioration in an insurer's financial condition, risk management professionals should monitor insurers' rates of growth. A net premiums written to surplus ratio (NPW/S) exceeding 3:1 is generally considered dangerous.

Managerial Practices

The quality of leadership has major implications for the long-term viability of any organization. Most industries, including insurance, have their highest failure rates in the first 5 years of operation. Inexperience plays a key role in this statistic, but age is not in and of itself an indicator of poor managerial skills. However, survival over the long haul does indicate at least a *strategy* of success. Nevertheless, every company has to have its beginning, and avoiding "young" insurers may not be necessary. The better approach would be to exercise an extra degree of caution and exert a little more energy finding out about the degree of experience in the company's upper management. New companies are often started by people with years of experience in the insurance industry, in which case concern over the level of management expertise would be unfounded.

The integrity and longevity of an insurer's key personnel are important considerations in any comprehensive evaluation of an insurer's long-term financial outlook. A high rate of management turnover could be indicative of a multitude of problems, ranging from blatant dishonesty and unethical practices to poor management skills at top management levels. It could also be a sign of managers' concern about the company's future. Whatever the cause, high turnover in upper levels of management is cause for concern and investigation.

Significant attention has been given to the role of intentional mismanagement, i.e., ethical violations and outright fraud, in insurer insolvencies. Clearly, fraud is a concern in the insurance industry, as it is in many industries, and examples of blatant fraud can be cited. Unfortunately, both the nature of the contract (exchanging cash for a "promise") and the general public's ignorance of insurance operations and insurance contracts create a ripe environment for dishonest individuals. By properly monitoring insurers' practices and performance, risk management and insurance professionals should be able to avoid most of the schemes that snare "laypersons."

Sources of Information

With all of the attention devoted to the issue of insurer solvency in the wake of the early 1990s life insurer failures, insurer evaluation services have become a hot commodity. New services have appeared on the market, and well-established services have changed their rating methods to reflect more subtle differences in financial conditions and developed new products that facilitate access to specific information. The National Association of Insurance Commissioners (NAIC) also performs tests of insurers' financial stability. In 1994, a new system for measuring the adequacy of insurers' capital (that expands the old Insurance Regulatory Information System (IRIS)) was introduced. This section provides an overview of some of the major players in the rating services industry.

Rating Services

Analyzing insurers' overall performance and financial strength is a task that requires specialized skills and an in-depth understanding of all aspects of insurance operations. For many years, A.M. Best was the sole source of this type of analysis. Since the early 1980s, a handful of additional firms have joined the property-casualty insurer rating and financial analysis industry. Figure B.4 provides a list of the more prominent rating agencies along with their addresses, telephone numbers, and Web sites. While a number of firms now provide this service, A.M. Best and Standard & Poor's rate the largest number of property and casualty insurers. Their ratings are available free of charge over the Internet. Risk management and insurance professionals should view all of the agencies as complementary—rather than competitive—sources of information.

Making Use of Insurer Ratings

Wisdom suggests that professionals responsible for insurance purchasing decisions should look at as many ratings as possible before drawing a conclusion as to an insurer's financial condition. Unfortunately, the lack of a uniform rating scale can be misleading when comparing ratings of different agencies. Figure B.5 provides a side-by-side matching of ratings based on the descriptions of the ratings published by each rating firm. The comparisons should only be used as a rough guide because some of the rating organizations use philosophies that are much more conservative than others. The ratings at the high end of the scales match up relatively easily; however, the lines are less clear at the bottom end of the scale. As a general rule, insurers falling into these categories should be closely scrutinized. Any that are highly suspect should be avoided.

Sources of Insurer Financial Information

A.M. Best Company
Ambest Road
Oldwick, NJ 08858–9988
Telephone: (908) 439–2200
http://www.ambest.com
http://www.trac.com (A.M. Best Canada)

Demotech
2941 Donnylane Blvd.
Columbus, OH 43235–3228
Telephone: (800) 354–7207
http://www.demotech.com

Fitch Ratings
One State Street Plaza
New York, NY 10004
(212) 908–0500
http://www.fitchratings.com

Moody's Investors Services
99 Church Street
New York, NY 10007
Telephone: (212) 553–1658
http://www.moodys.com

Standard & Poor's Corp.
55 Water Street
New York, NY 10041
Telephone: (212) 438–7200
http://www.standardandpoors.com
Standard & Poor's insurer ratings are available free of charge at www.IRMI.com.

Ward Financial Group
8040 Hosbrook Road, Suite 100
Cincinnati, OH 45236–2908
Telephone: (513) 791–0303
http://www.wardinc.com

Weiss Ratings
4176 Burns Road
Palm Beach Gardens, FL 33410
Telephone: (800) 289–9222
http://www.weissratings.com

Read each organization's descriptions of its ratings to get a better understanding of the extent of confidence the rater really has in the ability of the insurer to meet its policyholder obligations. Ratings based on purely quantitative analyses are useful sources of additional information; however, they overlook key aspects of an insurer's overall prospects for future stability. Consequently, risk management and insurance professionals should not base insurer selection solely on a quantitative measure, however stringent its standards may be.

Trends in ratings are also very important. Changes in ratings over the most recent 5 years (or as many as are available, if less than 5) should be factored into the judgment of future stability. When a few insurers are relied on heavily in providing coverage (by either a single firm or a producer that places a large volume of business with the insurer), more detailed analyses should be obtained (and are available from most of the rating agencies) and reviewed. Ratings of key insurers should be monitored closely throughout the coverage period.

Financial Strength Ratings Comparison

	A.M. Best		S&P[1]	Moody's[2]	Demotech
	(Best's Ratings)	(FPR's)			
Secure {	A++, A+		AAA	Aaa	A"
	A, A–	9	AA	Aa	A'
	B++, B+	8, 7	A	A	A
		6, 5	BBB	Baa	S
Vulnerable[3] {	B, B-	4			
	C++, C+	3	BB	Ba	M
	C, C–	2	B	B	L
	D	1	CCC		
				Caa	
	E		R	Ca	
	F		R	C	
	S				

[1]A + or – indicates that an insurer falls closer to the top or bottom of this category, however, all insurers within the category are considered to have similar claims-paying ability.

[2]A numerical qualifier of 1 (highest), 2, or 3 further distinguishes where an insurer falls within its class.

[3]Lower-end rankings do not match up quite as easily based on verbal descriptions.

When concerns about adverse financial performance arise, research the causes of the trouble and try to assess the probability that the problems can be reversed. (This kind of information is available through many of the products described in this section.) While the rating agencies are all quite reputable, each risk manager, broker, or agent must ultimately make a personal judgment as to his or her degree of confidence in a chosen insurer's financial reliability.

Summary

Insureds whose insurers become insolvent during—and in some cases after—the coverage period may suffer substantial costs as a result. Examination of insolvent companies has revealed a number of common traits in the months or years leading up to the eventual bankruptcy. Being aware of these "warning signs" can alert you to insurers with an unacceptable level of financial risk.

A variety of reliable external resources are available to assist insureds and their agents and brokers in making quality insurer selections. Monitoring changes in financial ratings should be part of the job description of someone within the risk management department, especially when a single insurer provides a large percentage of the insured's total coverages. If all of these precautions fail, good risk management techniques can help to minimize the financial impact of an insurer insolvency on a firm.

Appendix C

THE IRMI HARD MARKET SURVIVAL GUIDE 2002

THE U.S. PROPERTY-CASUALTY INSURANCE MARKETPLACE began firming in 2001 and by the summer of 2002 could be considered a truly "hard market"—the first in nearly 20 years. A "hard market" is a time when the demand for insurance is greater than the supply. Insurers typically raise rates (often substantially), reduce coverages, and increase deductibles in a hard market. Hard markets are also a time when the workloads of agents, brokers, and underwriters increase substantially, causing long processing delays.

During hard markets, insurance buyers and their agents and brokers need to get back to risk management basics. It is time to reinvigorate safety and risk control programs and to retain more risk through deductibles, retentions, or alternative market mechanisms. Insurance purchasing must also be very proactive. The process should begin early and should include a comprehensive and extremely well prepared underwriting submission. Additionally, a contingency plan should be prepared in case the terms quoted are unacceptable.

The following action list was developed by the IRMI research analysts during the summer of 2002 and should give you ideas for surviving the hard market of 2002–2003 or any future hard insurance market.[1]

1. If you have a great safety and loss control program, document it succinctly and clearly for your underwriters.

2. If you don't have a great safety and loss control program, get senior management commitment to put one in place.

3. Review your claims information to assure it is correct and up to date. If there have been frequency or severity problems, describe steps taken (e.g., loss control program) to address the problem.

4. Develop a comprehensive database for the past 5 years. Include claims, payroll, sales, and other needed underwriting data.

5. Pay particular attention to reserves on open claims. Meet with adjusters to review any that appear questionable. If there has been substantial development on open claims during the past 12 months, consider commissioning a claims audit.

6. Check your experience modifier calculation to make sure it is correct. Prepare a test modifier well in advance of your renewal.

7. Analyze your concentrations of risk by location and be prepared to show underwriters plans for dealing with catastrophic events that can affect major locations.

8. Prepare a high-quality, thorough underwriting submission using the data and information discussed above. Include a great deal of detail, using it to distinguish your account from others.

9. Begin the renewal process early—at least 4 months prior to the anniversary date.

---

[1] A version of this action list was first published in the September 2002 issue of *The Risk Report*.

10. Even though you prepare and submit your renewal submission several months out, be prepared for last-minute quotes. Make sure that you are in a position to quickly analyze the alternatives offered, have a contingency plan in place in case the terms are unacceptable, and are able to access all necessary decision makers as soon as you have the renewal quotes.

11. Analyze your risk retention capability and prepare to assume higher deductibles or move into a loss sensitive insurance program.

12. Determine what are your minimum liability limits requirements in case you need to reduce limits because of lack of capacity or unacceptable pricing. Don't forget to consider your contractual commitments.

13. Review your property insurance values to make sure that they would be adequate even if the insurer insists on scheduled per-location limits. Remember to factor in debris removal costs when selecting limits.

14. Meet your underwriters and review your company's risk management program, financial position, and business plans for the coming year.

15. Proactively demonstrate the reliability of your company's financial statements to underwriters, particularly D&O underwriters. Consider involving your CFO in these discussions.

16. Explore the feasibility of using a single parent, group, or protected cell captive insurance company to cover your liability exposures.

17. Develop a strategy for dealing with terrorism exclusions. Be sure to determine if contracts with lenders, customers, or other business partners require you to purchase terrorism coverage.

18. Carefully review the financial position of your insurers to assure that they are likely to be around when you need them. At a minimum review the 3-year trends in Best's ratings and S&P ratings.

19. Be diligent about obtaining certificates of insurance from all contractors, subcontractors, suppliers, vendors, and other business partners.

20. Prepare senior management for higher premiums and deductibles. The people responsible for the bottom line don't like surprises.

Glossary

101 Insurance Acronyms and Abbreviations

ACV	Actual cash value	**ELP**	Excess loss premium (factor)
AL	Automobile liability	**EPLI**	Employment practices liability insurance
ALAE	Allocated loss adjustment expense	**E&O**	Errors and omissions (liability)
AOP	All other perils	**ERISA**	Employee Retirement Income Security Act
BI	Bodily injury, business interruption	**ERP**	Extended reporting period
BPF	Basic premium factor	**E&S**	Excess and surplus (lines)
CCC	Care, custody, or control (exclusion)	**FCAS**	Fellow of the Casualty Actuarial Society
CCIP	Contractors controlled insurance program	**FC&S**	Free of capture and seizure
CEBS	Certified employee benefits specialist	**FM**	Factory mutual
		FOB	Free on board
CERCLA	Comprehensive Environmental Response Compensation and Liability Act	**FR**	Fire-resistive
		FSA	Fellow of the Society of Actuaries
ChFC	Chartered financial consultant	**FTCAC**	Fire, theft, and combined additional coverage
CGL	Commercial general liability		
CIC	Certified insurance counselor	**GL**	Garage liability, general liability
CIF	Cost, insurance, and freight	**HO**	Homeowners (insurance)
CLU	Chartered life underwriter	**HPL**	Hospital professional liability
C/O	Completed operations	**HPR**	Highly protected risk
CPCU	Chartered property casualty underwriter	**IBNR**	Incurred but not reported
		IDBI	Industrial development bond insurance
CSP	Certified safety professional		
DIC	Difference-in-conditions (insurance)	**IGF**	Insurance guaranteed financing
		IH	Industrial hygiene
D&O	Directors and officers (liability insurance)	**IIAA**	Independent Insurance Agents of America
EAP	Employee assistance program	**IRIS**	Insurance Regulatory Information System
EEOC	Equal Employment Opportunity Commission	**IRMI**	International Risk Management Institute, Inc.
EIL	Environmental impairment liability	**IRPM**	Individual risk premium modification
EL	Employers liability		

ISO	Insurance Services Office, Inc.
JSA	Job safety analysis
K&R	Kidnap and ransom (insurance)
LCF	Loss conversion factor
LOC	Letter of credit
MGA	Managing general agency
MIB	Medical Information Bureau
MOP	Manufacturers output policy
MORT	Management oversight and risk tree
MP	Minimum premium
MTC	Motor truck cargo (insurance)
MVR	Motor vehicle record
NAIB	National Association of Insurance Brokers
NAIC	National Association of Insurance Commissioners
NCCI	National Council on Compensation Insurance
NIOSH	National Institute for Occupational Safety and Health
NOC	Not otherwise classified
NP	Named perils
NPD	No payroll division
NPV	Net present value
OASDHI	Old age, survivorship, disability, and health insurance
OCIP	Owner-controlled insurance program
OCP	Owners and contractors protective (liability insurance)
OCSLA	Outer Continental Shelf Lands Act
OD	Occupational disease
OEE	Operators extra expense (insurance)
OL&T	Owners, landlords, and tenants (liability insurance)
OPIC	Overseas Private Investment Corporation

OSHA	Occupational Safety and Health Act
PD	Property damage
PI	Personal injury
P&I	Protection and indemnity (insurance)
PIA	Professional Insurance Agents (association)
PIP	Personal injury protection
PL	Professional liability
PMI	Private mortgage insurance
PRIMA	Public Risk and Insurance Management Association
RC	Replacement cost
RFP	Request for proposal
RIMS	Risk and Insurance Management Society
SIR	Self-insured retention
SMP	Special multiperil (package policy)
TM	Tax multiplier
UCR	Usual, customary, reasonable (reimbursement)
UL	Underwriter's Laboratories, umbrella liability
UM	Uninsured motorist
U&O	Use and occupancy
USL&H	United States Longshore and Harbor Workers (Compensation Act)
V&MM	Vandalism and malicious mischief
VSI	Vendors single interest (insurance)
WC	Workers compensation
XCU	Explosion, collapse, underground

101 Insurance Definitions

─────────────── **A** ───────────────

Accounts receivable coverage Insures against loss to accounts receivable that may be uncollectible through damage to records caused by an insured peril. Included in this coverage is interest on loans to offset collections and additional expenses resulting from impaired records. This coverage may be written on a monthly reporting basis for large organizations or on a nonreporting form for smaller firms.

Actual cash value (ACV) A term used in property insurance to denote the measure of recovery at the time of loss. ACV equals the cost to replace the damaged property less depreciation of that damaged property. The depreciation used is not the same as that used for accounting purposes but is an estimate of actual physical depreciation. "Book value" should never be used to establish insurable values because depreciation schedules used for accounting purposes do not correlate with physical depreciation.

Actuary An individual, often holding a professional designation, who computes statistics relating to insurance. Actuaries are most frequently used to estimate loss reserves and develop premiums. Professional designations are awarded by the Casualty Actuarial Society and the Society of Actuaries.

Additional insured An individual or entity that is not automatically included as an insured under the policy of another, but for whom the named insured's policy provides a certain degree of protection. An endorsement is typically required to effect additional insured status. The named insured's incentive for providing additional insured status to others may be a desire to protect the other party because of a close relationship with that party (such as employees or members of an insured club) or to comply with a contractual agreement requiring the named insured to do so (customers or owners of property leased by the named insured, for example).

Admitted company An insurance company licensed to do business in a specified jurisdiction. For example, a company licensed to do business in Georgia is an admitted company in that state.

Aggregate The maximum amount payable by an insurer on behalf of a policyholder during any given annual policy period. Aggregate limits may be equal to or greater than the per occurrence or per accident policy limit. An insurance policy may have one or more aggregate limits. For example, the standard commercial general liability policy has two: the general aggregate that applies to all claims except those that fall in the products-completed operations hazard and a separate products-completed operations aggregate.

Agreed amount clause A provision in fire insurance policies covering certain classes of property, whereby the coinsurance clause is suspended if the insured carries an amount of insurance specified by the company (usually 90 percent or more of value).

Allocated loss adjustment expense (ALAE) Loss adjustment expenses that are assignable or allocable to specific claims. Fees paid to outside attorneys, experts, and investigators used to defend claims are examples of ALAE.

All risk insurance Protection from loss arising out of any unexpected cause other than those perils or causes specifically excluded by name. This is in contrast to other policies that name the peril or perils insured against. All risk insurance is usually preferred over named perils insurance because it provides broader coverage and because it places a greater burden of proof on an insurer wishing to deny a claim.

Alternative risk transfer (ART) Risk financing mechanisms that do not primarily involve a commercial insurance company, such as captive insurers, risk retention groups, pools, and individual self-insurance.

Annual aggregate deductible A situation that occurs when a policyholder agrees to assume the payment of claims incurred up to a stated aggregate amount. Once the policyholder makes claims payments up to the agreed amount during a policy year, any additional claims are paid to the insured by the "excess aggregate" insurer on a monthly or quarterly basis as reported.

Assigned risk pool A method of providing insurance required by state insurance codes for those risks that are unacceptable in the normal insurance market. Assigned risk mechanisms are most frequently associated with commercial workers compensation insurance and personal automobile liability insurance.

Associate in risk management (ARM) A designation conferred on individuals who successfully complete three written comprehensive examinations administered by the Insurance Institute of America. The three exams are essentials of risk management, essentials of risk control, and risk financing.

B

Basic limits The minimum limits of liability of auto insurance or commercial general liability insurance that can be purchased by a policyholder. The manual rates are for basic limits, and increased limits factors are used to increase the rates for higher limits of liability.

Basic premium factor A factor used in the retrospective formula to represent expenses of the insurer, such as acquisition, audit, administration, and profit or contingencies other than taxes.

Basket retention Used in connection with self-insurance. This excess liability insurance is triggered (attaches) when retained losses for several lines of coverage (such as workers compensation and general liability) reach a certain specified level.

Binder A legal agreement issued by either an agent or an insurer to provide temporary insurance until a policy can be written. It should contain a definite time limit, be in writing, and clearly designate the company in which the risk is bound as well as the amount, the perils insured against, and the type of insurance.

Blanket coverage Policy coverage applying a single limit to any number of scheduled or nonscheduled locations.

Boards, bureaus, and taxes In retrospective rating, a term used to refer to those outside charges, such as state premium taxes, that are levied against an insurer's written premium. Such costs are ordinarily passed through to the insured in the retrospective plan factors.

Bodily injury liability coverage Protection against loss arising out of the liability imposed on the insured by law for damages as a result of bodily injury, sickness, or disease sustained by any person or persons (other than employees). This is one of the types of coverages (property damage liability being the other) provided by general and auto liability insurance.

Boiler and machinery insurance Insurance against loss arising from the operation of boilers and machinery. It may cover loss suffered by the boilers or the machinery itself, or it may include damage done to other property and business interruption (use and occupancy) losses.

Builders risk Indemnifies for loss of or damage to a building under construction. Insurance is normally written for a specified amount on the building and applies only in the course of construction. Coverage is usually on an all risk basis. The builders risk policy also may include coverage for items in transit to the construction site (up to a certain percentage of value) as well as items stored at the site.

Business auto policy (BAP) A standard automobile policy that can be used to insure physical damage to owned or hired autos and liability arising from owned, hired, or nonowned commercial automobiles. The BAP's physical damage coverage can include collision, comprehensive, and/or named perils coverage. Uninsured motorists coverage and medical payments coverage may be added by endorsement.

Business income insurance Protection against loss of earnings sustained by a business during the time required to rebuild or repair property damaged or destroyed by fire or some other insured peril. The coverage is also called use and occupancy or business interruption. Business interruption losses are often greater than the direct damage losses that cause the interruption, and careful consideration should be given to insuring this exposure. Business managers should also determine if they have, and should insure, a contingent business interruption exposure. This type of exposure arises when the business is dependent on a key supplier or key customer that could experience a fire or major catastrophe that would make it unable to continue supplying component parts or purchasing the insured business products.

C

Captive An insurance company that has as its primary purpose the financing of the risks of its owners or participants. Typically licensed under special purpose insurer laws and operated under a different regulatory system than commercial insurers. The intention of such special purpose licensing laws and regulations is that the captive provides insurance to sophisticated insureds that require less policyholder protection than the general public.

Care, custody, and control (CCC) A standard property damage liability exclusion found in most liability insurance policies. This exclusion precludes coverage for property that is in the care, custody, or control of the insured. This exclusion may be worded so that it applies either to personal property only or to all property. Some companies will occasionally consider removing or modifying the exclusion on a specific or blanket basis.

Cash flow program Any insurance rating plan that allows the insured, rather than the insurer, to hold and benefit from loss reserves—such as deferred premiums, self-insurance, and paid loss retros—until paid as claims.

Certificate of insurance A document that proves that an insurance policy has been issued and shows the amount and type of insurance provided. Certificates of insurance are often required by lenders to show that financed property is insured. Contractors and subcontractors providing services to a company should also be required to provide insurance certificates. It is important to note that an insurance certificate is not a contract and does not place any obligations on the insurance company. Certificates are only a statement that insurance policies are in effect on the date they are issued.

Chartered property casualty underwriter (CPCU) A professional designation within the insurance industry identifying an individual who has satisfactorily completed 10 college-level examinations and met ethical and experience requirements. The 10 examinations cover the following topics: commercial liability insurance, commercial property insurance, personal lines insurance, risk management, insurance issues and professional ethics, insurance company operations, insurance law, management, accounting and finance, and economics.

Claims-made A liability policy that will cover claims made (reported or filed) during the year the policy is in force for any incidents that occur that year or during any previous period the policyholder was insured under the claims-made contract. This form of coverage is in contrast to the occurrence policy, which covers today's incident regardless of whether a claim is filed 1 or more years later.

Coinsurance A policy provision requiring the insured to maintain insurance equal to a specified percentage of the value of the property covered. It provides for the full payment, up to the amount of the policy, of all losses if the insured has insurance at least equal to the specified percentage of the value of the property covered, or if the loss is equal to or exceeds the coinsurance percentage of the value of the property covered. The loss payment, in the case of most partial losses, is reduced proportionately if the amount of insurance falls short of the named percentage. The formula is as follows: amount of insurance purchased divided by the amount required multiplied by the loss equals the amount paid.

In health insurance and some other specialized property and liability insurance, the coinsurance clause requires the insured to pay a percentage of any loss. In these situations, the clause is used to discourage malingering in the hospital or, in the case of property and liability policies, to encourage loss control.

Commercial general liability (CGL) policy A broad form of liability insurance that covers business organizations against liability claims for bodily injury and property damage arising out of their operations, products and completed operations, and independent contractors (but excluding coverage for liability arising out of the use of automobiles). Contractual liability and personal injury/advertising liability coverages are also usually covered by the CGL. Contractual liability coverage insures the liability of others for which the insured agrees to be responsible in a business contract or lease. Personal injury/advertising injury liability coverage insures against false arrest and libel, slander, defamation of character, and disparagement of goods communicated by the insured's employees or in its advertising activities.

Contractual liability Liability that is passed from one party to another in a hold harmless or indemnity agreement. For example, a tenant in a building may hold the landlord harmless for any bodily injury sustained by the public in the premises. If an injured party sues the landlord, the tenant will have to hire an attorney to defend the landlord and pay any judgments made against the landlord. Contractual liability insurance covers this exposure.

Cross liability A situation that can arise when more than one organization is insured by a liability policy, such as commercial general liability (CGL) insurance. In that situation, one insured may injure or damage the property of and become legally liable to another insured. It may therefore be important for the insurance policy to cover the cross liability of one insured to another. Most CGL and umbrella liability policies contain a severability of interest clause that allows coverage for cross liability suits by stipulating that the policy covers each insured as if each were insured by a separate policy (except with respect to the policy limits).

───────────── **D** ─────────────

Deductible An amount specified in an insurance policy that is subtracted from a loss in determining the amount of an insurance recovery. In property insurance, the entire policy limit typically applies once the deductible is met. In liability insurance, the deductible amount typically reduces the policy limit. When deductibles are used with liability or workers compensation insurance, the insurer pays the entire claim and is then reimbursed by the insured for the amount of the deductible. This contrasts with a self-insured retention, in which the insurer's payment is net of the retained amount.

Deposit premium The premium deposit required by the insurer on forms of insurance subject to periodic premium adjustment. Also called "provisional premium."

Difference-in-conditions (DIC) insurance An all risk property insurance policy that is typically purchased in addition to a named perils property insurance policy to provide coverage for perils not insured against in the named perils property insurance policy (usually collapse, flood, or earthquake).

Dividends The return of premium to an insured by the insurance company. Policies on which dividends may be paid are often called participating insurance. Dividends are most commonly used with workers compensation insurance, but general and automobile policies can also be participating policies. There are different types of dividend programs. A flat dividend involves the payment of a flat percentage of the premium. A sliding scale dividend program bases the percentage to be paid on the insured's loss experience; the lower the losses, the higher the dividend. A retention plan is essentially the same as a sliding scale dividend plan, but the mechanics are slightly different.

It is important to note that it is illegal for insurers to guarantee that dividends will be paid. Consider the possibility that the dividend will be reduced or omitted entirely when evaluating dividend plans. Research into the insurer's dividend-payment history can facilitate this analysis.

Drop down provision A clause in umbrella policies providing that the umbrella will "drop down" over reduced or exhausted underlying policy aggregate limits. Some umbrella policies maintain their own coverage terms when they drop down; others assume those of the primary policy.

E

Employers liability coverage A coverage that becomes effective when, for one reason or another, an injured employee's claim is not covered under workers compensation law. In such a case, the employee usually files a lawsuit against the employer. This type of suit is not covered by the workers compensation coverage of the policy (which applies only to benefits required under workers compensation law). It is also excluded by the commercial general liability policy. To avoid a potential gap, employers liability coverage is included in the workers compensation policy. It pays on behalf of the insured (employer) all sums that the insured becomes legally obligated to pay as damages because of bodily injury by accident or disease sustained by any employee arising out of and in the course of his or her employment.

Experience modifier A factor developed by measuring the difference between the insured's actual past loss experience and the expected loss experience of that type of business. This factor may be either a debit or a credit. A debit increases the premium, while a credit decreases it. When applied to the manual premium, the experience modification produces a premium that is more representative of an insured's actual past loss experience. It is most frequently used in connection with workers compensation insurance.

Exposure base Basis to which rates are applied to determine premium. Exposures may be measured by payroll (as in workers compensation), receipts, sales, square footage, area, or worker-hours (as in general liability), per unit (as in automobile insurance), or per $1,000 of value (as in property insurance). The exposure base for a particular insured is multiplied by the manual rate to determine the manual premium.

Extended reporting period (ERP) A designated period of time after a claims-made policy has expired during which a claim may be made and coverage triggered as if the claim had been made during the policy period. An ERP covers only claims that stem from accidents or events that took place prior to the policy's expiration date and after its retroactive date, if there is one.

Extra expense insurance Coverage for businesses that would probably not shut down in the event of major physical damage to the property and would find it imperative to remain in operation. If a business is such that it could lose most of its customers during the temporary curtailment of its services, or if its services are vital to the public, then it needs extra expense coverage to insure against the extra cost of keeping the business operating despite damage to or destruction of existing facilities. Common examples of businesses that purchase extra expense insurance are newspapers, hospitals, banks, oil and gas distributors, and public utilities. Coverage can be combined with business interruption insurance.

F

Flat cancellation The cancellation of a policy as of its effective date, before the company has assumed liability. This requires the full return of paid premiums.

Fronting company An insurance company that issues an insurance policy to the insured and then reinsures all or most of the risk with the insured's captive insurance company or elsewhere as directed by the insured. The fronting company may or may not provide claims adjusting or other services. A percentage of the premium is retained by the fronting company as a fee. This approach allows the insured to issue certificates of insurance acceptable to regulators and lenders and avoids the burden of licensing the insured's captive in all states or of becoming a qualified self-insurer.

G

Guaranteed cost insurance Premium charged on a prospective basis but not on the basis of loss experience during the policy period. While an experience modifier derived from loss experience in past years may be used, there are no adjustments made to recognize the current year's loss experience. The only adjustment to the premium made after the policy year is to recognize the insured's actual exposure during the year. In other words, the premium is estimated at the beginning of the policy period based on estimated payroll, receipts, or whatever exposure base is determined, usually by a premium auditor, and is multiplied by the appropriate rate to yield the actual premium.

H

Highly protected risk (HPR) A term referring to industrial and commercial risks that meet high property protection standards. Risks of this kind are almost always protected by sprinklers. The Factory Mutual Insurers and Industrial Risk Insurers will only insure highly protected risks.

I

Incurred but not reported (IBNR) Recognition that events have taken place in such a manner as to eventually produce claims but that these events have not yet been reported. In other words, IBNR is a loss that has happened but is not known about. Since it is impossible to know the value of a case not yet reported or investigated, a subjective estimate is often used by insurance companies to recognize losses incurred but not reported.

Incurred losses All open and closed claims occurring within a fixed period, usually a year. Incurred losses customarily are computed in accordance with the following formula: losses paid during the period plus an estimate of the value of outstanding claims at the end of the period minus outstanding losses at the beginning of the period. Incurred losses include reserves for open claims.

Inland marine Insurance originally developed by marine underwriters to cover goods while in transit by other than ocean vessels. It now includes any goods in transit, except transocean, as well as insurance for certain types of personal property, with the essential condition being that the insured property be movable. For example, floater policies covering equipment, tools, musical instruments, cameras, or jewelry are considered as inland marine policies. Bridges and tunnels are also considered as inland marine because they act as instruments of transportation.

Insurance department A regulatory department charged with the administration of insurance laws and other responsibilities associated with insurance. Insurance regulators determine or approve acceptable rates and policy forms for many lines of insurance and monitor the financial position of insurers operating in their states. They may also help members of the public who have disputes with an insurer. The commissioner of insurance is the head of this department in most states.

Insurance Services Office, Inc. (ISO) A nonprofit insurer-owned association that collects statistical information, develops and files insurance rates with regulators, and drafts standard insurance policy forms for most lines of insurance (except workers compensation and surety). Insurance Services Office is supported on an assessment basis by its member insurance companies.

─────────────────── L ───────────────────

Lloyd's of London One of the oldest professional risk bearers in the world, Lloyd's of London is not an insurance company. Instead, groups of individuals or companies join "syndicates" that assume liability through an underwriter. Each individual independently and personally assumes a proportionate part of the insurance accepted by the underwriter. While Lloyd's is best known for the unusual policies it often writes for entertainers, it is a very significant part of the world reinsurance community.

London Market A term that refers not only to Lloyd's of London, but also encompasses the entire group of insurers, reinsurers, and brokers doing business in London, a world insurance hub.

Longshore and Harbor Workers Compensation Act (LHWCA) A federal act requiring employers to compensate injured longshoremen and harbor workers. LHWCA benefits are higher than those of most states, which makes insurance coverage under the Act more expensive than for state compensation acts. This exposure may be insured commercially, or the employer can file to become a qualified self-insurer. The classifications of persons falling under the provisions of this Act are broadening with time.

Loss costs Also called "pure premium," the actual or expected cost to an insurer of indemnity payments and allocated loss adjustment expenses. Loss costs do not include overhead costs or profit loadings. Historical loss costs reflect only the costs and allocated loss adjustment expenses associated with past claims. Prospective loss costs are estimates of future losses, which are derived by trending and developing historical loss costs. Rating bureaus have begun to develop and publish loss costs instead of insurance rates. Insurers add their own expense and profit loadings to these loss costs to develop rates that are then filed with regulators.

Loss limitation for retrospective rating and retention plans A limitation possible under retrospective rating plans; the losses used in computing the premium are limited to a selected amount. The effects of shock losses that would otherwise fall into the calculations of final retrospective or retention plan premium are thereby reduced. There is an additional premium charged for the loss limitation.

Loss reserve An estimate of the value of a claim or group of claims not yet paid. A loss reserve is an estimate of the amount for which a particular claim will ultimately be settled or adjudicated. Insurers will also set reserves for their entire books of business to estimate their future liabilities.

Loss trending Predicting future losses through an analysis of past losses. Past loss data must span a sufficient number of years (5 or more) with a preference for the most recent years, since they most closely approximate current exposure. Loss history must be considered in the light of exposure data, any anticipated changes in company operations or structure, inflation, workers compensation benefit changes, and any other input relevant to projection of future losses.

M

Manual rates Full rates as published in an insurance company or bureau "rating manual" before application of any credits or deviations. The rates are determined by looking them up in a rating manual, hence their name. By law, these rates are supposed to be adequate, reasonable, and nondiscriminatory.

Minimum premium The lowest premium that may be charged for an insurance policy. The minimum premium is charged for a policy when the manual premium (manual rate times exposure basis) is lower than the minimum premium. Sometimes policies, particularly umbrellas written in the excess and surplus lines marketplace, are subject to a quoted "minimum and deposit premium." This is the minimum premium to be charged for the coverage, and even cancellation of the policy by the insured will not result in a return of the premium.

Mobile equipment Equipment such as earthmovers, tractors, diggers, farm machinery, and forklifts that, even though self-propelled, is not considered an automobile for insurance purposes. Liability arising from mobile equipment is covered by the commercial general liability policy. Normally, it should not be insured in the auto policy. Physical damage coverage is usually provided by an "equipment floater."

Monopolistic state funds Compulsory funds in jurisdictions where employers must obtain workers compensation insurance from the state. Such insurance is not subject to any of the procedures or programs of the National Council on Compensation Insurance. Insurance companies may not write workers compensation insurance in the monopolistic fund states: Nevada, North Dakota, Ohio, Puerto Rico, Washington, West Virginia, and Wyoming.

Mutual insurance company An insurer owned and operated by and for its policyholders. Every owner of the company is a policyholder; every policyholder is an owner. Any profits made are usually returned to policyholders as dividends.

N

Named perils Perils that are insured against by specific mention in named peril policies. These are distinguished from all risk policies, which insure against all perils except those that are specifically excluded. Named perils often include fire, lightning, smoke, vandalism, malicious mischief, windstorm, hail, explosion, collision, and collapse. Some optional perils that may or may not be insured include flood, earthquake, volcanic eruption, sinkhole collapse, and damage from molten material.

National Council on Compensation Insurance (NCCI) A voluntary nonprofit unincorporated association formed in 1915. Its duties are the promulgation and administration of workers compensation insurance rates and policy forms. Its membership is comprised of stock and mutual insurers, reciprocals, and state funds. The National Council is a filing agency and rating organization in 34 jurisdictions, and it serves as an advisory or service organization in many states where independent or state bureaus exist.

—————————————————— **O** ——————————————————

Occupational disease An impairment of health caused by exposure to conditions arising out of or in the course of one's employment. This is distinguishable from impairment of health caused by accident. State workers compensation laws vary as to the compensability of occupational disease.

Occurrence insurance Coverage for an occurrence, usually defined in liability policies as an accident, including continuous or repeated exposure to conditions, which results in bodily injury or property damage neither expected nor intended from the standpoint of the insured. Occurrence policies cover injury or damage that occurs during the policy period irrespective of when the claim is made against the insured. This is in contrast to a claims-made policy that covers only claims made during the policy period.

—————————————————— **P** ——————————————————

Paid loss retrospective rating An insurance cash flow plan that allows the insured to hold loss reserves until they are paid out in claims. It is used most frequently with workers compensation and other liability lines. It utilizes the standard and retrospective rating formulas, but only paid claims, rather than incurred (paid and reserved) claims, are plugged into the formula. Because the insurer has a substantial credit risk, these plans are usually collateralized with a letter of credit.

Payout profile A schedule illustrating the percentage of loss dollars actually paid in settlement of claims over time. On the average, less than $.28 of the total loss dollar for workers compensation claims is paid during the first year of coverage. Even less is paid on the average for general liability claims. It may be 7 to 10 years later before $.99 of the loss dollar is paid. Therefore, unpaid loss reserves can generate significant investment income to the holder.

Peril The cause of a loss (such as fire, windstorm, explosion, hail, riot, vandalism, strike, malicious mischief, earthquake, flood, sinkhole collapse, volcanic eruption, etc.).

Pool An organization of insurers or reinsurers through which particular types of risk are underwritten with premiums, losses, and expenses shared in agreed ratios.

A group of organizations not large enough to self-insure individually can form a shared risk pool.

Premium audit A review of the records of the insured company by an insurance company representative, the premium auditor, to determine the actual exposure base and premium due on a policy such as workers compensation. At policy inception, the premium is based on an estimate of the exposure base. The purpose of the premium audit is to determine what the exposure actually was during the insured period. The actual exposure is then applied to the previously agreed-on rates to determine the final premium.

Premium discount A volume discount applied to standard premium for workers compensation insurance and, in some states, automobile and general liability insurance when rated on a guaranteed cost basis. The amount of the discount is determined by using a table approved by insurance regulators. As the premium increases, so does the discount. Basically, the discount recognizes that the cost of writing and issuing an insurance policy does not rise in proportion to the premium once premiums reach a certain level (say, $1,000).

Products-completed operations aggregate The maximum limit of liability payable by an insurer on behalf of an insured for all products and completed operations losses during any given annual policy period.

Products-completed operations liability The liability for bodily injury or property damage incurred by a merchant or manufacturer as a consequence of some defect in a product sold or manufactured or the liability incurred by a contractor for bodily injury or property damage arising from a completed job. This coverage is provided by the standard commercial general liability policies unless excluded by endorsement.

Professional liability The professional person's or the organization's liability for damages. The purpose of professional liability insurance is to protect this person or organization against liability for damages (and the cost of defense) based on his or her alleged or real professional errors and omissions or mistakes. This is also called errors and omissions insurance. Some of the forms available cover architects/engineers, medical personnel, attorneys, law enforcement officers, pharmacists, trust department, escrow agents, accountants, and veterinarians.

R

Rate In fire and marine insurance, the cost of a unit of insurance. In other words, the fire insurance rate is applied to the insured value. In casualty insurance, rate is the annual cost per unit of the insurance company's exposure to loss. In other words, a casualty insurance (such as workers compensation or general liability) rate is applied to an appropriate exposure base (payroll or sales, for example).

Rating bureau An organization that collects statistical data on losses and exposures of businesses and promulgates rates for use by insurers in calculating premiums. Rating bureaus include American Association of Insurance Services (AAIS), National Council on Compensation Insurance, Surety Association of America, and the Insurance Services Office, Inc. In addition, a number of states also use their own rating bureaus.

Reinsurance Insurance in which one insurer, the reinsurer, accepts all or part of the exposures insured in a policy issued by another insurer, the ceding insurer. In essence, it is insurance for insurance companies. It allows insurers to spread the risks of one policy among themselves and thereby write limits higher than one company would feel comfortable doing alone. Facultative reinsurance involves a one-time reinsurance transfer arranged specifically on a single policy. Treaty reinsurance involves an agreement in which a certain amount of the exposures of all policies written by the ceding company are automatically reinsured; in return, the reinsurer receives a percentage of all the premiums on the reinsured book of business.

Replacement cost coverage endorsement A property insurance provision that changes the valuation of covered property from actual cash value to replacement cost, the cost to replace it today with property of like kind and quality without deduction for depreciation.

Retention plan A rating plan normally used in writing workers compensation insurance. This plan provides that the net cost to the policyholder is equal to a "retention factor" (insurance company profit and expenses) plus actual incurred losses subject to a maximum premium equal to standard premium less premium discount. With a retention plan, the full guaranteed cost premium is paid to the insurer. At the end of the policy period, the calculation is made and the premium is adjusted. If a return premium is indicated, it is paid as dividends to the insured.

Retroactive date A provision found in many claims-made policies. The policy will not cover claims for injuries or damages that occurred prior to the retroactive date even if the claim is first made during the policy period.

Retrospective rating A rating plan that adjusts the premium, subject to a specified minimum and maximum, to reflect the current loss experience of the insured. Retrospective rating combines actual losses with graded expenses to produce a premium that more accurately reflects the loss experience of the insured. The adjustment, of course, is performed after the policy has expired.

Risk and Insurance Management Society (RIMS) A nonprofit association dedicated to the advancement of professional standards in risk management. Its membership consists of corporations, institutions, and governmental entities in the United States, Canada, and abroad. RIMS sponsors an annual educational conference and publishes educational materials used by risk managers.

Risk management The practice of analyzing all noncompetitive (nonproduction, pure risks) exposure to risk of loss (loss by fortuitous or accidental means) and taking steps to minimize those potential or real losses to levels acceptable to the organization. It provides a systematic process for treating pure risk: identification and analysis of exposures, selection of appropriate risk management techniques to handle exposures, implementation of chosen techniques, and monitoring of the results. Methods for treating pure risks include retention, contractual or noninsurance transfer, loss control, avoidance, and insurance transfer. A risk manager is an employee whose duty it is to establish and administer a risk management program for his or her employers.

Risk purchasing group A group formed in compliance with the Risk Retention Act of 1986 to negotiate for and purchase liability insurance from a commercial insurer. Unlike a risk retention group that actually bears the group's risk, a risk purchasing group merely serves as a vehicle for obtaining coverage, typically at favorable rates and coverage terms.

Risk Retention Act Federal legislation that facilitates the formation of purchasing groups and group self-insurance for commercial liability exposures.

--- S ---

Self-insurance A formal system whereby a firm pays out of operating earnings or a special fund any losses that occur that could ordinarily be covered under an insurance program. The moneys that would normally be used for premium payments may be added to this special fund for payment of losses incurred.

Self-insured retention The amount of each loss for which the insured agrees to be responsible before an umbrella or excess liability insurer begins to participate in a loss. A policy's full limit of liability applies in excess of a true self-insured retention. This is in contrast to a deductible that is subtracted from the policy limit.

Short-rate cancellation A term used in insurance and bonding to describe the charge required for insurance or bonds in place for less than 1 year. It also denotes the penalty assessed on the return premium for insurance or bonds canceled by the insured before the end of the policy period or term of the bond. Insurance policies provide that returned premiums be subject to short-rate cancellation if the insured cancels, but a pro rata return is provided if the insurer cancels.

Specified perils coverage An alternative to comprehensive coverage on automobiles that provides named perils rather than all risks physical damage insurance. The named perils typically include fire, theft, flood, earthquake, windstorm, vandalism and malicious mischief, hail, and explosion. This coverage is slightly less costly than comprehensive coverage.

Standard premium The premium developed by multiplying the appropriate rate times the proper exposure unit. This figure is then modified by experience rating, if applicable. If the risk is not subject to experience rating, the premium at manual rate is the standard premium.

Subrogation The assignment to an insurer by terms of the policy or by law, after payment of a loss, of rights of the insured to recover the amount of the loss from one legally liable for it. After the insurer pays the insured's claim, it subrogates against the party that caused the loss to recover the amount paid. Make certain that subrogation recoveries from third parties are subtracted from loss data used in experience rating or retrospective rating calculations.

―――――――――――――――― **T** ――――――――――――――――

Tax factor An amount applied to an insurance premium to increase it to cover state premium taxes. This is one of the factors used in the retrospective rating formula.

―――――――――――――――― **U** ――――――――――――――――

Umbrella liability insurance A form of excess liability insurance available to protect against claims in excess of the limits of other primary policies or for claims not covered by the primary insurance program. This latter coverage requires the insured to be a self-insurer for a specified amount ($10,000 to $25,000). It generally provides excess coverage over the insured's auto liability, commercial general liability, and employers liability policies. Care must be taken to coordinate all primary and excess policies to avoid coverage gaps.

Underwriter The employee of an insurance company or managing general agency who has the responsibility for determining whether or not the insurer will write insurance that has been applied for, the amount of coverage the insurer will write, and the premium that will be charged.

―――――――――――――――― **W** ――――――――――――――――

Wet marine insurance Insurance covering goods in transit while waterborne. Wet marine insurance is to be distinguished from inland marine insurance, which applies to goods in transit being transported by land conveyances.

Workers compensation Compensation—required by laws in all states—to workers injured while on the job, whether or not the employer has been negligent. Benefits vary according to state laws but generally require the payment of medical expenses and partial wage continuation. The workers compensation laws apply to all individuals except those specifically excluded. Employers are required by law to purchase insurance for their exposure unless they file for and obtain permission to become qualified self-insurers.

Wrap-up insurance program Also called an owner-controlled insurance program (OCIP), this involves the purchase by a building project owner of workers compensation and liability insurance on behalf of all or most involved contractors. If properly designed and administered, this type of program can substantially reduce insurance costs compared to what the contractors would otherwise collectively pay and pass on to the owner.

For further research and study

For a more extensive list of key insurance definitions, refer to the *Glossary of Insurance and Risk Management Terms,* published by IRMI.

Index